Lecture Notes in Artificial Intelligence 513

Subseries of Lecture Notes in Computer Science
Edited by J. Siekmann

Lecture Notes in Computer Science
Edited by G. Goos and J. Hartmanis

Nelson Mendonça Mattos

An Approach to Knowledge Base Management

Springer-Verlag

Berlin Heidelberg New York
London Paris Tokyo
Hong Kong Barcelona
Budapest

Series Editor

Jörg Siekmann
Institut für Informatik, Universität Kaiserslautern
Postfach 3049, W-6750 Kaiserslautern, FRG

Author

Nelson Mendonça Mattos
Universität Kaiserslautern, Fachbereich Informatik
Postfach 3049, W-6750 Kaiserslautern, FRG

CR Subject Classification (1991): H.2.1, H.2.3-4, I.2.4-5, D.1.5

ISBN 3-540-54268-X Springer-Verlag Berlin Heidelberg New York
ISBN 0-387-54268-X Springer-Verlag New York Berlin Heidelberg

Printing and binding: Druckhaus Beltz, Hemsbach/Bergstr.
2145/3140-543210 - Printed on acid-free paper

... à compreensão, apoio e carinho de

Claudia,

Alexandre e

Melina

Preface

During the last few years, Artificial Intelligence (AI) technology has produced a variety of Knowledge-based Systems (KS). In spite of this apparent success, KS applicability is still extremely limited since appropriate systems for an efficient knowledge base (KB) management do not exist. Current AI techniques cannot provide efficient access to and reliable management of large, shared, or distributed KB, and existing Database Systems (DBS) lack knowledge representation and even the simplest form of reasoning capabilities.

This work addresses the development of a new generation of systems, called Knowledge Base Management Systems (KBMS) with the aim of filling this technological gap, providing the solution to this KS problem. So, it firstly investigates in detail the design process, the architecture, and the working methods of KS in order to point out key characteristics of the field as well as its current limitations, which serve as basis for an exact formulation of KS requirements. Several approaches to satisfy these requirements are then thoroughly analyzed, thereby providing the basic concepts for building KBMS. The work demonstrates that KBMS functionality is directly influenced by the most important aspects of KS development and application, i.e., the needs of the user, knowledge engineering support, and implementation issues, so that KBMS should integrate especial AI and DBS features in order to support knowledge modeling, manipulation, and maintenance. Further, an architectural approach is presented, advocating the division of KBMS into three different layers in which these distinct KS aspects are particularly considered. On the basis of this approach, the design and implementation of the multi-layered prototype KRISYS are thoroughly described. One main philosophy of the system is the idea of abstraction aimed at the independence of knowledge which is provided by treating the KB in a functional way by means of ask and tell operations. A second very important issue is the effective support of the needs of KB design and manipulation, achieved by the integration of descriptive, operational, and organizational aspects of knowledge into an object-centered model. Finally, a number of concepts focus attention on performance requirements. The system provides a framework for the exploitation of the application's locality, guaranteeing fast accesses to the KB. In closing, the work describes the development of KS in a KBMS environment and gives some concluding comments on the impact of this new technology.

This work was conceived while I was a Ph.D. student in the Computer Science Department of the University of Kaiserslautern. It was supported by DAAD, to which I am very grateful. Its development was enabled by Prof. Dr. Theo Härder, whom I thank for the opportunity to carry out this research and for his encouragement during this study, the useful discussions, and his numerous comments on my work. I am also indebted to Prof. Dr. Gerhard Barth for offering to analyze my results and for reporting his remarks.

Colleagues, friends, and undergraduate students helped me a great deal during the years in which I was working on this project and living in Germany. Among several colleagues, especially Andrea Sikeler, Bernhard Mitschang, Klaus Meyer-Wegener, and Stefan Deßloch were always prepared to help. They contributed, by means of their fruitful comments, to clarify and improve important issues. I am very grateful to them. In particular, I would like to thank the several students that participated in our Knowledge Base Management System project whose combined effort resulted in some of the analyses of Knowledge-based Systems requirements as well as in the implementation of KRISYS. I am also very grateful to the many friends, in particular Heike Neu, Yan Weixia, and Noemia Mesquita, who were always ready to listen and to encourage me during difficult situations. Finally, I would like to acknowledge the valuable comments of Ian Litter on the edition of the text.

Kaiserslautern, May 1991   Nelson Mendonça Mattos

Table of Contents

1. Introduction

It is a generally accepted view within the computer science community that the 1990's will be witness to a tremendous emergence of successful applications of Artificial Intelligence (AI) expertise as real world systems. High on the list of the new technologies that are going to be applied in the marketplace are Knowledge-based Systems (KS).

Certainly, what distinguishes KS from the more traditional computer systems is not readily apparent from their name's definition. Every computer system makes use of some kind of specialized knowledge in order to solve the problems of its application domain and is, therefore, in some sense knowledge-based [Na83]. The main difference between KS and traditional computer systems lies not in the use of knowledge but above all in the form in which it is organized within them: thus, in their overall architecture. In KS, the model of problem solving in the application domain is explicitly in view as a separate entity, called knowledge base (KB), rather than being buried somewhere (i.e., appearing only implicitly) in the program's code. The KB is manipulated by a separate, clearly identifiable control component, usually a general purpose inference engine that is capable of making decisions from the knowledge kept in the KB, answering questions about this knowledge, and determining the consequences implied by it [CJV83]. This means that the knowledge incorporated into the system is independent of the programs that manipulate it so that it is easily accessed by the users and potentially more easily modified or extended. Consequently, such a system architecture provides a convenient and flexible way to develop sophisticated application-oriented problem solvers for many different domains, such as:

- medicine, biology, organic chemistry,
- computer-aided design (CAD), computer-aided manufacturing (CAM), robotics,
- speech recognition, synthesis, and understanding,
- geology, geography,
- image retrieval, presentation, and processing,
- financial decision making, and
- text management and editing.

The most important aspect of KS is, however, not this new architectural approach but the effects of it, i.e., the manner in which KS are constructed. In some way, the model of KS development is dictated by the often-quoted motto of AI researchers:

"knowledge is power",

which means that the KB component of an KS is the most important part of it since it contains the whole knowledge specific to an application. Therefore, the development of KS can be viewed practically as a KB construction task [My86]. In other words, it is almost restricted to a modeling activity involving

- knowledge acquisition,
- KB structuring, and
- KB evaluation with feed-back,

rather than to the traditional activity of programming.

This shift of viewpoint is bound to have a tremendous impact on all research areas of computer science since a new technology for one of the most important activities within this science, i.e., software development, is being established.

In practice, this new software development paradigm leads to an incremental approach to KS design. Usually, a simple KS prototype is developed just after making a brief analysis of the application context. This is then successively refined in a process of examining its behavior, comparing it to that of the people who used to do the work, and correcting its reasoning processes by modifying its KB. This process continues until the system performs at a level of expertise that approximates that of the people. At this point, the system is then ready to be used. However, just as a person, who never stops developing or expanding his expertise, the KS will be continuously growing and expanding its capabilities, by including new expertise into the KB [CJV83].

These observations make clear that without knowledge of the application environment, KS can not properly execute their tasks. For this reason, AI research has been preoccupied with the development of suitable ways to represent such knowledge for the last three decades. Since the 1960's several different approaches to knowledge representation have been developed, allowing KS to be able to express with great accuracy all types of existing knowledge: knowledge about objects, about processes, heuristics and common sense knowledge about goals, motivation, causality, time, actions, etc.

The success in representing the knowledge of even the most complex application areas encouraged AI researchers to develop several KS at the beginning of the 1970's. By the end of the decade, several projects had accomplished significant results [Ha87]:

- MYCIN incorporated about 400 heuristic rules to diagnose and treat infectious blood diseases and impressed the AI community with its ability to explain conclusions or questions it generated [Sh76,DBS77,BS84].
- HEARSAY-II employed multiple, independent, cooperating KS that communicated through a global control structure called blackboard to understand continuous speech for a vocabulary of a thousand words [EHLR80].

- R1 incorporated about 1000 IF-THEN rules needed to configure orders for Digital Equipment's Vax computers - a task that had resisted solution by conventional computer techniques [Mc80a,Mc82,MB84,MS81].

- INTERNIST contained nearly one hundred thousand judgments about relationships among diseases and symptoms in internal medicine and began to approach a breadth of knowledge and problem solving performance beyond that of most specialists in internal medicine [PMM75,Po82,MPM82,Po77].

Beginning this decade, AI researchers decided that Knowledge Engineering (KE) (the subfield of AI responsible for the development of KS) had matured to the point where KS could leave the laboratories to come out and be applied in the real world.

While some applications indicated the feasibility of the field, many other ones showed that their requirements lie beyond the current technology of this field. In other words, it became clear that expressiveness (concerning knowledge representation) is not sufficient to make KS a really widely applicable technology. Current limitations arise above all from the growing demands on managing the KB appropriately:

- efficient management of large KB

  Traditionally, KB were not large enough to be worth the investment in their organization or in their efficient management. Usually, they did not exceed 1MB in size so that they could be kept in virtual memory and manipulated by very simple search algorithms (e.g., sequential search) without affecting the KS's performance. However, when KS are used for large-scale applications, virtual memory sizes are not large enough to store the knowledge to be handled so that KB have to be maintained on secondary storage devices.

- adequate multi-user operation

  Most existing KS have no adequate facilities for allowing the KB to be shared among several applications. Typically, each user has his own private copy of the KB in multi-user environments. This leads to a considerable redundancy in stored knowledge with a resultant waste in storage space and consistency problems caused by updates in the KB.

- suitability for server/workstation environments

  Nowadays, powerful workstations offer the interactive computing features required by KS. However, when KS running on such workstations use a centralized KB maintained in a remote server, they exhibit very low performance due to the communication and transfer overhead between the two machines involved in this environment.

- high reliability and availability

  In order to be applicable in a production environment, KS must guarantee that their functions are performed correctly even if the system crashes or a loss of storage media interrupts their operation in an uncontrolled fashion.

- new inference mechanisms

  Existing inference mechanisms have been designed to work with KB kept in virtual memory. When used for large KB resident on secondary storage, they are computationally intolerable.

- distribution of the knowledge base

  KS for large applications involving several geographically dispersed locations should provide facilities for distributing the KB across multiple machines in order to guarantee efficiency of processing and increased knowledge availability.

- knowledge independence

  Most present-day KS are knowledge representation dependent. This means that the way in which the KB is organized on a storage device and the way in which it is accessed are both dictated by the requirements of the KS and, moreover, that the information about the organization and access technique is built into the KS logic (i.e., embedded in their program's code). In such KS, it is impossible to change the storage structures or access strategies without affecting them, more than likely drastically. Clearly, with complex KS and very large KB on the horizon, this knowledge dependence promises to be very problematic.

These new requirements lead today to similar considerations as those made 25 years ago as the demands on data management tasks of commercial applications began to become more complex. At that time, people realized that these demands were very similar in all applications so that the most reasonable solution was to efficiently implement data management tasks only once in a separate system, removing them from the application programs and delegating them to this independent new system. This led to a generalization and standardization of functions to define and manipulate data as well as to control access and different aspects of data integrity, resulting in the emergence of what we today call Data Base Management System (DBMS) [Da83,Ul82, LS87].

Like the solution found for commercial applications, the answer to the existing KS limitations is also the delegation of knowledge management tasks to an independent system, where they are achieved in an efficient and adequate way.

In trying to create such a system, the first effort made was to attempt applying DBMS for this purpose. Nevertheless, approaches combining KS with existing DBMS have failed for several reasons. The deficiencies of DBMS support for KS may be summarized as follows [Ma86a]:

- DBMS cannot support the incremental KS construction process.

- Classical data models are not satisfactory for knowledge modeling (lack of abstraction concepts, strict distinction between object types and object instances, weak object-orientation, etc.) [La83].

- DBMS provide insufficient operational support for typical knowledge processing requirements (lack of reasoning and explanation facilities).

- Integrity control mechanisms are too weak (lack of an automatic maintenance of semantic integrity).

- Coupling DBMS and KS generally yields very low performance [HMP87].

The deficiency of the DB support for KS endorses what many DB researchers have been united upon since the mid-1980's:

"The general purpose database management systems are general only for the purpose of commercial applications, and their data models are general only for modelling commercial views of the world" [HR83b, p. 453].

The solution to the KS problem is then to develop a new generation of systems aimed at the effective and efficient management of KB. Following the development of DBMS, which stemmed from data management demands, these systems, originating from knowledge management demands, are called Knowledge Base Management Systems (KBMS).

KBMS should in analogy to DBMS

- allow a description of knowledge, independent of the application programs,

- exhibit some degree of knowledge independence (i.e., the isolation of representational aspects of knowledge from the applications) when changing storage structures, access techniques, etc.,

- offer adequate operations for knowledge manipulation,

- guarantee the maintenance of the semantic integrity,

- support multi-user operation, as well as

- allow the distribution of the KB.

Furthermore, KBMS should support KS characteristics not ordinarily found in traditional computer systems and, consequently, unusual for DBMS. As such, in addition to the above points KBMS should extend DBMS features and so also

- support the development of KS,

- provide means for the incremental KB construction process,

- allow for an expressive and exact representation of knowledge, and

- support appropriate reasoning capabilities.

Therefore, KBMS should integrate selected features from AI and DBS technologies in order to be capable of supporting powerful knowledge-based processing and at the same time efficient KB management.

This work addresses the above integration with the final goal of filling the technological lacuna existing between these two fields, thereby defining a complete and appropriate environment for the KB management, i.e., the support of construction, manipulation, and maintenance of KB. Following this issue, we investigate the concepts to be provided by such an environment in order to obtain an exact specification of KBMS

- requirements,

- functionality,

- knowledge representation capabilities, as well as

- design and architectural issues

in terms that are understandable to both AI and DBS communities.

Before outlining KBMS issues, we examine in chapter 2 the focal points of KBMS applications: expert knowledge and human problem solving process. This description serves then as basis for the understanding of the current KS technology which is presented in chapter 3. After showing the characteristics of the field, we discuss in chapter 4 its limitations, thereby assembling the functions to be provided for KB construction, manipulation, and maintenance. On the basis of these requirements, several approaches for KB management are investigated in detail, providing the foundational concepts of KBMS. In chapter 5, we then specify an architecture for KBMS and show how the features provided by each of the system's components fulfil KS requirements. After that, we illustrate in chapter 6 how this architectural approach may be applied to build practical KBMS. This chapter focuses on the design and implementation of our *multi-layered prototypical KBMS* called *KRISYS*. Finally, we demonstrate in chapter 7 how to employ our KBMS approach to construct KS. After this closing description of KS development under KBMS environment, we give in chapter 8 some concluding remarks concerning AI and DBS integration.

2. Knowledge and Human Problem Solving

KS may be roughly defined as

"computer programs which use knowledge represented explicitly to solve problems".

Based on this definition, one can argue that the two most important focal points of KS are *knowledge* and the *process of solving problems.* For this reason, before describing KS character-istics, it is important to understand the meaning of knowledge as well as its involvement in the problem solving process and to recognize the existence of some important activities underlying this process in order to comprehend the working method and the architecture of KS. We do not intend, however, to give a detailed survey of these two themes but just to introduce some impor-tant definitions and some foundational concepts which will be used throughout this work. Because of this, the contents of this chapter might ignore some important considerations, reflecting, in some sense, the view of the author as to the most relevant aspects necessary for KS understanding.

2.1 Knowledge

The word 'knowledge' adopted in this work derives its meaning from the signification ascribed to it in the current literature on KS:

"Knowledge is the sum of perceptions of an individual about aspects of some named universe of discourse at a particular time".

As such, we regard knowledge as being everything that an individual (e.g., a person) "knows" about a specific universe at a given time. The universe of discourse (also denoted application domain or simply domain) may be any part of the actual universe or some non-actual universe such as a universe in the future, a make-believe universe depicted in fiction, a universe existing in an individual's beliefs, etc. [Fr86]. Thus, a "particular knowledge" must always be associated with these three different things (an individual, a domain, and a time) in order to be distinguishable.

This is quite an obvious observation. Two different persons generally have different knowledge of the same domain. Distinct domains generate clearly distinct knowledge. And the domain knowl-edge of an individual usually changes with the time since people commonly observe new things, make conclusions, etc. so that they change their perceptions of the aspects of this domain.

The above definition of knowledge ignores some interesting philosophical considerations as, for example, what we really mean by saying that one "knows" something. Is "knowing" associated with a kind of individual's beliefs? Does it translate only conscious things? However, these and other philosophical considerations are beyond the scope of this work. The definition of knowledge chosen here is in some sense not a philosophical one but a working definition which is in reasonable agreement with the meaning ascribed to it in everyday usage and above all in the current literature on KS. The interested reader is for this reason referred to [BS79] for a readable account of these philosophical considerations.

2.2   An Overview of the Cognitive Cycle

Knowledge is for us, people, important because almost everything that we do is in some way based on the knowledge which we have stored in our brains. In other words, people apply knowledge in order to achieve their goals. Hence, the process of problem solving is, for this reason, also a routine of applying knowledge, in this case, with the purpose of finding out problem solutions.

The ability of applying knowledge consciously is surely one of the most obvious skills that set people apart from the other creatures which inhabit this planet. However, people can only apply the knowledge that they have, i.e., people are not able to execute tasks with which they are not familiar.

This observation suggests that application might be the most important but is not the only human activity involving knowledge, which is significant in this context. In truth, application is just one of four activities which together build what we are going to call a cognitive cycle (figure 2.1): a sequence of human activities through which knowledge passes when people apply it to solve problems. Because of this, in trying to understand this process, it is also necessary to analyze the other phases of this cycle. However, it is not purpose of this work to describe this in fullest detail. Since this is closely linked with the aim of the related fields of cognitive science [Py84] and cognitive psychology [Ne67,LLB79,GH86,An85], we refer to the above sources for a detailed description of these activities.

Furthermore, the above observations suggest that several kinds of knowledge exist and are used differently depending of the goal to be achieved. For example, the knowledge applied to solve mathematical problems is completely different from that used to acquire the mathematical knowledge and even more to that utilized to bake a cake. Since we are focusing on KS (see above definition), only the kind involved in the human problem solving process is of interest for this work. For this reason, we disregard the several existing kinds of knowledge concentrating on those involved with problem solving.

As such, the first important phase in this context is the process of acquiring knowledge, i.e., the methodology of enriching someone's expertise (the set of knowledge used to solve problems). This involves collecting knowledge from many sources and assimilating it (in some sense corresponding to the cognitive psychology subareas of perception and attention [Ho87]).

As knowledge is being assimilated, the second phase comes in play. Knowledge must be represented and organized in some form in our brains so that we are able to find and apply it when needed. We denote this phase as the process of knowledge memorization (cognitive psychology subarea of memory [Ho87]).

Once memorized, it is then ready to be applied in the next phase: the human problem solving process itself. People basically solve problems by thinking (cognitive psychology subarea of thinking [Ho87]). This means the active transformation of memorized knowledge to create new one that is, in turn, used to achieve a goal.

Once the goal has been achieved, people usually automatically assimilate the new knowledge that they have inferred during the solving process. However, assimilation is not enough to keep this information available over many years. It is also important to transmit it to other people.

The transmission of new knowledge generally involves explaining to people how one came to this acquaintance. Explanation is therefore the fourth and last phase in this context. As people are having things explained, knowledge is once again being acquired so that the whole cycle is then completed (figure 2.1).

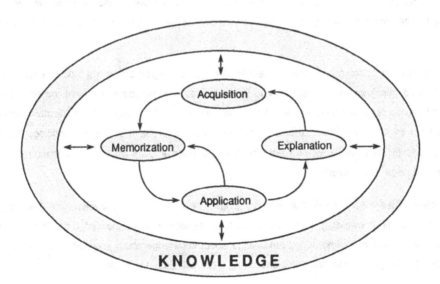

Figure 2.1: Cognitive cycle

2.3 The Human Problem Solving Process

Problem solving methodologies and inference strategies

In order to understand the human problem solving process, we need to distinguish between two different types of operations that are applied during a thinking process [Ho87]. The first one can be translated as the human capability of reasoning, i.e., drawing inferences from current knowledge. In other words, making conclusions (i.e., generating new knowledge) by interpreting the knowledge stored in our brains.

Clearly, making conclusions is not sufficient to solve problems in an adequate way. It is above all necessary to make the right conclusions at the right time. This is achieved by using the second capability, that we have, of guiding our reasoning processes. In some way, people also have the capability of determining a sequence of reasoning operations which, when applied over a domain, derive the expected solutions.

Surely, this second capability is the most important one for solving problems. By purely reasoning making, people would also come to the expected result, however, in a very inefficient way since many unnecessary conclusions would be also made. In order to solve problems in a fast and clear manner, it is therefore necessary to guide our reasoning process so that only the relevant conclusions are inferred.

We associate this guiding operation with a form of solving methodology which we are going to denote *problem solving methodology* for the purpose of this work. In the same scope, we are going to call *reasoning strategies or inference strategies* the different existing reasoning operations.

It is important to observe here that problem solving methodologies are also a kind of knowledge: in this case, the knowledge about how to solve problems. A particular domain knowledge (i.e., the individual's domain expertise needed to solve specific problems within this particular domain) should not be confounded with the first one. Note that the problem solving methodology lies at a higher level than the individual's domain expertise since it commands the application of this expertise to work out problems.

The above observations show that different levels of knowledge (meta levels) exist: knowledge (e.g., the domain knowledge), meta knowledge (i.e., knowledge about knowledge like the problem solving one), meta meta knowledge (knowledge about knowledge about knowledge as, for example, the knowledge about different problem solving methodologies) and so on.

The inference strategies are, however, not to be viewed as a kind of knowledge. Indeed, they should be understood as a natural capability of human beings of interpreting what we have stored in our brains. Clearly, the capability of guiding the inference process or choosing the best inference strategy to achieve particular goals is knowledge. However, as already mentioned, this is not part of the inference strategy itself but of the problem solving methodology.

According to the above observations, we can say that human problem solving may be compre-hended as the process of knowledge interpretation at two different levels: a problem solving methodology is interpreted at a higher level which, in turn guides the interpretation of the domain expertise at a lower level, generating the desired results (figure 2.2).

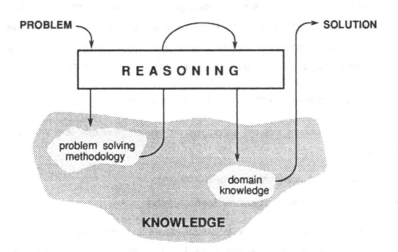

Figure 2.2: Overview of human problem solving at two levels

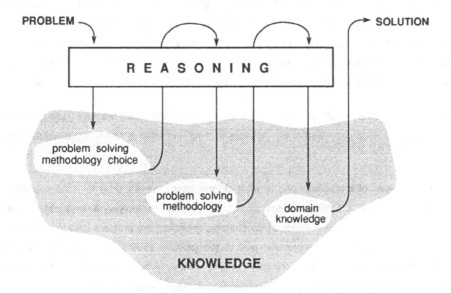

Figure 2.3: Overview of human problem solving at three levels

Clearly, we could also imagine that people may use their acquaintance with the different solving methodologies that they know and so dynamically guide the application of these methodologies choosing one or more of them during the problem solving process. In this case, we would have three levels of knowledge interpretation (figure 2.3).

Problem solving strategies and heuristics

Up to this point, we have analyzed problem solving methodologies treating them as a kind of algorithm or strategy applied over human inference strategies to achieve goals. However, in practice, people rarely solve problems purely by making use of algorithms. Actually, these algorithms, denoted *problem solving strategies*, are just one portion of the knowledge underlying problem solving methodologies. Generally, people combine such strategies with heuristics, i.e.,

"rules of good judgement or rules of thumb used by decision making".

Problems or parts of problems that are candidates for heuristic methods commonly fall into two classes [Ko87]:

- those for which no exact algorithms are known at all, and
- those for which the known exact algorithms are not feasible.

An example of the second class is chess. In principle, there is an exact deterministic algorithm for always making an optimal move in a chess game. This requires generating (mentally) all possible moves and countermoves in the game until only won, lost, and drawn positions remain, and propagating the ultimate outcomes of these positions back to the current position in order to choose the optimal move (see [Ma87, Ba87a]). Unfortunately, the number of generated positions by such an algorithm could be as large as 10^{120} so that no human being could be able to exploit it. Thus, although an exact solution is known in this case, it is impossible to use it. As such, people would solve this task by applying heuristics, like, for example, their chess playing experience.

Heuristics provide approximate methods for solving problems with practical resources (e.g., one's capacity to keep generated chess positions in mind) but often at some cost in solution quality.

Exactly the quality of one's heuristics is what differentiates people's skills for solving problems. Usually, people learn a solving strategy at first theoretically. In applying it, they obtain experience, which is then gradually added to this strategy, improving the problem solving methodology as a whole. Heuristics is, therefore, the part of the problem solving knowledge that is mostly enriched with practice. Thus, since distinct persons commonly have different experiences, their skills and, consequently, their whole problem solving knowledge will be also different.

Dependencies of the problem solving knowledge

The knowledge involved in the problem solving process (figure 2.4) may depend on two different factors: the type of the problem to be solved (i.e., problem class) and the application domain.

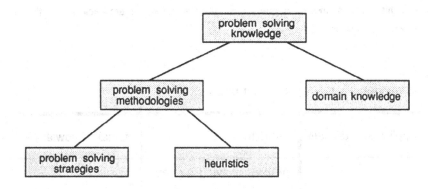

Figure 2.4: Knowledge involved in a problem solving process

The domain knowledge is obviously application dependent and problem class independent (see definition of knowledge in section 2.1).

Problem solving strategies are domain independent since they frequently cover many different domains. For example, the strategy somebody uses to find out the defect of a car (e.g., hypothesizing different faults and testing them to check which one might be) can also be exploited to determine a refrigerator's defect. However, problem solving strategies are problem class dependent. For example, the above strategy for discovering a defect cannot be used to plan somebody's vacations since this would mean hypothesizing different places and traveling to each one of them in order to prove whether this person would enjoy a stay in those places or not. This might be a good idea but is not practicable in the present day. Note that although the car and the refrigerator problem involve distinct domains, they are from the same type: diagnosis. For this reason, it is possible to make use of the same strategy. The vacation one is, however, of another problem class (planning) and, because of this, could not be solved in the same manner (an overview of some existing problem classes is given in section 3.1).

Heuristics are generally either problem type dependent or problem type and domain dependent. For example, the heuristic that one uses to determine in a diagnosis process which hypothesized defect he is going to check first, might be to begin checking the hypothesized fault that occurs most frequently. In this case, it is problem class dependent but domain independent. In contrast to this, the heuristic used to find out optimal game moves is problem type and domain dependent since it is quite different in a chess and in a checkers context.

As one can see, the three different types of knowledge involved in a human problem solving process (domain knowledge, problem solving strategy, and heuristic) are intrinsically related to each other either by means of the application domain or of the problem type. Hence, knowledge classifications based on these two factors are also very helpful for understanding how knowledge is involved in this process and, consequently, for understanding the architecture and the working method of KS later (see table 2.1).

dependence on	problem class	
application domain	heuristic	domain knowledge
	problem solving strategy heuristic	

Table 2.1: Factors on which problem solving knowledge may depend

2.4 Resume

Human problem solving is to be comprehended as the process of knowledge application, i.e., the active interpretation of knowledge by using reasoning or inference strategies to make conclusions at different levels.

Involved in this process are three different knowledge types, which may depend on the application domain and/or on the class of problem that has to be solved.

At a higher level, some problem type dependent and domain independent problem solving strategies together with some problem type dependent and occasionally also domain dependent heuristics are interpreted. This guides, in turn, at a lower level the interpretation (inference process) of the domain dependent domain knowledge yielding expected solutions.

Closely related to this process, there are some other processes which together with it build the cognitive cycle, i.e., the sequence of activities that knowledge undergoes from the point when it is acquired by the interaction of human beings with their environment. These processes are acquisition, memorization, application, and explanation.

3. A Survey of Knowledge-based Systems

Artificial Intelligence (AI) has achieved considerable success in the development of knowledge-based systems or KS for short. This area has concentrated on the construction of high-performance computer programs in specialized domains to solve problems that ordinarily require human intelligence [HWL83].

Starting in the early sixties, the first period of AI research, several efforts emerged to build general purpose problem solvers based on the at that time dominant naive belief that a small amount of knowledge coupled with some reasoning strategies supported by powerful computers would produce expert performances. Among these efforts were GPS (the General Problem Solver built at Carnegie-Mellon University) [EN69,NS63], STRIPS (a general problem solver for the SHAKEY robot at Stanford) [FN71] and several programs for chess. None of these efforts was particularly successful with respect to the solving of significant problems.

In reaction to this failure, many researchers began to work on narrowly defined application problems. Within a few years, the key role played by knowledge in the problem solving process became then apparent. As a consequence, people began to understand that the reason why the early AI systems could not solve any very difficult problem lay in their lack of knowledge. In other words, those systems exploited a general problem solving mechanism which, however, was supported by a very small amount of knowledge about the application domain in which it worked. The impulse given towards the importance of knowledge was particularly provided by MYCIN [BS84,Sh76,DBS77] by the mid-1970s, which was designed and implemented to diagnose and recommend treatment of infectious blood diseases. Since most people cannot do this task because they lack the appropriate expertise, the need for knowledge in this application domain was more obvious than it was in the domains of the earlier programs. Throughout the years, AI researchers learned to appreciate the great value of knowledge as a basis for solving significant problems, realizing that although computers may have many advantages over human beings (e.g., speed, consistency, etc.), they cannot compensate for ignorance. In order to construct systems that perform as well as human experts, it is necessary to provide these systems with specialized know-how comparable to that which experts possess.

Thereby, a new set of principles, tools, and techniques has emerged forming the basis of knowledge engineering as a significant subfield of AI. Professor Edward A. Feigenbaum, one of the leading researchers in KS, defines the activity of knowledge engineering as follows:

"The knowledge engineer practices the art of bringing the principles and tools of AI research to bear on difficult applications problems requiring experts' knowledge for their solution. The technical issues of acquiring this knowledge, representing it, and using it appropriately to construct and explain lines-of-reasoning, are important problems in the design of knowledge-based sys-

tems.... The art of constructing intelligent agents is both part of and an extension of the programming art. It is the art of building complex computer programs that represent and reason with knowledge of the world." [Fe77, pp.1014-1016].

His view suggests that knowledge engineering is closely linked to human problem solving and therefore also to cognitive psychology, the field that investigates how people acquire knowledge, remember it, put it to use to make decisions and solve problems, and explain the new knowledge inferred.

For this reason, we investigate in this chapter the characteristics of KS by drawing a parallel to the human problem solving process which was previously discussed. In the following sections, we summarize what is known about KS architecture and working methods, presenting the concepts that are central to knowledge engineering. In order to achieve this goal, we make use of several existing expert systems (XPS) since they are the best known examples of KS. Throughout this work, we might use XPS and KS as synonyms, but we actually refer to XPS as just one of the many types of KS which exist. Some other examples of KS might be:

- packages for computer-aided design (CAD), and/or computer-aided manufacturing [Li85, Be84b],
- speech recognition systems [EHLR80],
- components of other complex computer systems like query optimizer in Data Base Systems (DBS) [GD87,LFL88] and operations planner in robotics [FN71],
- image processing systems, and
- intelligent programs for information retrieval [Jü87].

3.1 KS Problem Classes

In the previous chapter, we showed that human problem solving methodologies are strongly dependent on the classes of problems which people wish to solve. Consequently, the human problem solving process exhibits different peculiarities depending on these problem classes.

Just like human beings, the characteristics of KS are also mostly determined by the particularities of the problem class in which the system is going to be employed. Hence, it is important to investigate some of the most significant classes, before starting to analyze KS in depth.

An overview of these classes is given in table 3.1 (for a complete description see [St82 or St83]).

PROBLEM CLASS	GOAL
Interpretation	Inferring situation descriptions from data
Diagnosis	Fault-finding based on collected symptoms or classifying situations according to given characteristics
Simulation	Forecasting consequences of given situations
Monitoring	Invoking actions by observing particular situations
Instruction	Bridging student's knowledge weaknesses
Planning	Determining actions to achieve a given goal
Design	Configuring object's specifications under given constraints

Table 3.1: Generic problem classes of KS

Interpretation

Interpretation is the analysis of data to determine their meaning. An example is mass spectroscopy, i.e., the interpretation of mass spectrometric data [BSF69,LBFL80,FBL71,BF78,St78]. In this case, the data are the measurements of the masses of molecular fragments and interpretation means the determination of the chemical structures. Other examples included in this category are image processing, speech recognition [EHLR80,Lo76], legal consulting [BALLS85,Le83], analysis of measurements in mineral [HDE78,DR84,Ga82] or oil prospecting [SB83,Da81,Ge82], and analysis of electrical circuits [SS77a].

The key problem in this class is that data are often noisy and error prone. As such, KS must be able to

• deal with partial information,

• hypothesize which data are believable since they may seem contradictory,

• identify where information is uncertain, incomplete, and where assumptions were made in order to avoid producing an unreliable interpretation, and

• explain how the interpretation is supported by the evidences.

For these reasons, the analysis process should be rigorously complete. This means considering possible interpretations systematically and discarding candidates only when there is enough evidence to rule them out.

Diagnosis

Diagnosis is the process of fault-finding in a system given some set of symptoms. The best example for this problem class is the determination of a disease state in living systems. Most KS falling into this problem class are medical applications: internal medicine [PMM75,Po82,MPM82,Po77, Pu86a,Pu84], glaucoma [KW82,We78,WK79], liver [CM83, Ch79] and kidney [PGKS76] malfunctions, infectious blood diseases [Sh76,DBS77,BS84], diagnosis of lung tests [AKSF82], and others [Sz82,Pu83,Re80]. Some other examples are fault-finding in machines [FLK83,Bo83,BH81] and diagnosis of plant diseases [CJM76]. The difficulties found in this category are that

- symptoms, and consequently their faults, might be masked by other symptoms,
- faults can be intermittent,
- important information is sometimes inaccessible or too expensive or even dangerous to be retrieved, and
- especially in living systems, their physiology (e.g., human body) is, in general, not fully understood.

Because of the above observations, KS for diagnosis must understand the organization of the system in which fault-finding will be done and the relationships and interactions between its subsystems in depth. Furthermore, KS should combine several partial models of this system, stressing them and deciding which measurements are practicable to take during the diagnosis process.

Monitoring

Monitoring is the process of continuously observing system behavior in order to take actions when particular situations occur. Although most KS for this problem class have not left the laboratories yet, many other computer-aided monitoring systems already exist. Examples of application areas where monitoring KS can be utilized are nuclear power plants, air traffic control, and medicine (e.g., monitoring patients after or during surgeries [Fa80,FKFO79,Os79]).

The requirements for monitoring KS are very similar to those of diagnosis since the particular situations to be recognized usually correspond to fault or malfunctions in predicted states. The key problem with which monitoring KS must usually deal is that not only the situation recognition but also the corresponding actions must be carried out in real time, and that the system must guarantee very high availability.

Planning

Planning is the process of determining a sequence of actions to be carried out to achieve a given goal. The best examples for this problem class come from the field of robotics: planning robot operations [Sa74,Sa77,FN71]. Others are planning experiments in molecular genetics [St81a, St81b,Fr79,Ma77] and planning military actions.

Planning problems are usually so large and complicated that they have to be solved in parts or subgoals. Since there are often dependences between different subgoals, planners must be able to cope with these interactions. Furthermore, they should construct their plans, without consuming excessive resources or violating constraints. Finally, they must be able to operate with some degree of uncertainty and time varying data because most planning contexts and requirements are only approximately known and change with time.

Design

Design is the development of object's specifications that satisfy some given set of requirements. Such objects include circuit layout [LSG82], structural engineering objects [FN78], computers [Mc82,MS81,MB84,Mc80a], and even computer programs [BOR81].

Design, as well as planning, belongs to the most difficult problem classes of KS since here the solution cannot be found in a set of possible ones but has to be constructed. The key problems that are involved in this process are, for this reason, numerous:

- Design problems are generally so large that the designer cannot immediately understand the consequences of its decisions.
- Usually, design constraints come from different sources and there is no theory that integrates them.
- Just like planning, design problems have to be solved by factoring them into subproblems which, however, frequently depend on each other.
- Design KS should keep a protocol of design decision justifications in order to be able to reconsider these decisions intelligently during a redesign process.
- Many design problems require reasoning about space, which demands considerable computational resources.

As a consequence of the above observations, design KS must be able to explore design alternatives tentatively, coping with subproblems' interactions, and taking the given constraints permanently into account. Additionally, they must keep in mind that the consumption of resources should be minimized as far as possible .

Instruction

Instruction means tutoring students in order to eliminate weaknesses in their knowledge [SB82]. This involves several teaching activities in many different subject areas as, for example, electronics troubleshooting [BBK82,BBB74,BB75], medical diagnosis [CI79a,CI79b,CSB79,CI83], and programming languages [BBA75,Mi79,Ge79,So83,JS85].

Typically, tutoring KS begin by diagnosing the weaknesses of the student's knowledge based on an analysis of the student's behavior. This leads to the major requirement of tutoring KS, namely, that they must have a kind of student model. Finally, they plan a tutorial interaction intended to convey some new knowledge to the student. In order to determine what instruction to present next, it is necessary to have a good idea of what the student knows and has already learned. This is achieved by interpreting the aspects of the knowledge currently understood by the student. For these reasons, the requirements of KS for instruction involve those of diagnosis, interpretation, and planning.

Simulation

Simulation can be translated as the process of forecasting consequences or some course in the future from some given initial situation. Examples are weather forecasting, prediction of the development of diseases [PGKS76], and prognosis of effects of a change in economic policy.

Prediction KS must be able to make reasoning about time since many of the given situations change over and are ordered in time. Therefore, predictors must have precise models describing how changes in the situations modify the state of the environment over time. Consequences which may be inferred from this model form the basis of the predictions. Additionally, KS in this area must deal with incomplete and uncertain information (note that when information is complete and certain, it is not necessary to guess anything and, consequently, KS do not constitute the best software technology to solve these problems).

3.2 Expert Systems

3.2.1 Definition and Basic Concepts

Expert systems (XPS)

"are computer programs which attempt to reach a level of performance by means of solving problems comparable to that of a human expert in some specialized application domain".

The task of solving problems in particular domains is actually the goal of any computer program. Most existing conventional programs (i.e., those out of AI fields) perform this task according to a form of decision making logic embedded into their code which cannot really accommodate significant amounts of knowledge. Generally, these programs manipulate two types of knowledge organized respectively in two different forms: data and algorithms. The latter determines the ways in which specific kinds of problems are worked out, and data defines values for parameters that characterize the particular problem at hand.

As shown in chapter two, human knowledge and problem solving process do not fit this model. Firstly, people organize their knowledge in a separate entity (our brain) and access it to reason out specific problems. And secondly, the human problem solving process involves at least three types of knowledge: domain knowledge, heuristics, and problem solving strategy, organized on two or three levels, depending on the existence and use of meta knowledge or not.

XPS follow this human model. They collect their "pieces" of knowledge in a separate entity, called knowledge base (KB), which is manipulated by a separate clearly identifiable reasoning component. Furthermore, they split their knowledge in three types: data, rules, and control (corresponding to domain knowledge, heuristics, and problem solving strategy) organizing them on three different levels (figure 3.1). Consequently, almost the whole model of problem solving in the application domain is, in XPS, explicitly in view in the KB rather than appearing only implicitly as part of the coding of programs as in conventional computer science.

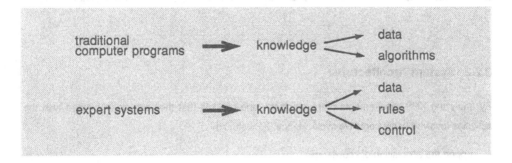

Figure 3.1: Knowledge organization in computer programs

Additionally, since most tasks performed by experts demand the exploitation of significant amounts of knowledge, ways to accommodate these large amounts, preferably explicitly, are necessary in order to permit finding the relevant knowledge easily when needed. In other words, new ways to organize decision making fragments different to those of conventional programs are required, where knowledge is lost somewhere in the code.

The knowledge organization approach of XPS fulfils this requirement. Actually, it is also the most important feature of them. Since knowledge is stored in a separate entity, XPS storage capacity is theoretically unlimited. Moreover, since KB contents are stored declaratively by means of some assertion language, knowledge can be accessed straightforwardly as well as very easily modified and extended.

The demand for this new knowledge organization approach, and consequently also for XPS, arose from the limitations of the traditional technologies to fulfil this requirement. In many different areas like medical diagnosis, equipment repair, computer configuration, chemical structure elucidation, speech comprehension, image recognition, mineral and oil prospecting, legal consulting, VLSI design, financial decision making, chemical experiments planning, and robotics, program developers need not only to

- incorporate large amounts of knowledge to work out problems, but also to
- solve them automatically by following whatever reasoning processes seem most appropriate to the case at hand,
- gradually integrate new knowledge to improve system's performance, and
- build systems able to give meaningful explanations of their behaviors when requested.

All these points are, therefore, the requirements of XPS. They reflect also the differences between XPS and traditional programs, i.e., XPS

"... differ from conventional programs in the way they are organized, the way they incorporate knowledge, the way they execute, and the impression they create through their interactions. XPS simulate expert human performance and present a human-like facade to the user." [Ha84, p. 11].

3.2.2 System Architecture

By analyzing XPS requirements more precisely, one realizes that they are closely linked with the activities involved in the cognitive cycle. Hence, XPS should

- support the acquisition of knowledge,
- assume its storage and management,
- apply it to solve problems, and
- explain their solving process.

Naturally, their architecture reflects these requirements as is clearly to be observed from figure 3.2.

Knowledge Base (KB)

A KB usually contains, in a declarative form, three different things. Firstly, the knowledge about the particular application domain (i.e., domain knowledge). Secondly, the current state of the affairs in the attempt to solve the problems (e.g., specific data about the case being analyzed, partial results, new knowledge that was dynamically inferred, etc.). And thirdly, the heuristics

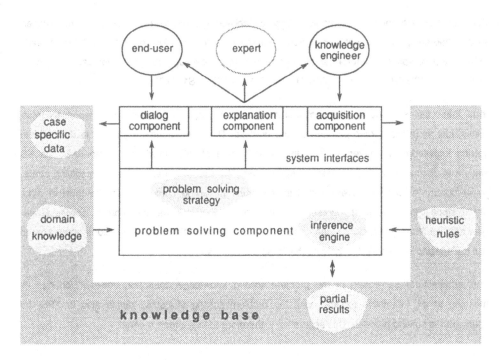

Figure 3.2: Overall XPS architecture

specific to the application domain and to the particular class of problem that the XPS is set up to solve. This latter knowledge type together with part of the domain knowledge is used by the system to make inferences about the problem and is, for this reason, generally represented in the form of pattern-invoked programs (i.e., programs which are not called by other programs in the ordinary way but are instead activated by the control structures whenever certain conditions hold in the knowledge) as for example rules. Any number or even no rules may be applicable at any time. When applied, they produce changes in the KB contents, generating new knowledge which will be also stored in the KB (in form of partial results), and, in turn, used in the inference process until a satisfactory solution has been found.

Problem Solving Component

The KB knowledge is mostly interpreted by a general purpose inference engine which is part of the problem solving component. As mentioned above, this interpretation involves applying heuristic rules to domain knowledge in order to deduce logical or probable consequences and prove that these ones satisfy the goal. Such actions correspond to the basic propositional calculus mechanisms of inference and proof. Although most XPS today do not actually employ formal logic programs, they achieve the same effects. Propositional calculus provides, therefore, just a formal foundation for their informal and generally more limited inference and proof capabilities [Ha84].

Such an inference engine implementing these capabilities can be, for example, a pattern matcher, simple theorem prover, or network search mechanism customized for one XPS, or it may already exist in the compiler or interpreter of a corresponding knowledge representation language such as OPS-5 [Fo80], PROLOG [Ko79,CM81], EMYCIN [vM79], or S1 [Te85].

In all these cases, some additional control mechanism is required to cut down unnecessary inferences, just as in the human problem solving process. This corresponds, therefore, to the problem solving knowledge. However, in XPS the heuristic part of this knowledge is stored in the KB since it is desirable to have it explicitly represented. The rest of it, i.e., the problem solving strategy or control knowledge, is embedded in the problem solving component in the form of algorithms since this is the best representation scheme for it. (Note that the problem solving strategies are algorithmic procedures, see chapter two). These algorithms make decisions about how to use the specific KB knowledge, guiding the reasoning process.

This architectural separation of the problem solving knowledge does not, however, change its meaning at all. Heuristics together with the problem solving strategies define also in XPS the course of the solving process. This separation is therefore merely organizational.

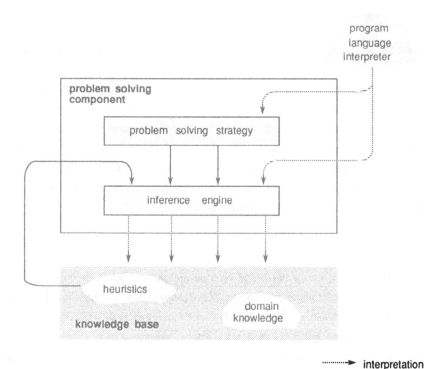

Figure 3.3: Interpretation schema of XPS

Hence, since the problem solving strategy is usually implemented by means of a programming language, it is not, like the heuristics, interpreted by the inference engine but by the language interpreter itself, that also generally interprets the inference engine programs. As a consequence, XPS present the interpretation schema sketched in figure 3.3.

The contents of the problem solving component can, therefore, be summarized as being computer programs that implement particular problem solving strategies and a general purpose inference engine.

System Interfaces

The other components of XPS are a number of various user interfaces for different purposes.

Through the knowledge acquisition component, the knowledge engineer inserts, updates, and checks the knowledge maintained in the KB. Frequently, this is made by means of comfortable editors that allow the knowledge engineer to do these tasks very easily.

The explanation component communicates with the knowledge engineer or directly with the experts and sometimes also with the end-users, giving them justifications about their results that elucidate the XPS lines of reasoning. (A line of reasoning shows how a starting set of assumptions and a collection of heuristic rules produce a particular conclusion). Although these explanations only show the chaining of single inferences or the relationships between different rules and are therefore too weak to be denoted "explanations" by means of the semantics of this word, they are the only mechanisms available in existing XPS to permit knowledge engineers to validate that the system has reached the right conclusions and that it did so for the right reasons.

The dialog component is used by the end-users to consult the XPS. This component can be found in many different forms varying from menus oriented towards natural language interfaces.

These communication capabilities are certainly a very significant aspect of XPS. Because of their interaction with three distinct persons (end-user, knowledge engineer, and eventually human expert), supporting, as a consequence, completely different tasks, XPS can possess particular characteristics that differentiate them even more from traditional computer programs: their expertise can be made available to train new human experts, and they could, just like human beings, use the results of their solving process to learn and thereby improve their knowledge.

3.2.3 Construction of XPS

3.2.3.1 The Model of XPS Development

The previous discussion about the architecture and the basic concepts of XPS have certainly made it clear that the KB is at the heart of any XPS. Since it is the storehouse of almost all expert's knowledge, its construction deserves special attention during the XPS development.

In [Ha84] it is maintained that almost 50 percent of the system development period is devoted to building the KB. If we add to this 50 percent the time spent with knowledge acquisition and many design decisions that involve the KB in some way (e.g., developing an appropriate representation scheme to express the knowledge, defining the means of the KB organization, etc.), almost the whole XPS construction process can be viewed as a KB construction task. In other words, XPS development is almost restricted to a modeling activity rather than to the traditional activity of programming. For example, Mylopoulos affirms

"... I believe that it is time to reconsider the software development paradigm in favour of one that views software development primarily as knowledge-base construction. This shift of viewpoint is bound to have a tremendous impact on large and established research areas within Computer Science concerned with software development. Moreover, the shift can only come about when KBMSs become widely available." ([My86, p. 8]).

This viewpoint has been supported by the various knowledge engineering tools (i.e., XPS building tools and XPS shells, see next section) that are emerging in the market during the last years. These tools already contain predefined knowledge representation schemes, inference engine, and often also problem solving strategies so that the knowledge engineer just has to integrate into them the knowledge of the application at hand to build an XPS.

This new software development paradigm leads in practice to an incremental approach to XPS construction. Usually, by working in small teams consisting minimally of the domain expert and a knowledge engineer, a small XPS prototype is rapidly developed. After this, the prototype is successively refined by means of a process of examining its behavior and comparing it to that of the human experts. By modifying the contents of the KB correspondingly, its reasoning process is then corrected in steps until the prototype presents a level of expertise that approximates that of the human expert. At this point, the development is completed, and the prototype becomes an XPS, entering in operation. However, just as a human expert, who is continuously improving, refining, and expanding his/her expertise by means of the activities involved in the cognitive cycle (see chapter 2), the XPS is in continued growth and expansion of its capabilities [CJV83]. Based on a permanent XPS evaluation, new expertise (acquisition) will be included into, and obsolete expertise will be removed from the system by making the corresponding changes in the KB (memorization). This new KB is, in turn, exploited to solve problems (application), providing a new system behavior as well as better justifications for the proposed problem solutions (explanation).

3.2.3.2 The Phases of the Construction Process

In [Ha84,Ha87] the XPS construction process is divided in four distinct phases where the knowledge engineer performs respectively the four types of activities identified in table 3.2. The table provides term definitions for these development phases and identifies the key products of each one.

Engineering Activities	Products
Knowledge Acquisition	heuristic rules domain knowledge
XPS Design	knowledge representation scheme inference engine problem solving strategy
Knowledge Modeling	knowledge base
Knowledge Refinement	revised heuristic rules revised domain knowledge

Table 3.2: Activities of the XPS development process

Knowledge Acquisition

Knowledge does not come off-the-shelf, prepackaged, ready to be used. Because of this, knowledge engineers must first of all collect it by analyzing the expert's working method in the application domain. Knowledge acquisition is, just like in the cognitive cycle, the process of eliciting from different sources, here mostly a human expert, the knowledge involved in the problem solving process in a particular application domain. The key product of this extraction is the problem solving heuristics. Note that algorithms, like the problem solving strategies, and the domain knowledge are easily found in different sources (e.g., in the literature of the field). However, experience (i.e., heuristics) is not described anywhere.

The knowledge extraction occurs by means of a two-way communication where the knowledge engineer interrogates the expert for insight into how he solves problems and views the objects important for the solving process, and he then explains this to the knowledge engineer. Unlike system analysts who try to translate this to an algorithm immediately, knowledge engineers just seek to capture the existing problem solving method at hand in order to create a model that directly reflects the way experts think about and solve problems in that domain, i.e., a model of expertise. This model will then, when implemented, behave just like the experts (for an analysis of system analysts and knowledge engineers roles see [CK88]).

The extraction process continues until enough problem solving knowledge has been obtained that enables the knowledge engineer to build a simple prototype, expressing a first version of the model of expertise. However, before constructing it, the knowledge engineer must design an architecture for the XPS which will support this model.

XPS Design

XPS design involves establishing an appropriate scheme for representing the KB knowledge, specifying the overall KB organization, materializing the problem solving strategy, and developing the inference engine which will be later fueled by the KB contents.

Knowledge representation options include formal logic, semantic networks, frames, object-oriented schemes, rules, etc. These will be analyzed in a separated section (see 3.3). Problem solving strategies are, for example, constraint-propagation, hypothesize-and-test, establish-and-refine, and generate-and-test, and are discussed in section 3.5.

Although this seems to be a very important phase of the XPS development process, it almost does not exist. As already mentioned, most XPS are nowadays constructed by exploiting a knowledge engineering tool (i.e., XPS building tool or XPS shell), which already contains most when not all of the above points.

XPS building tools, or tools for short, are software packages that have as purpose to facilitate XPS construction, reducing its development time. Generally, they offer various schemes for representing knowledge, an inference engine for reasoning, and interfaces for knowledge acquisition and explanation. As such, by using a tool to build XPS, a knowledge engineer just has to incorporate a problem solving strategy to give special instructions to the tool's inference engine in order to achieve the goals of this phase. Examples of such tools together with a summarized description of their features are given in table 3.3, and evaluations of some of them are found in [Ge87,Ri86,WABGO86,Me87].

ATTRIBUTE / XPS TOOL	ART	BABYLON	KEE	KNOW-LEDGE CRAFT	LOOPS
KB REPRESENTATION					
Frames	yes	yes	yes	yes	yes
system-defined relations	yes	yes	yes	yes	yes
user-defined relations	no	no	no	yes	no
inheritance	yes	yes	yes	yes	yes
Object-orientation (methods)	limited	yes	yes	yes	yes
Demons	limited	yes	yes	yes	yes
Rules	yes	yes	yes	yes	yes
hierarchical organization	no	limited	yes	no	limited
integrated with frames	no	no	yes	no	no
certainty factors	no	no	no	no	yes
INFERENCE ENGINE					
Forward Chaining	yes	yes	yes	yes	yes
Backward Chaining	yes	yes	yes	no	no
Context (viewpoints, worlds)	yes	no	yes	limited	no
Truth Maintenance	yes	no	yes	no	no
DEVELOPMENT AIDS					
Internal Editor	yes	no	yes	yes	yes
Help Menus	yes	yes	yes	yes	yes
Trace	yes	yes	yes	yes	yes
Break points	yes	yes	yes	yes	yes
Performance Measurement	yes	no	no	no	yes
Graphic Interface	yes	limited	yes	yes	yes
Cross Referencing	no	no	no	no	yes
Version Control	no	no	no	no	yes
DELIVERY					
Company	Inference	GMD	Intellicorp	Carnegie Group	XEROX
Cost	$65.000	$3.000	$50.000	$50.000	$15.000
MACHINES					
SYMBOLICS	LISP	LISP	LISP	LISP	-
LMI	LISP	-	LISP	-	-
TI Explorer	LISP	LISP	LISP	LISP	-
VAX	C	LISP	LISP	LISP	-
XEROX	-	-	LISP	-	LISP
IBM PC/RT	-	LISP	LISP	-	-
APOLLO	-	-	LISP	LISP	-
SUN	LISP	LISP	LISP	LISP	-
REFERENCES	[Cl85] [ln87a] [Wi84b]	[GMD87] [GWCRM86]	[FK85] [ln84] [Fi88]	[Ca87] [FWA85]	[BS83] [SB86]

Table 3.3: Summary characteristics of some XPS building tools

ATTRIBUTE \ XPS SHELL	INSIGHT	KES	MED2	M.1	Nexpert Object	Personal Consultant	Picon	S.1	TIMM
PROBLEM CLASS									
Interpretation	limited	limited	limited	limited	yes	limited	yes	yes	limited
Diagnosis	yes	yes	yes	yes	yes	yes	yes	yes	yes
Monitoring	no	no	limited	limited	yes	no	yes	no	yes
Planning	no	no	no	limited	yes	no	no	no	no
Design	no	no	no	limited	yes	no	no	limited	no
Instruction	no	no	no	no	yes	no	no	no	no
Simulation	yes	no	no	no	yes	no	yes	no	no
KB REPRESENTATION									
Frames	no	no	no	no	yes	yes	yes	limited	no
Demons	no	no	no	yes	yes	yes	yes	yes	no
Rules	yes	yes	yes	yes	yes	yes	yes	yes	yes
INFERENCE ENGINE									
Forward reasoning	yes	no	yes	limited	yes	limited	yes	limited	yes
Backward reasoning	yes	yes	limited	yes	yes	yes	yes	yes	no
DEVELOPMENT AIDS									
KB editor	yes	no	limited	yes	yes	yes	yes	yes	no
Check for consistency	no	no	no	yes	yes	no	yes	yes	yes
Inference tracing	yes	yes	yes	no	yes	yes	yes	yes	yes
Explanation facilities	yes	yes	yes	yes	yes	yes	yes	yes	yes
DELIVERY									
Company	Level-5-R	Software A&E	Inware	Teknowledge	Neuron Data	TI	LMI	Teknowledge	GRC
Cost	~$500	~$4000	~$15000	~$5000	~$4000	~$3000	~$60000	~$50000	~$2000
MACHINES									
SYMBOLICS	no	no	yes	no	no	no	no	yes	no
LMI	no	no	no	no	no	no	yes	no	no
TI Explorer	no	no	no	no	no	yes	yes	no	no
VAX	no	yes	yes	no	no	no	no	yes	yes
XEROX	no	no	no	no	no	no	no	yes	no
IBM PC	yes	yes	yes	yes	yes	yes	no	yes	yes
APOLLO	no	yes	yes	no	no	no	no	yes	no
SUN	no	yes	yes	no	yes	no	no	yes	no
MACINTOSH	no	no	yes	no	yes	no	no	no	no

Table 3.4: Summary characteristics of some XPS shells

An XPS shell, or just shell, is a "complete XPS" to which the knowledge engineer just has to add the contents of the KB in order to build a new XPS. Therefore, shells already contain not only a specified knowledge representation scheme and an inference engine but also predefined problem solving strategies and the system's interfaces. For this reason, they tend to be used for solving a certain class of problems only, i.e., those that fit the implemented problem solving strategy. Consequently, they are not as general and flexible as tools, that allow the knowledge engineer to define his own control mechanisms. Nevertheless, they tend to be simpler and easier to learn than more general tools. Examples of such shells are given in table 3.4.

Summarizing the above observations, we can say that the XPS design phase is very short, involving just the materialization of the problem solving strategy when tools are used.

Knowledge Modeling

In order to build the model of expertise, the acquired knowledge must undergo some transformations before it becomes valuable. This corresponds to expressing it by means of the representation scheme chosen in the previous phase. As such, after having "designed" the XPS, the knowledge engineer can transform the extracted knowledge and insert it into the KB.

Knowledge Refinement

At the end of the modeling process, a first prototype is ready, and the knowledge refinement phase begins. Generally, prototypes perform poorly at the start because of an inexact understanding of the expert's behaviors, an erroneous transformation of abstract concepts of the domain, an incorrect definition of heuristic rules, or a neglect of some important aspects. This does not reflect, however, incompetence of the knowledge engineer or the expert. On the contrary, approaches free of errors hardly exist. Note that experts are denoted in this way because they have large amounts of knowledge and not because they think about or verbalize it. Actually, experts first analyze consciously how they work when they examine the behavior of the implemented prototype.

By diagnosing XPS weaknesses and deficiencies, the knowledge engineer can begin acquiring new knowledge, modeling it once again, and reevaluating the system. This leads to an incremental, evolutionary development with performance that first is typically away from human levels and then generally comes near to, and sometimes exceeds them. This evolutionary process is summarized in figure 3.4.

It might be important to point out here one of the most significant aspects in this developing context. Knowledge engineers extract knowledge from experts and integrate it into an XPS. Therefore, they are engineers who build special purpose systems out of elementary knowledge components. What is important in this process is that the way an XPS works, its results, and performance directly reflects how and what the knowledge engineer extracts and represents in order to build the model of expertise. In other words, XPS, just like any other computer system, depend directly on the skills of their developers and on the resources they have available to perform this task.

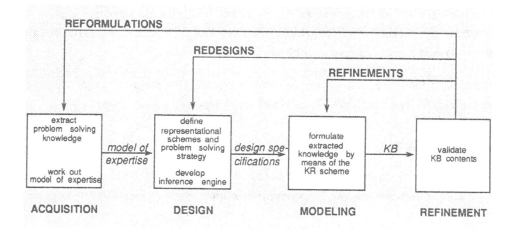

Figure 3.4: Evolutionary process of XPS development

Thus, it is important at this point to examine the resources available for an XPS development. These are certainly closely linked with existing methodologies which reflect the state of the art in the field. For this reason, we examine more closely in the rest of this chapter the three most important methodologies involved in the XPS context, namely, knowledge representation schemes, inference processes, and problem solving strategies.

3.3 Knowledge Representation

We have been arguing throughout this chapter that the solutions to AI problems depend more on the availability of large amounts of knowledge than on sophisticated algorithms. In other words, it has been argued that KS must "know" about the application world in order to be able to solve problems in this domain. Knowledge Representation, or KR for short, is the field of AI that studies ways of supplying programs with this necessary knowledge.

In our context, the knowledge made available to AI programs is referred to as the contents of the KB. As such,

"a KB constitutes a model of the real world, about which it contains specific informations pertinent to a particular application domain: i.e., the model of expertise."

The accurate representation of the model of expertise is exactly what underlies the efforts in the specification of KR schemes. In other words, this AI field has been working on the development of schemes that directly reflect the user's natural conceptualization of the universe of discourse.

By doing this, very powerful and sufficiently precise schemes to represent knowledge have been developed.

Some of these schemes emphasize the declarative characteristics of knowledge and are, for this reason, very appropriate in describing the passive parts of the domain knowledge because of its inactive nature. Others focus on the representation of procedural aspects and are, therefore, useful for expressing the behavioral (i.e., active) knowledge of the application world and of the human experts. A final collection is involved with structural aspects and is applied mostly for KB organization purposes.

With respect to the focus which they give to these three different aspects, KR schemes have been classified into declarative and procedural [Wi75] as well as structural schemes [Ra82]. Examples of declarative representations are logical and semantic network schemes. Procedural ones are production rules and the planner approach [He71,He72]. And structural KR schemes are frames [Mi75], units [St81a], and scripts [SA77].

In the following, we give a brief overview of some of these KR schemes. Other more extensive overviews are found in [My80,ML84], discussions about central issues on KR theory in [BC75,Ha74], and detailed papers on semantic network, production system, and logical representation respectively in [Fi79,WH79,GM78]. More recently, [BL85] have compiled an important collection of papers which give the interested reader a self-contained survey of the whole KR field.

While reading the description of the following KR schemes, the reader should keep in mind that very few of them fit neatly into one of the above categories. Actually, most schemes combine features from the three different aspects of knowledge.

Before starting our overview, we would like to focus on some points that are common to all of them. Each KR scheme, no matter if it emphasizes a declarative, procedural, or structural focus of the world, is characterized by the sum of constructs it offers to represent the model of expertise and the operations to work with them. Basically, KB operations do not essentially differ from KR scheme to KR scheme. Usually, they include storing and retrieving KB contents and deriving new knowledge in some form.

Therefore, the constructs offered to represent the model of expertise is what actually reflects the expressiveness of the different existing schemes. These constructs are connected to some notion of syntax to describe the world and with some semantics associated with them. The power of the semantics is exactly what differentiates poor KR schemes from good ones.

KR semantics are also particularly important because they define the ways to model the application world by using such KR schemes. For example, in a particular scheme, one has to obligatorily express car(auto1), whenever one wishes to represent that the object named auto1 is a car.

Despite the fact that the sense of semantics might only become clear at some later point during the course of this work, let us discuss briefly some important aspects related to it.

The meaning of objects and statements, i.e., the relationship between objects in the representation and entities in the world, is part of the semantics of a KR scheme. The meaning of such statements in a KB is usually taken to be true (T) or false (F). In this regard, an interpretation of a set of statements consists of a specification of a nonempty set of entities E and a mapping of the objects of the statements to the elements of E. If all statements in the KB are true in a particular interpretation, this interpretation is called a model of the KB [GMN84].

The specification of KB interpretations is very important because it allows the answering of several questions about the KB [KM87]:

- A KB is said to be inconsistent if there is no model of it. This results when contradictory information can be derived based on the KB contents. For example, a KB containing both person(Mary) and not person(Mary).

- With respect to a KB model, it can be proved that an inference scheme derives only true sentences. This is also called inferential validity or soundness.

- A KB is said to be complete when every true statement expressible with the KR scheme's constructs can be derived from the KB.

3.3.1 Logical KR Schemes

One well-known way to represent declarative knowledge is by means of formulas in some logic (first or higher order, multi-valued, modal, fuzzy etc.), from which the first-order predicate logic is the most popular one. Here, simple declarative facts can be represented as instantiated predicates. For example, "John gives Mary a car" can be adequately represented by GIVE (John, Mary, car). Thus, precise knowledge can be stated as assertions over objects that take the form of first-order predicates with functions and equality [Ko79].

According to this view, a KB is a collection of logical formulas providing a description of the world. Changes in the knowledge are therefore achieved by making modifications (i.e., insertion, deletion, etc.) of the logical formulas.

Logic has the advantage of offering a sound and complete set of inference rules. It is also purely declarative and therefore allows multiple uses of the same piece of knowledge, although it is represented just once in the KB. Furthermore, it usually possesses a well-understood and well-accepted formal semantics [Me64], and a very simple notation, which leads to a KB description that is easily understandable [My80].

Procedural knowledge can also be represented in first-order predicate logic, however, only if the logical formulas are suitably interpreted. The programming language PROLOG [Mc80b,vEK76, Ko74] is an example of such an approach. In PROLOG, the formula A1 & A2 & .... & An -> B can be thought of either as the logical statement that B is true whenever A1 A2...An are true or as a procedure for producing a state satisfying condition B. For inference purposes, PROLOG uses the resolution principle [Ro65], i.e., the negation of a theorem in causal form is added to the set of logical formulas and if the conjunction of them can be shown to be contradictory, the theorem has been proved.

A drawback of logical schemes is the difficulty in expressing clearly procedural and heuristic knowledge applied to guide the use of a large KB. An example might be the following heuristic rule: "If you are trying to reach A and situation B occurs THEN try strategy C first". The major drawback is, however, the lack of structural principles. In logical KR schemes, the knowledge about a particular real world object is spread out all over the KB. Furthermore, this KR scheme supports no structural facilities in any form. For these reasons, large KB represented in logic are mostly unmanageable making this approach often inadvisable.

3.3.2 Semantic Networks

In semantic networks, knowledge is expressed by a labeled, directed graph, whose nodes represent objects, concepts, or situations, and arcs define relationships between them. An example is shown in figure 3.5. The illustrated graph is intended to represent the white car of price of $1000 located on the 5th avenue that is owned by the person of age 23 called Mary.

By observing this structure, the first important advantage of network representations should become clear: all information about an object are integrated together around a labeled node and are directly accessed from it.

However, the crucial contribution of network schemes is the organizational axes they offer for structuring a KB. Some of these axes are discussed briefly below:

- Classification (member-of/instance-of)

  This axis relates an object (e.g., Mary, auto1) to its generic object type (e.g., person, automobile). The inclusion of such an axis in a KR scheme forces a distinction between objects and concepts or object types.

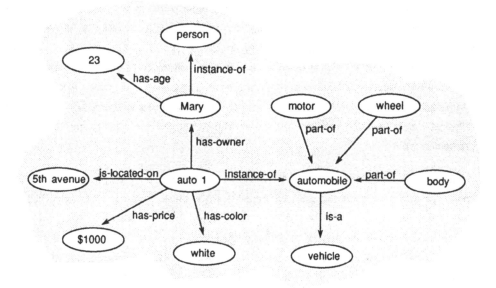

Figure 3.5: Example of semantic network

- Generalization (is-a)

  Is-a axes relate an object type (e.g., automobile) to more generic types (e.g., vehicle). The use of this type of axis has occurred mostly to minimize storage requirements by allowing properties of generic types to be inherited by more specialized ones.

- Aggregation (part-of)

  Part-of arcs are used to relate an object to its components. For example, the parts of an automobile are motor, body, and wheels.

The major drawback of network schemes has been the lack of a formal semantic and a standard terminology. This problem exists even in the most important constructs of these schemes (note, for example, the many existing meanings for the IS-A relationship [Br83]). This is at least partly due to the fact that semantic networks have been used to represent knowledge in very different ways [My80], e.g., to represent logical formulas [Sc76], to organize knowledge [Br79], to express the meaning of natural language sentences [Sc75], and to represent linguistic expressions [SHM77]. Furthermore, not all existing network schemes associate the different meanings of their organizational axes with different arcs. This certainly adds even more problems to the semantics of these axes. For an example of such a network see [Fa79].

Another disadvantage of this approach, which can be seen as a consequence of the lack of a formal semantics, is the difficulty in making the verification of the correctness of inference processes.

Semantic networks seem to be more popular in other AI fields (e.g., natural language processing) than in KS. Nevertheless, a number of XPS rely on network formalisms, among them very large systems such as INTERNIST [PMM75,Po82,MPM82,Po77], PROSPECTOR [HDE78,DR84, Ga82], and SOPHIE [BBK82,BBB74,BB75].

3.3.3 Procedural KR Schemes

3.3.3.1 Production Systems

In this approach, a KB is a collection of facts and degenerate pattern-invoked programs of the form "IF condition THEN action", that are called production rules, or just rules [DBS77]. The condition is usually the description of some state and the action mostly determines some changes in this current state.

This representation scheme has been the most popular form of KR in XPS. [Ch84] points out different interpretations for rules in such systems. From among these interpretations, the most important one is as a representation of problem solving heuristics or, in other words, as a simulation of the cognitive behavior of human experts. According to this, rules are not just a neat formalism to represent expert knowledge but rather a model of actual human behavior.

The major drawback of this and most procedural approaches is the lack of structural principles for the KB. For this reason, it is quite difficult to make changes in such KB as well as to localize desired information.

Here, it should be clear that the above construct is closely linked with the operation of retrieving intentional knowledge from the KB. Nevertheless, this activity is not provided by KR schemes supporting rules but by the inference engine.

Only in the last few years, did KR researches begin to realize that KB should not be seen simply as a passive repository of knowledge. Following this, the interpretation of such rules (i.e., inference) became part of the operations provided by some KR schemes. By using schemes with enough inference capability, KS developers could construct problem solutions simply by storing the necessary knowledge into the KB and defining a problem solving strategy to guide the inference process. This shift in viewpoint corresponds to one of the most important programming styles in the KS world: rule-oriented paradigm, which means defining such rules which are interpreted in order to derive new knowledge. As a consequence, rule operation (i.e., inference) is now seen as one of the most important operations to be provided by any KR scheme together with the traditional operations of storage and retrieval.

In spite of this recent view, we prefer to discuss inference in a later section (see 3.4) since most KR schemes of existing KS have been proposed without functions for deriving new knowledge, which used to be done in the inference engine.

3.3.3.2 Other Approaches for Representing Procedural Knowledge

The approaches discussed below are not actually seen as KR schemes but as programming styles used in AI. However, since they are also involved with the representation of behavioral knowledge of the application domain, it is important to discuss them briefly.

Object-oriented paradigm

This approach focuses on the description of "objects" which are data structures that combine the properties of procedures and data. The idea behind this is to define a kind of capsule whose contents cannot be seen from the external world. As such, all actions in this programming style are made by sending messages between objects. A selector in the message specifies the kind of operation to be performed corresponding to one of the object's (i.e., the receptor's) procedures, the so-called methods. After receiving a message, the receptor activates its procedure, which then provokes changes in its internal data, sends further messages, and/or returns a significant result.

Following this approach, no direct accesses to the properties of objects are possible. Everything occurs by activating their procedures by means of message passing. This idea, which has its roots going back to SIMULA [DN66] and SMALLTALK [GR83], supports a very important programming principle: data abstraction. It is to be contrasted with conventional programming styles by its uniform use of objects to represent both data and procedures, which is usually done separately in the conventional styles.

This approach offers a very appropriate framework for representing not only declarative but also behavioral characteristics of real world entities. For example, we might express a particular car with its behavioral property 'move' which, when activated, changes the amount of gasoline kept in the tank as well as the amount of miles already driven, just as it occurs in the real world.

In summary, the object-oriented paradigm is characterized by three different concepts which are centered on the keystone of this approach, i.e., objects. These concepts translate features of the objects and are: the ability to store information, the ability to process information, and the ability to communicate [Li87].

Data-oriented paradigm

As opposed to the previous style which explicitly activates procedures by sending messages, procedures are implicitly triggered in this paradigm when data is accessed. The access may be a put or a get access. Depending on the type of the access, the data-oriented paradigm can also be called data-driven (i.e., reactions to "put" accesses) or demand-driven (i.e., reactions to "get" accesses).

The idea is to define procedures, the so-called demons, that are able to be triggered when particular situations occur. Since the description of these situations is expressed by some declarative knowledge (i.e., data), the procedures are linked to data. This mechanism of associating programs to data is called procedural attachment. It is a very useful concept to represent intensional knowledge, to express very complex integrity constraints, or to provoke changes in the KB based on particular accesses.

The representation of intensional knowledge is, for example, important in order to express information whose value changes with respect to other data (e.g., the exact age of a person changes every day). In this case, it is interesting to have mechanisms that generate the extensional value of this information automatically each time it is accessed.

The last two uses of this concept are closely related with a desired maintenance of the KB in a consistent state, exactly reflecting the circumstances of the application world. This can be achieved by either rejecting operations that violate particular integrity constraints, or by provoking further changes in the KB that will bring it into a consistent state.

3.3.4 Frames

A frame is a KB data structure for representing stereotypical situations such as being of a certain kind of object type or going to a football game [Mi75]. The contents of the frame is a list of slots that define relationships to other frames which play significant roles in the particular situation at hand. Linked to a frame or to a slot are different kinds of information such as default values for its slots, constraint specifications, attached procedures etc. For example, a frame for a book, which is shown in figure 3.6, has slots for the author, title, publishing house, and publishing date. To describe a particular book, a "copy" of this book frame would be created, and the slots would be filled in with the information about the particular book being described.

Such a representation cannot represent any more concepts than first-order predicate logic can (see [Ni80]), but the integration of all information about a real world entity in a frame together with the support of some operational aspects make this KR scheme one of the most powerful ones.

```
frame :    book
author:_____
title:     _____
publishing house:_____
publishing date:_____
```

```
frame:      a particular book
author:     N.J. Nilsson
title:      Principles of AI
publishing house:   Springer
publishing date:    1982
```

Figure 3.6: Examples of frames

Additionally, some frame-based representation schemes give particular slots the meaning of the organizational axes (part-of, is-a, etc.) found in semantic networks, enabling KB structuring. A KB is now a collection of frames organized in terms of some slots which are very useful for modularity and accessibility of knowledge. Nevertheless, this approach suffers the same problems as network approaches, i.e., lack of formal semantics and terminologies for these organizational slots.

It is important to observe that the original frame proposal was nothing but a framework for developing other representation schemes. For this reason, this approach combined many of the ideas of semantic networks, procedural schemes, etc. Since the original proposal by Minsky, the notion of frame has played a key role in the KR research. This proposal has been adapted in several representation schemes from which FRL [GR77, GP77], KRL [BW77], OWL [SHM77], and KL-ONE [Br79,BS85] are good examples.

3.4 Inference

Inference in AI refers to various processes by which programs, in a similar manner to people, draw conclusions or generate new knowledge from facts and suppositions. As already mentioned, this is usually a subactivity of a more general task of problem solving, and the programs or KS components that perform in this way are called inference engines.

The most common types of existing inference methodologies are logical ones. A simple example is modus ponens, i.e., from p -> q and p, one may conclude q. By such scheme, the result is always true in any interpretation in which the premises are true. A very important subclass of logical inference is based on the resolution principle [Ro65], which was briefly discussed in section 3.3.1.

The most important aspect of the inference process is, however, not the inference methodology used but the kind of control or guidance that is available to direct the process to the desired conclusion [He87]. Such control mechanisms are crucial since, in most cases, the number of possible inferences at each particular time is vastly larger than the number of inferences that actually contribute to the problem's solution. For this reason, we concentrate in this section simply on the significant mechanisms that are used to control inference processes. For a readable account of detailed studies of logical inference methodologies in AI, we refer to either [CL71], [Lo78], or [WOLB84].

In the following description, we are going to use the term rule, which may be interpreted in many different forms: for example, as a method for deriving conclusions by means of modus ponens; as a formula in implicative form, i.e., A1 & A2 & ... & An -> B, which is generally expressed in an "if-then" form, etc. Since this last form is the most common in KS (see section 3.3.3), the reader should be conscious of this construct while reading the rest of this section.

The simplest way to control the application of rules acts as follows [Fr86]:

(1)   Evaluate the condition part of the rules with respect to the current state of the KB, identifying the applicable ones (applicable are those whose conditions are evaluated to be true).

(2)   If no applicable rule exists, terminate with failure. Otherwise, choose anyone and execute its action part.

(3)   If the goal has been achieved terminate with success, else return to (1).

Such an approach is said to be data-driven since the KB state is used as the basis for the identification of the applicable rules. Furthermore, it is said to be non-deterministic due to the arbitrary selection of the rule to be executed in the second step. Mechanisms used to identify applicable rules are denoted inference strategies [Pu86b]. Among these, data-driven and goal-driven are the most common. The mechanisms used to determine the rule to be executed are called conflict resolution strategies and are frequently further divided in search strategies and conflict solving strategies. In the following, we discuss the inference strategies and then the conflict resolution ones.

3.4.1 Inference Strategies

3.4.1.1 Forward Reasoning

The forward reasoning approach is also known as data-driven, bottom-up, forward chaining or antecedent reasoning. As mentioned above, whether a rule is applicable or not is determined by the data describing the current state of the KB. Thus, the inference process starts with an initial KB state and generates intermediate steps (or new KB states) by applying rules that change the previous state. When one of these intermediate states matches the goal, the problem is solved. This process is illustrated in figure 3.7 where the goal is achieved by successively applying rules R4, R8 and R17.

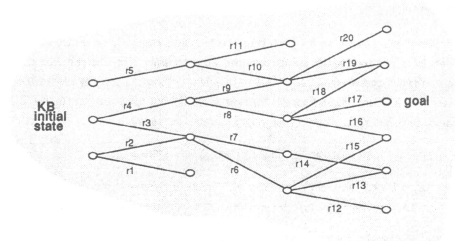

Figure 3.7: Example of forward reasoning process

As one can imagine, forward reasoning tends to generate very many intermediate states since some of the rules being executed are totally unrelated to the problem at hand. However, this strategy, in spite of its possibly enormous inefficiency, is very appropriate in situations in which the goal cannot be easily specified. This is, for example, the case in chess, where the goal is to make the best move in each game step. In such a situation, the best move can only be found by a form of evaluation that analyses the relative merit of intermediate states. For this reason, it is necessary to derive a lot of such states in order to compare one to another.

Other important situations in which this approach is highly recommended are in finding conse-quences of a particular state, i.e., one is interested in knowing what can be derived, based on a particular assertion. This is, for example, the case in medical diagnosis where the XPS or doctor should generate many suspicions about diseases based on identified symptoms. Examples of XPS that use this strategy are EXPERT [KW82,We78,WK79], R1 [Mc82,MB84,Mc80a,MS81], and PDS [FLK83] and are illustrated in table 3.5.

3.4.1.2 Backward Reasoning

This approach is also known as goal-driven, top down, backward chaining, or consequent reasoning.

The idea behind this strategy is to focus only on rules that are relevant to the problem at hand. As such, it starts with the goal specification and tries to find rules whose conclusions match this goal. After finding such rules, it formulates as new goals the problems of satisfying the rule conditions in order to apply them. Certainly, if there are several rules that match the current goal, the system has to decide which one it will try first, just as in the case of forward reasoning, i.e., by exploiting some conflict resolution strategy. Since a rule frequently has many conclusions, the process of satisfying a goal is usually transformed into the problem of satisfying many subgoals. In this respect, the goal is fulfilled when all its subgoals are satisfied, i.e., when they match some assertion of the KB.

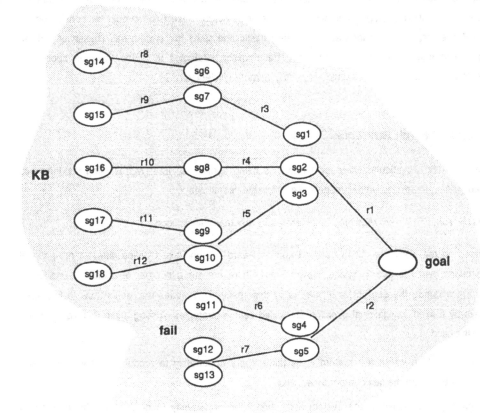

Figure 3.8: Example of backward reasoning process

Figure 3.8 shows a backward reasoning process in which the goal is fulfilled after the application of some rules and the satisfaction of the subgoals sg14, sg15, sg16, sg17, and sg18.

As one can observe, backward reasoning tends to generate less intermediate states than forward reasoning does since only rules that potentially contribute to the goal are applied. This is the strategy usually applied to check out particular hypothesis (possibly generated by forward reasoning) since, in these cases, the goal (i.e., such hypothesis) has already been well specified.

The best example of XPS using this approach is MYCIN [Sh76,DBS77,BS84] (see table 3.5).

3.4.2 Conflict Resolution Strategies

As pointed out above, at any given time, both backward and forward reasoning may have several rules for making the next inference step. The decision as to which rule to take is determined by a conflict resolution strategy, that defines the order in which these rules should be considered. In our first example, this order was a nondeterministic one since the system has chosen any of the applicable rules. Obviously, by exploiting deterministic strategies to define this rule application order, an inference process should reach its goal more efficiently.

3.4.2.1 Search Strategies

Basically, as a particular inference strategy is being applied, a "tree" representing the inference steps will be generated. In this respect, we define the search space

"as the sum of all trees that may be generated by any inference process".

Based on the above definition, forward and backward reasoning just define different navigational directions over the search space. Nevertheless, there are still a number of additional choices to be made during the search for a "way" over this space. Techniques that define how to find such ways by a fixed navigational direction are called search strategies. Among these techniques, there are the blind ones:

- depth-first, in which the system firstly takes every opportunity to produce a new intermediate state based on the last one produced, and

- breadth-first, in which the system firstly takes the opportunity to produce all the new states from a previous one.

They are called blind because they make no use of the characteristics of the generated states which may reflect some of their merits to contribute to the goal at hand.

As opposed to these, heuristic search gives the nodes of the search tree special weights that indicate their contribution to the goal and then choose the rule of highest usefulness. Usually, this kind of search strategy exhibits better performance than depth- or breadth-first because they make use of some problem specific information. This is quite an obvious observation. Heuristic search is the approach that is most similar to the way people search their problem space. Note that humans do not search without regard to the particular goal to be achieved. Nevertheless, all three search strategies have been combined with forward and backward reasoning to solve problems in different KS application areas. The result of such a combination is partially illustrated in figure 3.9.

3.4.2.2 Conflict Solving Strategies

This class of strategies is used to complete the decision of the search strategy in the case where it is not deterministic enough. For example, a left-most conflict solving would, when combined with depth-first, define a left-most depth-first search strategy. That is, the inference process would start at the root of the search tree and work down the left-most branch to the end node before embarking on any other branch.

Other examples of conflict solving strategies may include:

- select the right-most rule,
- choose rules arbitrarily,
- use heuristics to select them, and
- apply the first rule identified.

3.5 Problem Solving Strategies

In the previous section, we discussed some techniques for solving problems that, with exception of heuristic search, do not take any particular characteristic of the problem at hand into account in order to find out solutions. Both inference strategies take either the initial state of the KB or the goal to be achieved and begin to make conclusions in a blind sense, hoping to reach either the goal or the KB assertions in an acceptable time.

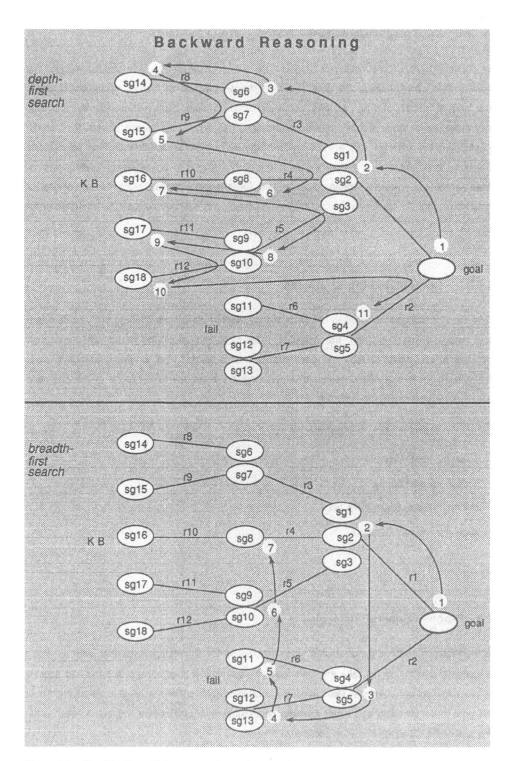

Figure 3.9a: Combination of inference and search strategies

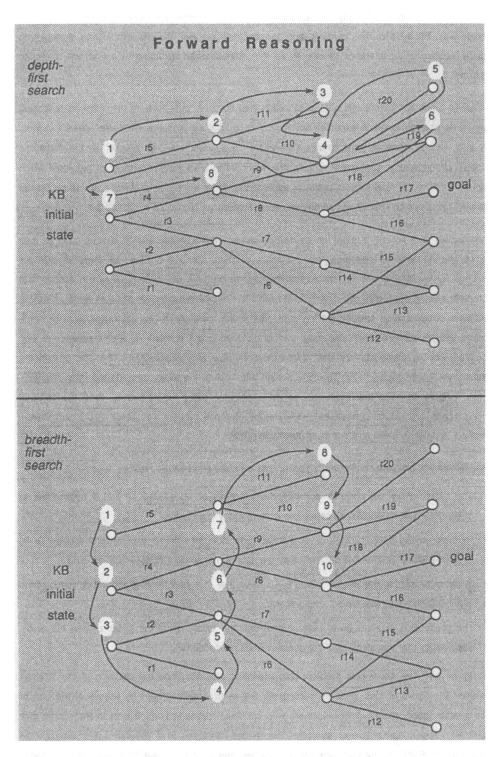

Figure 3.9b: Combination of inference and search strategies

As shown in chapter 2.3, only conclusion making is not sufficient to solve problems in an adequate way. Because of this, humans, and consequently KS too, use problem solving strategies to guide sequences of inference processes so that solutions can be found in a fast and adequate manner.

Actually, since computers are quite a bit faster than humans, pure forward or backward reasoning would be enough to reach expected solutions very quickly for problems with small search spaces. In such cases, the whole time spent on irrelevant conclusions would be masked by the machine's speed. Unfortunately, such small spaces are restricted to a very small number of problems which do not have much relevance in practical applications. Most KS problem classes are characterized by very large search spaces and some other complications as discussed in section 3.1.

The choice of a solving strategy is affected by characteristics of the search spaces such as their sizes, the reliability of their data, the availability of abstractions, etc. Since all these aspects are defined by the problem to be solved and not by the domain, (as already shown in section 2.3) problem solving strategies are closely related to the KS problem classes. In other words, they are problem or application specific solving strategies which, contrary to the neutral problem or application independent inference strategies, cannot be used in any domain. As a consequence of this, problem solving strategies are one of the most variable characteristics of XPS and one of the most investigated topics in AI. The idea behind this field is, therefore, to guide the reasoning process, keeping in mind that inference, as the application independent activity, is at the heart of this process and failure to organize sequences of inference properly can result in problem solvers that are hopelessly inefficient, naive, or unreliable [St82].

The difficulty of problem solving strategies increases in four ways [Ha84,Ha87]:

- The system may not possess accurate data sources or knowledge so that it might have to make assumptions which may cause it to explore many false paths.
- By time-varying data the system must base some decisions on its expectations and revise its decisions when the changes performed on the data do not confirm its assumptions.
- In some problems, the search space is so large that it is hard to find alternative formulations of the search space that simplify the problem.
- The elimination of alternatives may compromise the efficiency of the system when the methods available for this elimination are complex and time consuming.

In figure 3.10, we show how problem characteristics may influence the decision of the strategy to use. The figure divides these characteristics first in two major groups by means of the size of the search space. It then combines them with additional difficulties which lead to the choice of a particular design description or strategy. The reader interested in a detailed explanation should see [St82 or St83]. In the following, we only discuss the strategies useful for large search spaces since these are the most frequent in KS problem classes. For examples of XPS using such strategies see table 3.5.

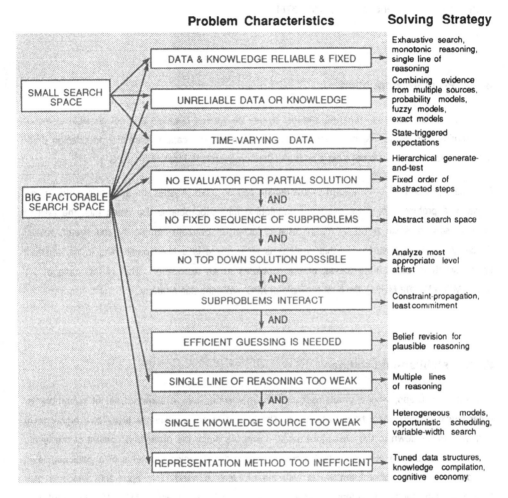

Figure 3.10: The influence of problem characteristics by the choice of a solving strategy
[Ha84,Ha87]

3.5.1 Generate-and-Test

Generate-and-test, also called reasoning by elimination, translates the idea of considering all possible solutions to a particular goal, and rules out those with low plausibility. The idea behind this strategy is to prune the search space as early as possible so that the system can reduce its search activities. To do this, the knowledge engineer must partition the search space in such a way that early pruning can be achieved. The difficulty often found in this approach is that sometimes there is no practical way to consider all possible solutions to the goal at hand. DENDRAL [BSF69,LBFL80,FBL71,BF78] is the best known XPS that uses generate-and-test to perform its interpretations. Another example is GA1 [St78].

3.5.2 Problem-Reduction

In some problem classes, generate-and-test cannot be applied because it is not possible to evaluate solutions since they do not exist. This is, for example, the case in planning and design problems in which the plans do not exist a prior and their creation is the task of the XPS.

In these types of problems, a form of abstraction can be used. Abstraction emphasizes the importance of a problem and its subsequent partitioning into subproblems. By doing this, the task of problem solving is simplified by means of a reduction of problem complexity and search space. Certainly, the best case to use this strategy is when there is a fixed partitioning in the abstract space which is appropriate for all of the problems in an application. This is the case of R1 [Mc82,MB84,Mc80a,MS81], the best example of XPS exploiting this strategy.

3.5.3 Establish-and-Refine

In application areas, whose problems cannot be partitioned into a standard set of subproblems, other levels of abstraction have to be used. The idea is to solve problems firstly at a higher level and then move down to the next more detailed one. As such, the order and content of the levels (i.e., its subproblems) are predefined. However, the order in which problems of a particular level are partitioned into subproblem varies with the problem at hand. This approach, which is also known as top down refinement, is used by various XPS from which MDX [CM83,Ch79] and ABSTRIPS [Sa74] are good examples.

3.5.4 Hypothesize-and-Test

The previous strategies work out problems by using a kind of abstraction hierarchy whose levels are the steps of the solving process. Particularly, the last one allows a variation of problem partitioning sequences within the levels, but it requires a top down solution. In some application areas, from which the class of diagnosis is the best example, problems cannot always be solved top down. In such classes, it is often most appropriate to solve problems at a lower level first and then to investigate the higher levels of the problem solving abstraction hierarchy. In the diagnosis case, the idea behind this approach is to analyze the diagnose (general or specific) that is the most suspicious one at each particular time. This may still be viewed as a hierarchical problem solution which, however, may now start at any level of the hierarchy. Contrary to the previous strategies, this demands the existence of knowledge to produce suspicions that are generated in a previous hypothesize phase, following a test phase as described above. Examples of XPS applying it are PROSPECTOR [HDE78,DR84,Ga82], MODIS [Bo83], PIP [PGKS76], and MED2 [Pu86a].

3.5.5 Constraint-Propagation

The last three strategies assume that certain types of decision should always be made at the same point or at a particular level of abstraction, and/or that subproblems are independent of each other. Some problem classes do not allow, however, the making of decisions in a predefined order due to lack of data. Others possess subproblems whose decisions may turn out to be inconsistent because of other decisions made in subsequent subproblems. In such cases, decision making must be coordinated with the availability of data and postponed as long as possible. The basic idea behind this is that the search space should not be reduced arbitrarily or prematurely but only when there is enough information to assume that some part of it can be eliminated with security. This strategy, which is best found in MOLGEN [St81a,St81b,Fr79,Ma77] and NOAH [Sa77], is also called least commitment.

3.5.6 Guessing

Up until now, all previous strategies assume that it is always possible to make decisions at any point in the problem solving process. However, there are circumstances in which decision making is not possible so that an XPS has to guess. The difficulty with guessing is that sometimes the system makes wrong guesses. In such cases, an identification of them as well as an efficient recovery from them must be performed. There are various approaches to be used here. The simplest ones are backtracking and theories for dealing with uncertainty. In the last few years, the use of non-monotonic reasoning to construct the so-called belief-revision or truth-maintenance systems has been proposed [Do79,dK86,Mc83,MS83] that keep inferred information together with the guess used to derive it. In these systems, when a guess turns out to be inconsistent, the whole information derived from it is then automatically withdrawn. An example of an XPS using this approach is EL [SS77a]. Recently, the XPS building tool KEE [FK85] has been expanded with a truth-maintenance component [Fi88]. It is likely that all future XPS will make use of this technique.

3.5.7 Multiple Lines of Reasoning

When problems are very complex, experts generally use multiple lines of reasoning to provide different views of the problem so that they can take advantage of the particular strengths of the different views to solve the problem. This approach is also used by XPS that solve the problem at hand by integrating various lines of reasoning in such a form that the weak points in one line are covered by strong points of others. The difficulty associated with this approach is knowing how to create adequate views and to combine them appropriately.

XPS	application domain	developed at/in		problem class	problem solving strategy
ABSTRIPS	planning robot actions	SRI Int.	1974	planning	establish-and-refine
DENDRAL	mass spectroscopy	Stanford	1969	interpretation	generate-and-test
EL	analysis of electrical circuits	MIT	1976	interpretation	guessing + backtracking
EXPERT	glaucoma	Rutgers	1976	diagnosis	pure forward reasoning
GA1	mass spectroscopy	Stanford	1976	interpretation	generate-and-test
HEARSAY-II	speech recognition	Carnegie-Mellon	1976	interpretation	blackboard architecture
MDX	liver diseases	Columbus/Ohio	1979	diagnosis	establish-and-refine
MED2	internal medicine	Kaisers-lautern	1986	diagnosis	hypothesize-and-test
MODIS	fault-finding in motor	Kaisers-lautern	1983	diagnosis	hypothesize-and-test
MOLGEN	experiments in molecular genetics	Stanford	1979	planning	constraint-propagation
MYCIN	infectious blood diseases	Stanford	1976	diagnosis	pure backward reasoning
NOAH	planning robot actions	SRI Int.	1975	planning	constraint-propagation
PDS	process diagnosis of machines	Carnegie-Mellon	1983	diagnosis	pure forward reasoning
PIP	kidney malfunctions	MIT	1976	simulation	hypothesize-and-test
PUFF	analysis of lung tests	Stanford	1981	interpretation	pure backward reasoning
PROSPECTOR	mineral exploration	SRI Int.	1976	interpretation	hypothesize-and-test
R1	computer configuration	Carnegie-Mellon	1980	design	problem-reduction

Table 3.5: Realization of problem solving strategies in some XPS

3.5.8 Multiple Sources of Knowledge

Several very complex problems are best solved not by a single expert but by a group of them. In such cases, each expert makes use of his own knowledge to analyze a different aspect of the problem. This approach is also used in XPS which exploit the so-called blackboard architecture [Ha85] to control the communication between the different XPS integrated to solve the problem. The best example of the use of this approach is given by HEARSAY-II [EHLR80].

4. Approaches Towards KB Management

"For years it remained little more than a bold experiment, an avant-garde technology with matchless capabilities but with painfully restricted applications. Since 1981, however, the emerging field of expert and knowledge-based systems has changed dramatically. No longer the exclusive property of diagnosticians and a few other medical specialists, the systems are finally starting to broaden their user base and wriggle their way into mainstream, commercial applications. Like infants taking their first halting steps, expert and knowledge-based systems are slowly toddling out of basic research laboratories and making places for themselves in big business " [Be84a].

The above observation translates the idea that knowledge engineering faces a promising but still a very long road; promising because of its first successful applications, and long since the confrontation with the practical world has just begun.

Most KS mentioned in the previous chapters were successful research prototypes, however, without much practical significance. Up to the beginning of this decade, real world KS were few and concentrated on restricted problems of some special application areas. Most commonly, they were diagnosis KS, from which those exploited for medical consultations have shown the best feasibility.

Since the early 1980's, however, these few applications have made clear the practical as well as the economic importance of the field, provoking the occurrence of a number of significant events with the purpose of accelerating the field's development:

- In Japan, the Ministry of International Trade and Industry launched a US $500 million, 10 year program for the development of fifth-generation computers based on the belief that the country's future economic viability requires leadership in KS technology [FM83].

- The European Economic Community set up the ESPRIT program funding the development of a necessary infrastructure for this technology [ES85].

- In the USA, the Department of Defense claimed that KS would become the front line of US defense in the 1990's and initiated a US $500 million, five year strategic knowledge engineering program.

- A major push forward in KS technology has also been determined by the British Government, following a recommendation by the UK's Alvey Commission.

- In Germany, similar pushes have been enacted with the foundation of several AI research centers dispersed over the country [CM88].

The acceleration of KS development revealed the enormous size of the field for potential applications, stimulating rapidly the introduction of KS in the marketplace. However, the diversification of KS as real world applications brought new demands which exceeded the field's ability to supply them. KS were faced with problems of managing very large volumes of knowledge, for which they were not prepared. In other words, it became clear that expressiveness and exactness to represent human knowledge were not sufficient to make KS a really widely applicable technology. The growing demands on managing the KB appropriately required the following [Ma86a]:

Efficient management of large KB

Early KS were characterized by a large variety, but a small quantity of knowledge. For this reason, they emphasized the richness, flexibility, and the accuracy of the KR schemes and ignored the efficient access and manipulation of the KB contents [VCJ84]. Mostly, KS applied very simple search algorithms (e.g., sequential search) and delegated all KB management tasks to the programming language interpreter being used. Nevertheless, the inefficiency of knowledge handling was not a critical issue because it was compensated by the small sizes of the KB, which could be kept in virtual memory.

However, real world applications require the use of large amounts of knowledge for solving problems. KB contents exceed in these cases virtual memory sizes so that they must be maintained on secondary storage devices. As a consequence, inefficiency in knowledge management becomes apparent and critical, restricting KS applicability significantly.

We have investigated the case of diagnosis XPS [Pu83,Pu84,Pu86a,Bo83] which delegate all KB management tasks to the LISP interpreter [Wi84a,SG84]. In the investigated systems, KB contents are represented by means of frames, which (because they have been mapped to LISP objects) are accessed only by two LISP operations "getproperty" and "putproperty" (i.e., get slot of a frame and put frame slot). As consequences of this realization, KB accesses are mainly to tiny granules, referring to individual slots of the frames rather than to the frame as a whole. Hence, during XPS consultation, an excessive number of KB accesses are necessary since a very small amount of knowledge is provided in each access. For example, a sequence of accesses to the slots of a frame is executed when the whole object is needed.

The results of our investigations showed that when KB are moved from virtual memory onto secondary storage devices, making apparent the inefficient knowledge management of the XPS , the performance of the system may worsen by a factor of approximately 170 [Ma86a,St86].

It is important to observe here that most existing KS present KB management schemes very similar to the investigated one. The majority of the existing KS are LISP-based and delegate their management tasks to this interpreter. Other KS, from among which PROLOG-based XPS are the best examples, should perform badly even when large KB are kept in virtual memory since their programming language interpreter manages the KB much more inefficiently than LISP

[Ba87b,AB85,Ca84]. For these reasons, KS technology, at best, might be exploited as long as KB fits into virtual memory.

New inference mechanisms

Existing inference mechanisms have been designed taking into account the fact that accesses to KB contents are not time consuming. However, when KB are resident on secondary storage, this is no longer valid. For example, searching applicable rules sequentially during an inference process turns out in such cases to be computationally intolerable. Therefore, the application of KS as real world systems requires the development of novel inference mechanisms based on the new circumstances of the running environment.

Adequate multi-user operation

In real world applications, we often find specialists interacting with distinct aspects of information. This is particularly evident in design problems, where it is very common to find many engineers working together on the development of a new product. In such environments, it is necessary to share KB among several users in order to permit and support design interactions. Unfortunately, most existing KS do not provide facilities for sharing the KB among several applications. When multi-user operation is necessary, each user has his own private copy of the KB so that design interactions can only be statically performed. Additionally, the redundancy of knowledge due to many copies of the KB results in waste of storage space and may cause consistency problems while KB are having their contents modified. These points lead to a hindrance of KS usage in such environments.

Suitability for server/workstation environments

KS typically require interactive computing environments. Nowadays, powerful workstations offer tailored support for such use so that it is possible to have several users being served by the same KS running on different workstations. Knowledge is however maintained centralized. For this reason, workstations are connected with a central processor complex (server) in which the KB is kept. In such an environment, knowledge is therefore extracted from the public KB and transferred to the workstation to be exploited for solving problems during KS processing. Clearly, this demands KS ensuring

- minimal communication between workstation and server,
- minimal volume of knowledge transfer, and
- avoidance of duplicated work.

High reliability and availability

A lot of environments require the use of systems that are continuously available and present a very high reliability since their application demands real time reactions often associated with dangerous situations. This is the case of the problem class of monitoring.

Reliability basically means fault tolerance. That is, if the KS fails, the operating system goes down, the computer crashes, or some storage device holding parts of the KB becomes inoperable, after restarting, KS must present a well-defined KB state which should be up-to-date and logically consistent [HR83a]. Availability means being in a continuous operable state.

Existing KS do not provide any mechanisms for increasing either their reliability or their availability. Usually, they do not assume any responsibility for controlling operation correctness, delegating all related tasks to the operating system. Consequently, they cannot be applied in production environments since they do not guarantee that they operate continuously nor that their functions are performed correctly if a fault interrupts their operation in an uncontrolled fashion. This is particularly reflected in the inexistence of monitoring KS (see section 3.1).

Distribution of the knowledge base

In order to achieve better performance and availability, KS should allow a distribution of their tasks and of the KB across multiple powerful computing modules. This is essential in applications involving a network of different locations which are geographically dispersed and only connected via some kind of communication net. KB distribution combines in such cases

- efficiency of processing since knowledge is stored close to the point where it is most commonly used, with

- increased accessibility since it is possible to access knowledge kept in different locations via the communication link.

Knowledge independence

Knowledge independence can be defined as the immunity of KS to changes in the organizational and access techniques of the KB. The basic idea behind this is to isolate KS programs from the representation of the knowledge. This permits lower KS components (i.e., those responsible for the KB management) to choose appropriate internal data structures and efficient access strategies to respectively keep and manipulate the knowledge as well as to change both of them at any time without affecting the higher KS components.

Most present-day KS do not provide this concept, being therefore knowledge dependent. In such KS, the information about the organization and access techniques of the KB are embedded in the program's code. As a consequence,

- changing the storage structures,

- modifying access paths,

- introducing new data structures more appropriate for the KB maintenance, or

- applying new techniques for accessing stored knowledge more efficiently

cannot be carried out without affecting KS programs, probably drastically. The thought of changing the KR scheme used, for example, from frames to semantic networks is considered a heresy since this means throwing the entire KS away and implementing a new one.

Knowledge dependence is particular critical in XPS tools and shells which, like any other computer system, should be continuously ameliorated. In such systems, improvements are, however, very limited since there is already a lot of implemented KS which are going to be affected by these changes. In order to support knowledge independence, KS must be strictly designed with a kind of knowledge representation concealing principle to guarantee local confinement of all modifications and improvements throughout the system lifetime.

The new KS requirements discussed above made clear as early as at the beginning of this decade, as KS started to leave the laboratories, that the applicability of knowledge engineering could turn out to be very limited if the growing demands on managing the KB appropriately and above all efficiently were not fulfilled. The search for solutions to these requirements lead to analogous considerations which 25 years ago gave the impulse for the development of Data Base Management Systems (DBMS) [HR83a]. This development was (and still is) stimulated by the rapidly growing demands of data management tasks in commercial applications. Since file management systems do not support these tasks conveniently, their shortcomings triggered the design and implementation of DBMS as a separate independent system where data management tasks are implemented in an efficient and appropriate manner. Since the management requirements were very similar in all applications, the corresponding tasks could be removed from the applications and delegated to the DBMS without any difficulty. So, the idea of data models was born [Br84] which, in turn, brought forth the notion of data independence [Se73]. The need for high-level user interfaces [Ch76] as well as for system enforced integrity control [EC75] was recognized.

Like the solution found for commercial applications, it became clear that the answer to the KS confrontation with new knowledge management requirements was also the delegation of management tasks to a separate and independent system, where they can be achieved in an efficient and adequate way.

In this chapter, we investigate different approaches for supporting KB management which, over the years, have converged to the idea of developing a new generation of systems for this purpose. These approaches are divided into two main groups, which we respectively denote homogenous and heterogeneous. Into the homogenous group fall the proposals based on single existing systems such as DBMS and XPS tools or on extensions of them. On the other hand, the heterogeneous group refers to proposals based on the cooperation of at least two distinct systems [MW84]. Before exploring these different approaches, we collect together the functions to be provided by such systems as well as show how KS architecture should turn out to be in this new environment.

4.1 Knowledge Management Requirements

Systems for knowledge management should integrate three different classes of functions which support the means for

- modeling the knowledge involved with a particular application, that is, constructing a KB,

- knowledge manipulation, i.e., exploiting KB contents to solve problems, and

- knowledge or KB maintenance, e.g., guaranteeing integrity control, efficiency, etc.

Clearly, such systems can only undertake tasks whose execution does not require any information about the particular application being supported. As such, they can only support KS operations that are application and problem class independent, leaving the dependent ones to be implemented in the KS themselves. In the light of the KS architecture and working methods discussed in chapter 3, this means the support of all functions provided by the KB and inference engine components, i.e., those associated with KR schemes. Problem solving strategies as well as KS interfaces are closely related to the characteristics of the real world applications and their problem classes and are, for this reason, to be kept within the KS. (Note that the tasks of the problem solving component have therefore been divided between KS and the system for knowledge management). Consequently, in this new management environment, KS present the overall system organization and architecture shown in figure 4.1.

Considering first of all the functions for the KB construction support, we can argue that they are *dictated by the model of KS development*. As such, systems for knowledge management should first of all provide *means for supporting the incremental KS construction process*. Since knowledge modeling is at the heart of this process, expressiveness and exactness to represent knowledge plays a central role in this context. In other words, such systems should

- offer KR schemes that permit an appropriate representation of all types of knowledge, and

- allow a description of knowledge which is independent of the application programs.

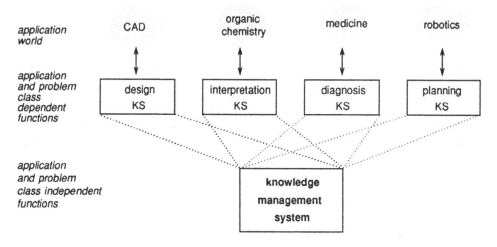

a) overall system organization

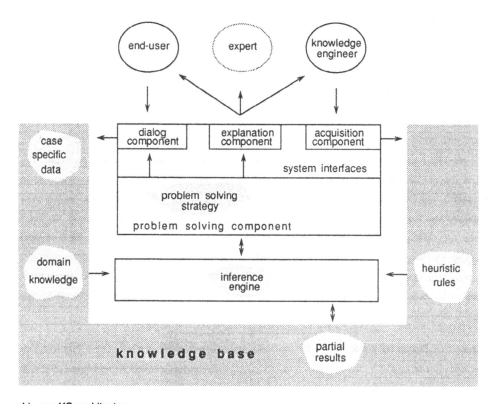

b) new KS architecture

Figure 4.1: Overall KS architecture and organization with independent KB management

It is important to observe here that this first class of functions is very similar to the purposes of existing XPS tools. These software packages embody functions to support XPS construction, reducing its development effort. Generally, they offer various KR schemes permitting quite an exact knowledge representation (see section 3.2.3.2). Furthermore, knowledge modeling functions are partially linked with the purposes of data models by means of knowledge independence and the modeling activity itself.

Knowledge manipulation support requires appropriate functions to make use of KB contents to solve problems. Thus, such functions *reflect the effective realization of an appropriate set of operations offered by KR schemes*. This set should include at least operations for

- storing,

- retrieving, and

- deriving new knowledge.

Its effective realization requires

- exhibiting some measure of isolation of representational aspects from the application, i.e., knowledge independence, and

- developing new inference mechanisms.

As such, this class of functions is related to the operations provided by XPS tools. Nevertheless, they are strongly dictated by efficient and adequate implementation requirements which constitute the last class of functions. Hence, they should reflect internal DBMS aspects as systems that very efficiently implement the tools associated with a data model [Br84].

Considering the last class of functions, we argue that they are mostly *dictated by the growing demands on managing the KB adequately*. As already discussed, their requirements are closely related to DBMS purposes and include, for this reason, features to:

- achieve efficiency translated by the design and implementation of suitable constructs to support knowledge modeling and manipulation operations such as storage structures, access techniques, etc.,

- support multi-user operation,

- guarantee the maintenance of the semantic integrity of the KB,

- exhibit high availability, and

- permit KB distribution.

Summarizing the above discussion, we can argue that the characteristics of the systems for knowledge management are dictated, on one hand, by knowledge engineering features aimed above all at the improvement of expressiveness and, on the other hand, by DBMS features stimulated principally by the improvement of efficiency.

4.2 Homogenous Approaches

4.2.1 Conventional Database Systems

As already mentioned, the development of DBMS during the last 25 years has been stimulated by the rapidly growing demands of commercial applications [HR83a]. In course of this development, three different types of data models (i.e., relational, hierarchical, and network-oriented) [Da83] have gained acceptance as DBMS interfaces for the application world. These models, just like KR schemes, provide the conceptual basis for thinking about commercial applications. They are also characterized by a collection of constructs with corresponding semantics and some operations to work with these constructs. As such, data models define the necessary concepts that help one to consider and express

- static properties such as objects, attributes, and relationships between objects,

- dynamic properties such as operations on objects and sequences of operations (e.g., to form transactions), and

- integrity rules about objects and operations [Br84].

Hence, all data model constructs and operations fall into one of these three categories. In representing an application, static properties are defined in a DB schema, whereas dynamic ones are defined as specifications for transactions and queries. A schema contains the sum of all object type specifications including attributes, relationships, and static constraints. Associated with a DB schema definition there is a data repository or database, where the collection of object instances are stored. An application has access only to the DB contents, which is achieved by using predefined operations offered by the data model. Transactions are generally used to define application events. They consist of a collection of operations which transform the DB contents from one logically consistent state to another logically consistent state [HR83a].

These observations should make clear the important role played by data models in the context of DBMS. Nevertheless, the corresponding modeling capability does not always turns out to be the crucial point taken into consideration when applying these systems. Actually, DBMS differ from other data managing systems in other characteristics as well. These include:

- efficient management of large data repositories,

- adequate support of multi-user operation,

- guarantee of data persistency,

- maintenance of data integrity,

- access control,

- high reliability and availability,

- means to support DB distribution, and

- high degree of data independence.

As such, in looking for systems to undertake knowledge management tasks, the KS research community arrived directly at the idea of applying DBMS for this purpose. Surely, when considering only knowledge maintenance, one may argue that DBMS are ideal for this task. The deficiencies found in KS for real world applications correspond exactly to the DBMS features. However, as shown in the previous section systems for knowledge management should also adequately support knowledge modeling and knowledge manipulation activities.

4.2.1.1 DBMS-based Knowledge Modeling

Considering the modeling activity, it is important to remember that DBMS were developed for applications in private business and public administration. Such applications present particular characteristics, which have been determining the lines of DBMS development over the last two decades. As a consequence, DBMS turned out to be oriented towards these special demands so that their application in practice assumes a collection of premises, corresponding to the particularities of the commercial world. These premises are the following [Hä88b,Re87]:

I. Certain degree of knowledge about objects' structure
DB schema specification presupposes the existence of knowledge about the structure of the application objects, otherwise it is not possible to define the object types, their attributes, integrity constraints, and relationships to other object types. For this reason, before building DB schemas, DB users should make a detailed analysis of the application world, reflecting upon the existing objects in order to determine exactly what they look like.

II. Very rare DB schema changes
After building a DB, restricted schema extensions (e.g., defining a new attribute for an object type) are possible but troublesome. Changes to the previously specified object types' structures are also possible but prohibitive since they require a more or less complete restructuring of the DB and an expensive adjustment of the application programs.

III. Rigorous object structuring

Each object instance is associated with a fixed and predefined structure which corresponds to its object type maintained in the DB schema. In other words, an object can only exist if it has an object type implicitly associated with it. As such, the insertion of an object into the DB is subject to the specification of the corresponding object type. Changing such association afterwards is not possible at all, i.e., the type of an object must remain the same for ever.

IV. Uniform and persistent object identification

Objects possess a unequivocal identification (primary key), which is uniform for an object type and is valid as long as the object is stored in the DB.

V. Attributes pertinent and applicable to all instances

The attributes as well as integrity constraints and relationships to other objects defined by an object type must be pertinent and applicable to all its instances. Therefore, the definition of particular attributes, constraints, or relationships for specific instances is typically not supported.

VI. Semantically disjoint object types

The types of the application objects must be semantically disjoint, otherwise a disjunction is forced during the DB schema specification. Moreover, each object instance must have one and only one object type.

VII. Big inhomogeneity among object types in contrast to big homogeneity within an object type

This premise is a consequence of the previous two. Object instances of the same type have exactly the same structure since the complete type specification is applicable to all of them. On the other hand, instances of different types are completely different, since object types are semantically disjoint.

VIII. Single-valued and static attributes only

Object attributes are mostly single-valued. Furthermore, they only represent passive properties of the real world entities. Dynamic properties cannot be expressed as operations of objects (i.e., in the form of attributes). In general, they must be defined outside the DBMS (i.e., in the application program) as operations on the objects by means of DB queries.

IX. No representation of temporal aspects

Attributes of an object express the knowledge about this object at the current time. The maintenance of versions of objects or a kind of history about object changes is not supported.

X. Small amount of data per object

Commonly, the sum of stored data per object instance is small (normally under 1KB).

XI. Few object types and many object instances per type

The number of object types (described in the schema) is very small when compared with the number of instances per type stored in the corresponding DB.

XII. Explicit object types/object instances separation

Object types are maintained in the DB schema and are not treated as objects of the DB. As a consequence, they cannot be manipulated by regular data model operations so that queries about the structure of the objects cannot be formulated.

XIII. Large amount of data per DB

Usually, a DB contains a large data set mostly varying between some MB and some GB.

Examining the above premises, one should be able to see clearly that DBMS do not satisfy management requirements concerning knowledge modeling (see section 4.1).

First of all, they do not provide ways to support the incremental KS construction process. On the contrary, DB applications are built only after the DB schema has been completely and exactly specified. Later on, extensions to the schema are hard to manage, changes of the structures of the objects are typically forbidden, object insertions are limited to the types already defined, and disassociations of objects from types are not possible. In other words, mistakes committed during the DB schema specification might turn out to be so catastrophic that DB users prefer to do without the flexibility of an incremental development.

Secondly, DBMS do allow for an application independent representation which, however, is a long way from being able to exhibit the expressiveness and the flexibility of KR schemes. Data models presume that the application world is quite structured, containing none or at most very few exceptions. The application world of KS directly contradicts this presupposition. Generally, it possesses a large number of object types and a small number of instances per type. Such instances are neither necessarily associated with just one object type nor must they keep these associations unchangeable for ever. They might contradict type specifications so that not all defined attributes, constraints, and relationships are pertinent to every instance. Furthermore, object types are not necessarily disjoint and might be very similar one to another. (Note, for example, those related by the organization principle of generalization found in semantic networks). Finally, object types cannot always directly represent the entities of the application world. For example, in representing complex or composite objects, i.e., those whose internal structures (the components) are also objects of the DB, the information about such objects has to be spread out among several object types. That is, they have to be mapped to a large set of meshed data structures, e.g., tuples connected by (n:m) relationships. As a consequence, operations over them are quite inefficient since they have to be split into thousands of related and serially executed 'tiny' DB operations, during which only rudimentary integrity constraints can be checked [Hä89a].

Additionally, data models only allow for the representation of a restricted view of the world. They do not provide constructs for specifying active properties of objects (as those found in the object-oriented paradigm). They are lacking in organizational principles provided by semantic networks and some frame-based schemes. They do not offer appropriate constructs for representing heuristic knowledge. And they do not permit the specification of meta knowledge as data in the DB. (Note, for example, the restrictive separation between DB and DB schema).

As a consequence of all these aspects, the semantics expressed in the data models are very limited. They provide ways to represent a restricted view of the application objects but without supplying DBS with any information about the existing events in the application world as well as about the sense of object attributes, relationships, or integrity constraints.

4.2.1.2 DBMS-based Knowledge Manipulation

Generally, data models provide primitives to define, manipulate, and query the data stored in the DB. In most existing DBMS, these are condensed into a Data Definition Language (DDL), a Data Manipulation Language (DML), and a Query Language (QL) [Br84]. Actually, the partitioning of these functions into three different languages is not necessary. Many database languages combine both query and manipulation, and others even integrate all three classes of primitives.

Typically, these languages together with their underlying implementation provide flexible and efficient accesses to DB contents, qualifying objects based on attributes or attribute combinations. Good performance can be expected even in the case of high data volumes. Data may be inserted, modified, and deleted with high frequencies also in multi-user mode. In such environments, DBMS guarantee the durability of DB changes, the consistency of the DB, and the isolation of users from each other. Furthermore, they provide mechanisms for access control, authorization, and recovery. Finally, they conceal all aspects of data accesses from the users so that operations simply specify the required set of data without any hints from the user as to how the data can be found [HR83a].

So, DBMS accommodate powerful operational features which are even beyond knowledge manipulation requirements with regard to storage and retrieval. However, considering the derivation of new knowledge, DBMS have only very limited reasoning capabilities. Derivation of new information is usually achieved by evaluating query expressions or view definitions in relational systems [Co70,As76].

A view is a virtual relation; that is, a relation not explicitly stored in the DB, but which is derived from one or more underlying relations. In other words, there is no stored data that directly represents the view per se. Instead, the DBS simply maintains the definition of the view, which specifies how the view is to be derived from the base relations [Da83]. After being defined, a view can be used in the query language in the same way as any other relation except for insertions, deletions, and updates [Da83,Ke81,Ma83]. Since a view is simply a kind of "window" to the DB contents and not a separate copy of them, changes performed on the DB are visible by means of the view. In the same sense, operations on the view should be converted into operations on the real DB. For select operations, such a conversion is always possible. However, the situation is quite different for update operations. For example, in System R [As76] updates through views are only allowed when the view is derived from a single relation. The view cannot be a genuine projection (with elimination of duplicates), neither can it be a join, nor a union, and cannot involve "group by", nor "computed fields" [Da83]. Similar or even more rigorous restrictions are also found in delete and insert operations.

A view corresponds to the goal of a backward reasoning inference process. (Note that both determine the termination criterion for stopping the evaluation process.) Nevertheless, its evaluation occurs in a forward sense since DBS always start it from the base relations. The specification of a pure forward reasoning process, in which no specific goal is known in advance, cannot be achieved in DBS. Such process would mean deriving all possible views based on the actual DB contents. For this reason, there is no way to generate consequences of DB contents (i.e., knowledge that can be derived based on particular assertions) if the user does not previously know the structure of these consequences and specifies the corresponding view.

Furthermore, the view mechanism does not possess the dynamics found in the AI inference processes. Note that during an inference process, the evaluation of rules may provoke changes on the KB, modifying the course of the inference process itself. As opposed to this, views are quite static. There is no way to make the course of their evaluation dependent on the execution of other views, nor on particular states of the DB expressed as a kind of condition for the view evaluation. Additionally, view definitions as well as query expressions are restricted to regular operations over the DB. Since DBMS typically do not provide user access to the schema, there is no way to reason about object structures, to make changes on such structures, to create new object types, or to delete them. Finally, special mechanisms which are often integrated into KS inference features such as belief-revision, certainty factors, contexts, etc. (see chapter 3) are totally disregarded by DBMS.

For all these reasons, we argue that DBMS fulfil only partially knowledge manipulation requirements. They provide very flexible and efficient ways to store and retrieve the explicit knowledge maintained in the DB, but adequate knowledge derivation primitives are simply ignored. (For further discussion about DBMS support for knowledge management see [Hä88b,La83,Ma86a]).

4.2.1.3 Resume

In this section, we have shown that the applicability of DBMS for knowledge management is very limited. DBMS became successful in the support of business and administration, the so-called standard applications; however, they failed to satisfy KS requirements. They might be adequate to satisfy knowledge maintenance requirements but are unable to support knowledge modeling and manipulation in an appropriate manner. The deficiencies of this support may be summarized as follows:

- DBS are inadequate for an incremental KS development environment.

- Classical data models are not appropriate for representing knowledge. They lack expressiveness, semantics, and organizational principles, impose a strict distinction between object types and object instances, and exhibit very weak object-orientation.

- DBMS provide insufficient manipulation support. They have only very limited reasoning capabilities.

- Integrity control mechanisms are too weak. DBMS cannot guarantee an automatic maintenance of complex semantic integrity constraints.

As a matter of fact, existing DBMS are not only unable to support KS. In reality, they also fail to meet the requirements found in a range of other emerging application areas such as CAD/CAM, geographic information management, VLSI design, etc. The inherent causes for this situation were illustrated already at the beginning of the 1980's [Ea80,Si80,Lo81,GP83,Lo83,HR85,Lo85] being pointedly characterized in the hypothesis proposed in [HR83b]:

"The general purpose DBMS are general only for the purpose of commercial applications, and their data models are general only for modelling commercial views of the world."

According to this hypothesis, the failure of DBMS for the support of knowledge management just endorses what most DB researchers already have known since the mid-1980's.

4.2.2 Non-Standard Database Systems

During the last 20 years, DBMS have been regarded as an adequate way of automating record keeping functions for business and administration data processing applications. Nowadays, it is however recognized that DBMS capabilities are needed in many other application areas having typically different requirements and constraints from those found in traditional commercial applications. Examples of such applications occur in engineering areas (CAD/CAM, geography, VLSI-design), AI, and others. As already discussed, attempts to use conventional DBS for these applications have generally failed to provide the required functionality. Furthermore, DBS in such environments do not show satisfactory performance [BMW82,GS82].

In order to eliminate these problems, considerable research efforts have been made to design a new generation of DBMS, the so-called Non-Standard Database Systems (NDBS). Their corresponding data models, denoted data models for non-standard applications or non-standard data models, are substantially more powerful than the classical ones (i.e., hierarchic, network, and relational). They provide much richer structures for representing the application world, incorporating, therefore, a kind of structural object-orientation [Di86,Di87]. This means the support of complex or composite objects, i.e., those whose internal structures (the components) are also objects of the DB. Such support comprises [Mi88a,Hä89b]

- modeling techniques to describe the structures of an object (i.e., its components) as well as the object as an integral entity,

- a corresponding operational semantics, including object management to deal with such complex objects,

- appropriate granulation of data structures and operations to dynamically compose and decompose objects (i.e., dynamic object handling),

- structural integrity checking,

- adequate object manipulation supporting both types of accesses: vertical (i.e., accessing the object as a whole with all constituting components) and horizontal (i.e., accessing objects of the same type), and

- a descriptive language that allows set-oriented processing of sets of heterogeneous records.

Non-standard data models may be classified in two main groups: those that are enhancements of the flat relational model (POSTGRES [RS87] and STARBURST [LMP86]) and new ones addressing the integration of complex object structures (MAD [Mi88a], EXTRA [CDV88], NF2 [SS86,Da86,RKB85], extended relational model [LK84]). Some of them support all the above issues, whereas others only consider some of these. Many of these data models only allow for a hierarchical representation of complex objects, and others support a symmetrical representation (i.e., in both "directions": downwards and upwards) of even recursive network structures.

Because of the large number and differences of such data models, their detailed analysis is beyond the scope of this work. For this reason, the interested reader is referred to [Mi88a,Hä89b,HK87,PM88] for a detailed description of the requirements of these new data models and to [PSSWD87,Si89,SR86] for comments about their implementation.

Considering knowledge management requirements, it should be clear that the improvement brought by these new data models does not eliminate all the deficiencies of DBS for KS. They do provide much richer structures for knowledge representation, which in some sense should contribute to more accurate knowledge modeling; however, they still lack

- KS development support,

- semantics,

- organizational principles,

- elimination of object types/object instances distinction,

- object-orientation,

- knowledge manipulation support, and

- integrity control mechanisms.

In reality, these deficiencies can be roughly expressed as "the lack of an orientation towards the application requirements" in such models. This observation, which was also made in the other non-standard application areas, lead to an architecture of NDBS, the so-called kernel architecture [HR85,Da86,PSSWD87]. In such an architecture (figure 4.2), the required orientation is achieved on the top of the supported data model interface in an additional NDBS component, called application layer (AL).

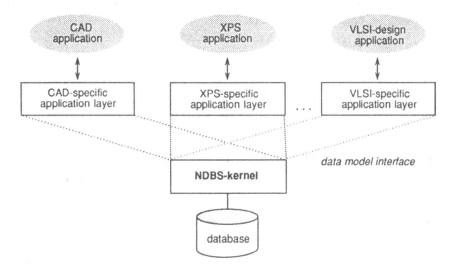

Figure 4.2: Overall architecture of NDBS

The basic idea behind this approach is to keep a strong separation between kernel and AL so that the kernel remains application-independent. That is, it efficiently realizes neutral, yet powerful mechanisms for management support of all types of non-standard application: storage techniques for a variety of object sizes, flexible representation and access techniques, basic integrity features, locking and recovery mechanisms, etc. In other words, the kernel can be viewed as the implementation of a non-standard data model which, in turn, characterizes its external interface. On top of this interface, there is an application-oriented AL, which is responsible for the realization of mechanisms useful for a specific application class. In our case, such an AL should support the above mentioned points (i.e., knowledge modeling and manipulation tasks). The clear division between kernel and AL is necessary for simultaneously using the kernel from different AL, as indicated in figure 4.2. Thus, the interface supported by the AL is at a much higher level than the data model interface. Its orientation is more towards the purpose of its application class, whereas the data model interface offers a more or less neutral support corresponding to the tasks involved with knowledge maintenance. Since these tasks are not only required by KS but by every non-standard application, it seems to be a reasonable approach.

Following this architectural conception, a lot of proposals for the realization of AL began to appear in the last few years. Some of them aim at the fulfillment of the required orientation by means of an AL module containing a set of programs that achieve specific mechanisms for an application class [Fi83]. Others follow the abstract data type (ADT) approach [HS88a], and some other ones address the integration of the object-oriented paradigm into a DBS environment.

The latter lead to the conception of so-called Object-Oriented Data Base Systems (OODBS) which in the last few years have been emerging in the literature as the solution for all requirements of non-standard applications. An overview of the characteristics of OODBS can be found in [Ba88,Di86,Di87], and a detailed survey on existing concepts and projects is provided by [Si89].

Unfortunately, the AL concept as well as the existing proposals for its realization have not yet been elaborated upon enough to permit a well-founded analysis of its applicability and its appropriateness for knowledge management support. There are only immature ideas to be found in the literature, without founded practical experience to confirm the indicated propositions. In some cases, DB researchers are still quarreling about the meaning and constructs of the AL concept (see for example the different opinions and views about OODBS [Si89]) so that the approach has still a long way to go until it may prove of practical significance.

We, in particular, do not believe that any of these existing AL proposals will ever be adequate for KS. It seems to be that not only OODBS but the whole research in the field is only directed by the concepts underlying the object-oriented paradigm. Therefore, they

• neglect KS incremental development support completely,

- try to incorporate the organizational principles of classification and generalization, however, disregard the existence and importance of the other ones,

- still maintain the strict distinction between object types and object instances (in spite of the resultant restrictions), and

- cannot incorporate the dynamism associated with reasoning operations.

Summarizing our ideas, we argue that the NDBS approach is adequate in satisfying knowledge maintenance requirements. NDBS kernels with the corresponding data models are much richer than conventional DBS and should, for this reason, achieve maintenance tasks in a more efficient and effective manner. Furthermore, since knowledge modeling and manipulation tasks are usually achieved at a higher level than knowledge maintenance tasks, NDBS architectural conception seems to be quite advantageous. Nevertheless, existing proposals for AL realization are still far from fulfilling knowledge modeling and manipulation requirements.

4.2.2.1 A Practical Investigation

With the purpose of validating our premises about the appropriateness of the architectural concept of NDBS, we have investigated the applicability of a non-standard data model as a neutral instrument for mapping application-oriented structures and operations at the kernel interface.

For this investigation, we have chosen a simple frame-based representation as an example of an orientation towards KS. Here, we summarize our results, referring to [Ma86b,HMM87] for a detailed description of the performed analysis. In the following, we first give a short overview of the Molecule Atom Data Model (MAD Model) [Mi88a], which together with its NDBS implementation, called PRIMA [Hä88a,HMMS87], served as foundation for our analysis.

Short Notes on MAD

The most primitive constructs of MAD are denoted atoms. They are, in analogy to tuples in the relational model, composed of attributes of various types, have their structure determined by an atom type, and possess an identifier. Atoms represent components of more complex objects, called molecules. The composition as well as the decomposition of molecules are performed dynamically following the specification of a molecule type. A molecule type is a structural composition of constituent atoms among which relationships exist. The specification of relationships is made in attributes of the atom types by using a special attribute type called reference. In MAD, each relationship is symmetrically modeled. That is, for each reference attribute there exists in the pointed atom type a back reference, whose inherent consistency is automatically maintained by the system. MAD allows for a direct representation of all existing relationship types (i.e., 1:1, 1:n, and n:m) achieved by combination of reference with the attribute type set_of. In this sense, atoms together with their references build a kind of atom networks over which special views (i.e., the molecules) may be dynamically defined. Such views (or molecules) may, in turn, be used to construct other more complex molecules, which may even occur recursively. Therefore, the specification of the molecule types can be defined in such a way that they directly allow for an appropriate mapping of the application objects (here frames) to their structures.

The Frame Representation Scheme

As described in section 3.3.4, frames may be viewed as objects containing attributes called slots used to represent either properties of real world entities or relationships between them. In our prototype scheme, each slot possesses name, value, type, and kind that specifies whether the slots were inherited or not. The type indicates whether an attribute represents characteristics of the frame itself or of its members. Characteristics of a frame are defined by the type ownslot whereas those of the members by memberslot. Associated with the slots, there can be aspects used to describe the slot more exactly. Each frame may possess several slots from which two are predefined. The scheme gives these particular two slots the meaning of the organizational axes of classification (member_of) and generalization (subclass_of), therefore permitting slots to be inherited by more specialized frames (see section 3.3.2). In our scheme, only memberslots are inherited since the ownslots represent characteristics of their frames. A frame therefore passes on its memberslots as memberslots to its subclasses and as ownslots to its members. A complete overview of our frame structure is shown in figure 4.3. The figure also illustrates a hierarchy of frame objects representing individuals of comics with their members Pluto, Goofy, Mickey, and Minnie.

```
frame_name
subclass_of:     list of frames
member_of:       list of frames
slot 1: value 1  type 1       kind 1
                 aspect 11    aspect_value 11
                 aspect 12    aspect_value 12
                    :            :
                 aspect 1m    aspect_value 1m
   :
slot n: value n  type n       kind n
                 aspect n1    aspect_value n1
                 aspect n2    aspect_value n2
                    :            :
                 aspect nm    aspect_value nm
```

a) structure of a frame

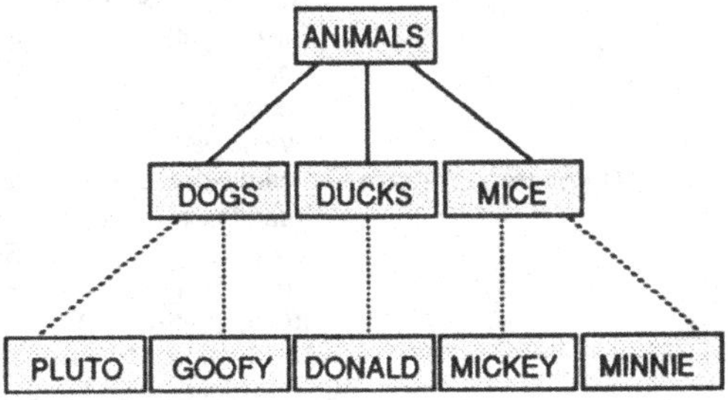

b) a frame hierarchy

Figure 4.3: Overview of the frame scheme

Mapping Frames to MAD Objects

In our frame representation scheme, one may observe the occurrence of three different constructs: frames, slots, and aspects, which are related to each other to compose the frames. From the structural point of view, frames are therefore composed of slots, which, in turn, consist of aspects, suggesting a MAD schema that contains three atom types (corresponding respectively to frames, slots, and aspects) connected by the references has_slots and has_aspects (figure 4.4). The specified schema defines just one aspect occurrence for each slot because aspect specifications have been grouped into one atom type (i.e., aspects) expressed as attributes of it. Additionally, aspect specifications are shared between several slots (think of slots being inherited), preventing redundancy. Organizational axes, as slots with special meanings, are not represented like ordinary slots but as recursive MAD references between the atom type frames. Since for each MAD reference there always exists the back reference, each organizational axis is represented by two reference attributes, namely, is_subclass_of and has_subclasses for generalization, and is_member_of together with has_members for classification.

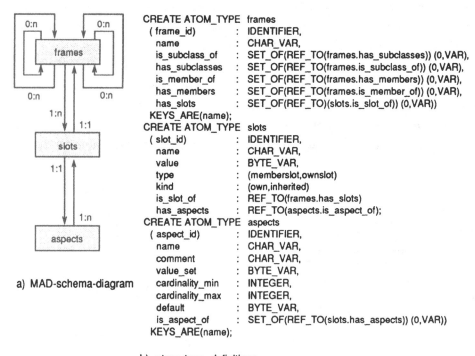

```
CREATE ATOM_TYPE frames
 ( frame_id)          :  IDENTIFIER,
   name               :  CHAR_VAR,
   is_subclass_of     :  SET_OF(REF_TO(frames.has_subclasses)) (0,VAR),
   has_subclasses     :  SET_OF(REF_TO(frames.is_subclass_of)) (0,VAR),
   is_member_of       :  SET_OF(REF_TO(frames.has_members)) (0,VAR),
   has_members        :  SET_OF(REF_TO(frames.is_member_of)) (0,VAR),
   has_slots          :  SET_OF(REF_TO)(slots.is_slot_of)) (0,VAR))
 KEYS_ARE(name);
CREATE ATOM_TYPE slots
 ( slot_id)           :  IDENTIFIER,
   name               :  CHAR_VAR,
   value              :  BYTE_VAR,
   type               :  (memberslot,ownslot)
   kind               :  (own,inherited)
   is_slot_of         :  REF_TO(frames.has_slots)
   has_aspects        :  REF_TO(aspects.is_aspect_of);
CREATE ATOM_TYPE aspects
 ( aspect_id)         :  IDENTIFIER,
   name               :  CHAR_VAR,
   comment            :  CHAR_VAR,
   value_set          :  BYTE_VAR,
   cardinality_min    :  INTEGER,
   cardinality_max    :  INTEGER,
   default            :  BYTE_VAR,
   is_aspect_of       :  SET_OF(REF_TO(slots.has_aspects)) (0,VAR))
 KEYS_ARE(name);
```

a) MAD-schema-diagram

b) atom_type definitions

```
DEFINE MOLECULE_TYPE frame_object
FROM frames-slots-aspects
```

c) frame specification by means of molecules

Figure 4.4: Frame scheme expressed in terms of the MAD-DDL

Mapping Frame Operations

Frame operations can be viewed on one hand as general functions to work on the frames as a whole, and on the other hand operations to directly manipulate slots or aspects exist. Here, we present just two of these operations together with the corresponding MAD statements (for other operations see [Ma86b]).

The first operation, which represents the function of reading a frame, can be directly mapped to one MAD statement as presented in figure 4.5.

Example: Selection of the frame 'goofy'

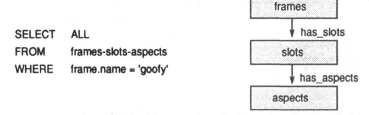

```
SELECT    ALL
FROM      frames-slots-aspects
WHERE     frame.name = 'goofy'
```

Figure 4.5: Selection of a frame expressed in terms of the MAD-DML

The second operation (insertion of a new memberslot) is a much more complex one; for reasons of clarity, it has been achieved in several steps. (For sake of simplicity, we insert the slots without aspects). Since the insertion of a member-slot (in the example habitat in the frame animals) provokes its inheritance by lower frames (i.e., dogs, mice, pluto, mickey, etc.), it is necessary to obtain each of these lower frames before inserting the slot. This is achieved by the first MAD statement shown in figure 4.6, which retrieves the whole hierarchy of frames under the object animal. Such a hierarchy is specified as a recursive molecule composed of the root atom named animals. From this atom, the subordinate classes are selected and used in turn as the root of new hierarchies to select further subclasses. Finally, the members of every class reached are also read. After this, the hierarchy is modified in the application program to reflect the introduction and inheritance of the memberslot habitat, as exemplified in the second step. Following this, the complete frame hierarchy is then updated in the DB via a modify statement. This operation changes the specified molecule in accordance to the given hierarchy, inserting atoms not yet stored (in this case the inherited slots) and modifying the corresponding connections (here the reference to the frames that received the slot just inserted).

Example: Insertion of the member-slot named 'habitat' to the frame called 'animals'

1. Retrieval of the whole subclass hierarchy
   with corresponding member frames

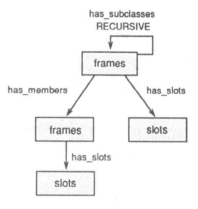

```
SELECT  ALL
FROM    frame-hierarchy
        (frames-(.has_slots-(slots),
                .has_members-(frames).has_slots-(slots))
        (RECURSIVE: frames.has_subclasses-frames))
WHERE   frame-hierarchy.frame(o).name='animals'
```

2. Modification within the application program:
   - addition of the member_slot in the root frame,
     that is the frame named 'animals'
   - inheritance as member slot to all
     subordinate classes
   - inheritance as ownslot to all subordinate members

3. Update of the database:
```
MODIFY  frame_hierarchy
FROM    frame_hierarchy
```

Figure 4.6: Insertion of a member-slot expressed in terms of the MAD-DML

Conclusions

Our investigation shows that the neutral NDBS kernel approach supports an application-independent structural object representation, permitting an effective exploitation of the DBS in several areas. Particularly in the case of KS, the generic constructs offered by non-standard data models (specially MAD) allow for an accurate and efficient mapping of the application-oriented structures. The semantics of such structures remains, however, outside of the NDBS kernel, i.e., in the KS. The main philosophy behind these models is to support a precise representation as well as a dynamic construction of complex objects (here frames), using elementary building blocks that are also represented as objects of the DB. In this sense, a direct and symmetric representation of relationships (including n:m) plays a very important role in this context. For further comments about the adequacy of non-standard data models (specially MAD) for KS see [Mi88b,HMM87].

4.2.3 Deductive Database Systems

In section 4.1, we showed that knowledge management requirements are grouped into three classes of functions from which knowledge maintenance can be well satisfied by DBS (section 4.2.1). Addressing the enrichment of DBS with better representational techniques, research efforts have been directed towards NDBS (section 4.2.2). Aiming at the integration of inferential or deductive capabilities, efforts move towards Deductive Database Systems (DDBS), i.e., *DBS in which new facts may be derived from other facts that are explicitly stored in the DB.*

Actually, every DBS can derive new facts from stored ones. As shown in section 4.2.1, the evaluation of both query expressions as well as view definitions provide DB users with new information. Nevertheless, only those that exhibit richer and more powerful mechanisms than conventional view processing offers will be classed as DDBS. Such mechanisms should focus on the efficient and adequate treatment of at least:

• recursive queries or views,

• negative data (i.e., keeping the negation of particular facts in the DB),

• null values (i.e., data whose value is missing), and

• indefinite data (e.g., one knows that 'q(x) or q(y)' is true, but not whether q(x) is true, q(y) is true or both are true).

Most DDBS are based on enhancements of the relational model viewed through logic [GM78, GMN84]. In this logical formalization, the DB consists of two parts: an extensional DB (EDB) and an intensional DB (IDB). The EDB is the set of all relations and tuples stored explicitly in the DB. As opposed to this, the IDB is the set of virtual relations that can be derived from the EDB. Usually, such virtual relations are defined as rules expressed by horn clauses. Hence, from the viewpoint of conventional DBS, the EDB corresponds to the contents of relations of a DB and the IDB to the defined views.

Every DDBS is constructed from a DB and a deductive component for evaluation of the virtual relations. Depending on the organization and the kind of cooperation existing between DB and deductive component, DDBS might be classified in three main categories:

• Database enhancement

This approach aims at the extension of DBMS capabilities towards deduction, where higher level operators are introduced for this purpose, e.g., fixpoint operators to deal with transitive closure and other recursive rules. Deductive features offered by POSTGRES [SR86] and PROBE [DS86] follow this approach.

• Deductive component enhancement

This second architecture consists of adding to the deductive part (e.g., PROLOG) techniques coming from the DBS world which permit effective access and management of large sets of tuples. This is the case of data access extensions for PROLOG [Pa83,Ch83].

• Coupling

In this approach, a DDBS is constructed by coupling DB and deductive component. Actually, this architecture cannot be considered a homogeneous approach since it consists of a connection between two independent systems. Nevertheless, it is one of the most successful approaches for constructing DDBS. Into this type fall for example DBCL [JV84,JCV84, VCJ83,VCJ84], some systems built at ECRC [GN87], as well as DBPROLOG [Ba87b]: a DDBS we have constructed for investigation purposes, which is described in section 4.3.3.1.

Independent of the category being considered, evaluation of recursive queries has been the most important feature focused on by the development of DDBS. Several proposals for strategies to evaluate recursion have been made (see [BR86] for an overview of them) although minimal or no practical experience about their application in real world DBS exists.

Nevertheless, it can be expected that efficient DBS with extensions of deductive capabilities will soon be available. Clearly, such systems might contribute to give a better support of knowledge manipulation tasks because of the powerful deductive capabilities already mentioned. However, such systems will be unable to support an appropriate modeling of knowledge since the data model provided (i.e., a kind of relational model extension) will still show the same deficiencies found in conventional ones (see section 4.2.1).

4.2.4 Expert System Extensions

Up until to this section, all approaches that we discussed were based on conventional DBS or enhancements of them. Parallel to these, other approaches may be traced by starting with KS technology. Following up this idea, we discuss in this section the use of an existing XPS or KS as the pivot for improvement towards an adequate knowledge management. Other approaches based on XPS tools will be introduced in the next section.

In the extension approach, attempts to deal with the growing demands for an appropriate management of large knowledge volumes are undertaken by improving existing XPS with DBS tasks. This is the concept adhered to most XPS that either have their KB overrunning virtual memory sizes or need to consult existing large DB to solve their problems. In a typical example, PROB-WELL [OL82], an XPS used to determine problems with oil wells, has a very important source of information stored under the IMS database system [Da83]. In another example, STROBE [La83], an XPS for CAD, is being extended to deal with secondary storage management.

This is surely the best strategy for fulfilling restrictions of XPS which have already been constructed since it requires a relatively short-term development. Consequently, it is also not a very expensive approach (considering isolated cases) and permits the implementation of knowledge management tasks that fit exactly and directly the requirements of the particular XPS being extended. However, such extensions result in special-purpose functions for knowledge management which are only appropriate to the particular domain at hand and are not readily generalized. For these reasons, this approach has only a short-term outlook and should be applied as long as general purpose solutions for knowledge management are not available.

4.2.5 Expert System Tools

Expert system tools can be also viewed as an approach towards knowledge management. Actually, they are the best attempt with regard to knowledge modeling and manipulation tasks. As opposed to XPS, tools present more general purpose KR schemes as well as knowledge manipulation operations. Furthermore, they are the only existing systems supporting KS development adequately. Hence, such systems fulfil knowledge modeling and manipulation requirements, but fail, however, to support knowledge maintenance.

Simple mechanisms to allow accesses to DBS may be found in some of the existing commercial tools. These mechanisms are mostly applied when some source of information for problem solving already exists under DBS control. This is for example the purpose of making use of the KEE extension, the so-called KEE connection [In87b], that supports accesses to relational DBS with SQL interface [Da83]. Nevertheless, such connections are developed bearing in mind that accesses will occur sporadically, therefore being away from the efficiency and the functionality provided by DBS, that is necessary to support knowledge maintenance in an adequate manner.

4.3 Heterogeneous Approaches

As already mentioned, heterogeneous approaches are characterized by the cooperation of at least two different systems rather than on enhancements of an existing technology. Generally, the concept underlying them refers to the cooperation of an expert system or a deductive system for knowledge manipulation and a DBS for massive data management. The key issue is therefore the interface that allows the two systems to communicate. In developing such an interface, there are essentially two possibilities that lead to a loose or a tight coupling [Va85].

4.3.1 Loose Coupling

In a loose coupling environment, data exchange between XPS and DBS occur statically; that is, the XPS extracts the necessary data to work on a particular problem from the external DBS before it begins to work. This data is then stored in an internal repository kept in virtual memory so that no further communications are necessary.

The major advantage of such an approach is the large degree of system independence. Both XPS and DBS maintain their identity, allowing for a simple portability to other environments. However, it does not make use of full DBS functionality being therefore insufficient for knowledge maintenance requirements. Additionally, the duplication of knowledge representations (in the XPS and in the DB) may introduce the usual problems associated with redundancy. Finally, the strategy cannot be exploited when the portion to be extracted from the DB is not known in advance, limiting its use excessively. XPS inference processes present a large degree of non-determinism so that making a prediction as to the portion of knowledge to be used during a consultation is almost impossible. These observations lead to the need for a dynamic data exchange between both systems in order to allow accesses to various portions of knowledge at different times. The support of such a dynamic communication is exactly the goal of the tight coupling approach.

4.3.2 Tight Coupling

In a tight coupling environment, interactions between XPS and DBS can take place at any moment. Queries can be generated and transmitted to the DBS dynamically, and corresponding answers can be received and transformed into the XPS internal representation. Thus, the DBS acts as a server to the XPS, supplying on demand the data that the latter requires. Depending on the moment when data requirements are transmitted, tight coupling may be referred to as the compiled or the interpretative approach [MMJ84].

The compiled variation [CMT82,KY82] is based on two distinct phases (deduction and evaluation) which may be repeatedly performed. Firstly, a deduction on the side of the XPS is executed by applying rules until a query containing no virtual relations can be sent for evaluation to the DBS. In other words, the evaluation is delayed until the query has been transformed into a conjunction of expressions involving only base relations which may now be translated to a DB query. The execution of the query on the side of the DBS and the subsequent delivery of the result to the former are then performed. To implement this variation in a PROLOG environment, several propositions have been made which may be classified in one of two main methods. In the first one, no modification is made in the PROLOG interpreter which operates on a meta-language program responsible for the query transformation [KY82,VCJ84]. In the second method, the PROLOG interpreter is slightly modified to delay the evaluation of queries by the DBS.

In the interpretative variation, deduction and evaluation phases are intermixed; that is, rule execution is interrupted as soon as a basis relation is needed. The corresponding query is then sent for evaluation to the DBS, which returns the result to the XPS, allowing for continuation of rule execution. The use of this variation in a PROLOG environment demands a modification of the PROLOG interpreter to deal with sets of values instead of individual values [MMJ84].

Both the compiled and the interpretative variations for tight coupling have advantages and drawbacks. Commonly, the compiled approach generates fewer DBS requests than the interpretative strategy; additionally, DBS queries that are better to optimize. On the other hand, XPS using the interpretative variation may execute their deductions without modifying the overall strategy. Finally, the compiled approach exhibits some problems in the evaluation of recursive virtual relations, and the interpretative one has limitations in the size of the retrieved relations that must be maintained by the XPS internally as long as a line of reasoning has not been completed.

Just as in the loose coupling, the major advantage of the tight coupling approach (no matter whether it is compiled or interpretative) is also the possibility of using existing DBS without any modification, to which the XPS can be connected as one of its application programs. In such a way, the DBS will continue to serve all users without the necessity of data replication. Furthermore, tight coupling tends to maintain the identity of each component, supporting, consequently, a large degree of system independence.

The principal drawback of this approach can be seen in the necessity to separate in a precise way the time at which deduction and data retrieval should occur. Moreover, if the selected data cannot be fully received by the XPS, additional mechanisms must be provided to support the transfer of sets of data in a stepwise manner.

From the user's point of view, the DBS is seen as an extension of his/her program, meaning that the decision as to when and how to access the DBS relies on the XPS. In this manner, the DBS is not provided with information about the XPS processing methods and purposes so that it can at best make use of its optimization potential by isolated complex queries. For this reason, such an interaction may cause a severe slowdown for XPS operations when used.

Finally, it is important to observe that coupling may perhaps solve KS limitations concerning virtual memory sizes but it (even when efficiently implemented) does not fulfil other knowledge maintenance requirements nor does it support knowledge modeling and manipulation tasks. It presents the same deficiencies shown by a DBS-based knowledge modeling and knowledge manipulation (see section 4.2.1).

4.3.3 Some Coupling Prototypes

In order to investigate the behavior of KS running on coupling environments, we have constructed two prototype systems using the compiled and the interpretative approach. In the first system (DBPROLOG), a DDBS has been implemented by means of the compiled variation on the
basis of PROLOG. The other prototype, called DBMED, has applied the interpretative strategy
to support a diagnosis XPS shell.

4.3.3.1 DBPROLOG

DBPROLOG [Ba87b] is a DDBS built of two components:

- a PROLOG interpreter for knowledge manipulation [CM81], and
- the relational DBS INGRES [SWKH76,Da87] for knowledge maintenance.

4.3.3.1.1 Deduction Process

Considering the interface between the two components, DBPROLOG uses the compiled
approach [KY82,VCJ84] in order to take advantage of the query optimization mechanisms of
INGRES. As a consequence, DBPROLOG cannot make use of the full expressive power of horn
clauses. It only allows those clauses free of functions as well as those without arithmetical and
logical expressions. Functions are not permitted because they cannot always be transformed into
valid DB query statements, and logical and arithmetical expressions because they may often provoke an infinitely long search for solution [Za86].

It is important to mention here that these limitations occur in every coupling approach using a
purely compiled strategy. Actually, the impossibility of evaluating recursive rules is also a drawback
presented by most existing implementations. However, we have extended the compiled approach
in order to deal with any type of recursive rules. To achieve this goal, the meta-language level of
the compiled approach was enlarged with algorithms to recognize recursive predicates and strategies to evaluate them.

Recursion is evaluated by using an efficient least fixpoint iteration algorithm [Ba85], that generates just one DB query for each recursion step. Therefore, during the deduction process, recursive predicates are recognized by the meta-interpreter and removed from the deduction tree. The
corresponding DB queries (following the applied algorithm for recursion handling) are evaluated
and their results are stored in temporary relations. After this, the recursive predicate is introduced in the deduction tree once more, however, this time representing a base relation. The
deduction process may then continue until a query containing only base relations can be sent for
evaluation to INGRES.

A complete overview of a deduction process is shown in figure 4.7, where the numbers indicate the sequence of the individual steps taken in the process. For a complete description of the system and details of its implementation we refer to [Ba87b]. The figure illustrates the evaluation of a recursive query, whose rules have been introduced into the DB during the first three steps. In this rule definition phase, axes two and three represent the communication between the control component and DBS in order to decide where and how to store the rule information. Evaluation begins with the fourth step when the control component received the query, sending it for transformation to the meta-language component (axes five and six). After being translated into the meta-language syntax, the deduction process is performed, during which accesses to the DB are made in order to get the necessary rules for evaluation. These are also sent for transformation in the meta-language component (axes eight, nine, and ten). By the time when the deduction process is completed, all recursive rules have already been recognized. The control component then activates the recursion handling component (axis 12), which requires the specification of DB queries to evaluate the recursive rules (axis 13). After this evaluation, the control component activates the DB query specification once again (axis 17) in order to complete the evaluation of the query (axis 18). The results return to the control component (axis 19) and from it to the user (axis 20).

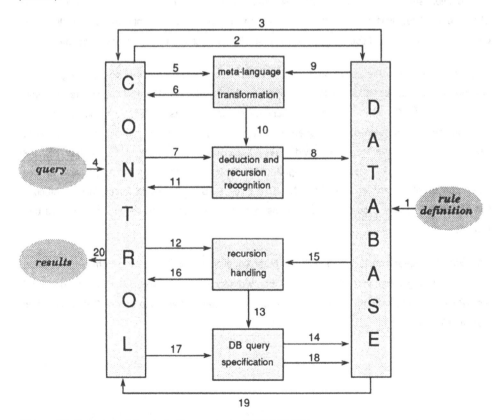

Figure 4.7: Overview of the deduction process of DBPROLOG

4.3.3.1.2 Investigation Results

A detailed analysis of the behavior of this prototype as well as many different performance measurements showed that inferences can be performed more efficiently by the DBS component.
This turns out to be particularly evident as the amount of manipulated data becomes larger. Unfortunately, DB query evaluation cannot provide all the inference capabilities of XPS. In essence, the
DBS is sacrificing flexibility in favor of increased performance.

As already mentioned, existing inference mechanisms have been designed to work on knowledge
kept in main memory so that they become very inefficient in secondary storage environments. In
spite of this fact, in every coupling environment, XPS inference mechanisms continue deciding
when and how to access the DBS, leaving the latter working in a "blind" way. This illustrates the
performance bottleneck existing in any coupling approach due to the slave role played by DBS in
such a situation. The solution to this problem is to achieve a kind of system integration where
DBS can "understand" the processing method of the XPS and the latter can "realize" the high
costs of secondary storage accesses. In such an integrated environment, the deductive component would then make use of inference mechanisms that take this new cost into account, moving
its deduction steps as far as possible down into the DBS. By moving more information to the
DBS, the DBS receives a higher-level specification of search requirements and above all knowledge about the purpose of such requirements so that it has much more scope for optimization.

Very similar results to the above ones were also found by [Sm84]. In this paper, it is argued that
the two principal performance bottlenecks when combining KS and DBS techniques are the inference process in KS and the access to secondary storage devices in DBS. In trying to solve the
first bottleneck, it is concluded that query evaluation can provide some but not all the inference
capabilities. However, since DBS provide these capabilities much more efficiently than KS, the
solution to this first bottleneck is to integrate both systems, allowing as far as possible for the
delegation of inference steps to the DBS. This gives DBS more margin for exploiting optimization as well as parallel processing, that seems to be the solution to the second performance bottleneck.

Following this integration idea, we built the other coupling prototype. Starting from a direct interpretative coupling between an XPS and a DBS, we successively exploited the information about
the XPS processing method in order to construct architectures that make use of DBS capabilities
more intelligently.

4.3.3.2 DBMED

DBMED is a DBS-based XPS shell prototype composed of

- the relational DBS INGRES [SWKH76,Da87] for knowledge maintenance, and
- the XPS shell MED1 [Pu83] for knowledge manipulation.

4.3.3.2.1 Overview of MED1

MED1 has been developed to support the construction of rule-based XPS for diagnosis in medical and technical areas [Pu84,Bo83,Pu85]. It uses hypothesize-and-test (see section 3.5.4) as problem solving strategy which, in turn, applies forward and backward reasoning respectively to create suspicions and to investigate them.

A consultation with MED1 always begins with an initialization of the KB. After this, the system addresses a sequence of general questions to the user (overview queries), whose answers are evaluated by forward rules in order to generate some preliminary suspicions. Following, there is a kind of general investigation (intermediate evaluation) when these first suspected diagnoses are evaluated and included into a control structure, called agenda, to be analyzed in the subsequent phase in a detailed manner. In this last phase, the most probable diagnosis is then removed from the agenda and investigated by backward rules. Thereby, it might be necessary to put new questions to the user, which after a new forward evaluation may generate new suspicions. For this reason, suspicions are evaluated in proper intervals and the analysis phase is started once again with the most suspected diagnosis. These control system cycles terminate either when there is enough evidence to establish one diagnosis or more or when there are no more suspected diagnoses to investigate.

MED1 differentiates particularly between knowledge about diagnoses and knowledge about associated symptoms. Diagnostic information is basically stored in an object type called diagnosis and in two others representing investigation steps (i.e., procedures) and technical investigations. Symptom information is divided into the object types questions and deducted symptoms. Finally, there are rules for expressing the heuristic relationships between diagnoses and symptoms.

Hence, a MED1 KB contains objects of six different types, namely, diagnoses, questions, procedures, technical investigations, deducted symptoms, and rules. Each of these object types is composed of three types of attributes:

- static attributes representing the knowledge of the human expert about the object,
- semistatic attributes expressing heuristic relationships among objects which are used as control information by the problem solving component, and

- dynamic attributes expressing either knowledge inferred during the consultation at hand or specific information about the case being analyzed in the consultation.

As one may observe, static and semistatic attributes together represent the whole expert knowledge. For a sake of simplicity, we will then refer to static attributes thereby meaning both.

The objects of a MED1 KB are manipulated by the following three operations:

- (get <object> <attribute>) to read the value of an object attribute,
- (put <object> <value> <attribute>) to write either the attribute or its value into the KB, and
- (remove <object> <attribute>) to delete the corresponding attribute.

These operations constitute the only existing interface between a MED1 KB and its problem solving component.

4.3.3.2.2   Coupling MED1 and INGRES

The coupling of MED1 and INGRES was implemented on the basis of the interpretative approach. Our goal in this first stage was to observe the access behavior of XPS and above all to investigate the adequacy of the coupling approach. For this reason, an important aim was to keep both XPS and DBS unchanged. The interface between MED1 and INGRES turned out, therefore, to be the existing interface between the KB and the problem solving component so that the corresponding operations could be mapped 1:1 to QUEL statements. This was achieved in two special modules as shown in figure 4.8.

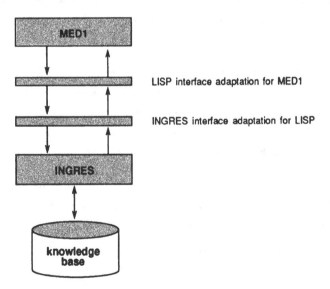

Figure 4.8: MED1/INGRES coupling overall architecture

The first results of our investigation were obtained as soon as we tried to represent a MED1 KB with the relational model. As expected, the inadequacy of conventional data models to represent knowledge (see section 4.2.1) became very evident. Such an inadequacy should be clear by observing the entity-relationship diagram of a MED1 KB presented in figure 4.9. It might be important to add that almost all relationships are n:m, that instances of the same object type do not always have the same structure (i.e., attributes), and that the length of the attribute values vary greatly (often it is not even possible to fix the maximal length of an attribute value).

These observations just came to confirm the necessity for the development of new data models supporting the complex structures found in non-standard application areas. When using a non-standard data model for representing MED1 KB, an adequate modeling could surely be achieved. (Note, for example, the support of an direct representation of n:m relationships).

The other expected result, i.e., the inability of XPS working methods to process KB on secondary storage, emerged when consulting MED1 in this new environment. Such an inability, which is described in detail in [HMP87,St86,Th87], may be characterized here in summary by the slowing down of the system by a factor of 170 when compared to the main memory-based version of MED1. In the coupling environment, the DBS works in a slave mode without knowledge about the XPS objects, about their relationships, as well as about the accesses of XPS so that it cannot make use of its optimization mechanisms.

4.3.3.2.3   First Step Towards Integration: Application Buffer

The results of our first DBMED version showed that coupling was not sufficient for an effective XPS support. For this reason, an optimization of the system should occur by a kind of integration where the DBS capabilities could be better exploited.

This was achieved by the introduction of an application buffer between XPS and DBS which provides for the exploitation of the locality of the XPS accesses (figure 4.10). Furthermore, the buffer enables the reduction of DBS calls as well as the reduction of the path length when accessing the objects of the KB. Additionally, the granules of the DB accesses could be enlarged (whole objects instead of attribute values) without provoking changes in MED1. A last, very important measure for optimization, was the complete delegation of the KB initialization (the first phase of a MED1 consultation) to the application buffer module. Thereby, the number of DB accesses was drastically reduced (from 2347 to 87) since the application buffer module applies few but adequate DB statements instead of initializing each attribute of each object sequentially.

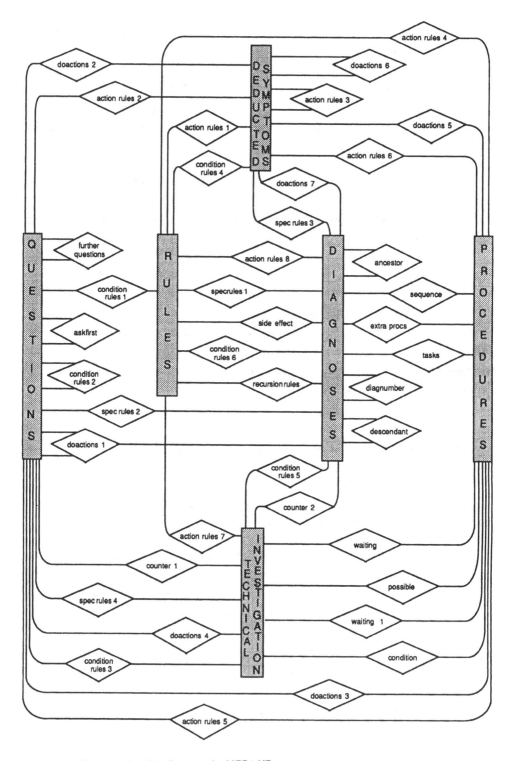

Figure 4.9: Entity-relationship diagram of a MED1 KB

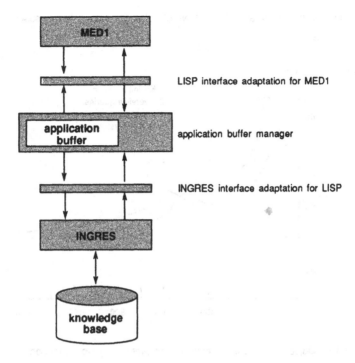

Figure 4.10: MED1/INGRES steps towards integration

The results of the above optimization measures can be characterized by the new performance of the system, i.e., a slowing down by only a factor of 18 which implies an improvement of a factor of 10.

4.3.3.2.4 Exploitation of Processing Characteristics

Further optimizations are possible by an increased integration of both systems so that the processing characteristics of the XPS may be exploited for performance improvement. In the previous version, the system does not make use of any knowledge about the reference behavior of MED1 to replace objects in the application buffer. The implemented buffer was managed by a simple LRU algorithm.

However, in each phase of the problem solving process, XPS typically need different parts of the KB. This became especially evident after observing that the object fault rate of the application buffer increases just after changes of processing phases (see figure 4.11). Consequently, XPS accesses concentrate on the attributes of just some objects of the KB. These objects represent in reality the knowledge needed to infer the specific goal of the phase. For this reason, we say that these objects together build a context. In MED1, an example of such contexts were the general questions together with associated forward rules to deduce some suspicions in the overview queries phase.

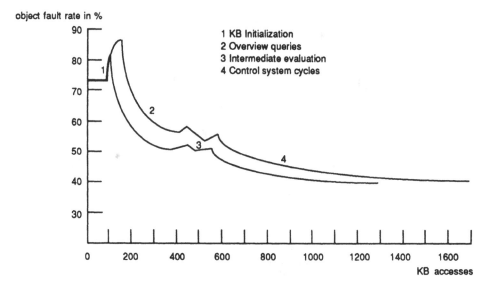

Figure 4.11: Object fault rate in the application buffer during two MED1 consultations

The context needed in each phase can, however, be neither static nor determined at the beginning of a consultation. As already discussed, this restriction is exactly what causes the drawback of the loose coupling approach. In general, the need for contexts is established by some information that the XPS deduces during the preceding phases (i.e., dynamic knowledge) so that it is possible to determine the next context required only at the end of a phase. This disables a static but enables a dynamic preplanning of the accesses to the KB used at this integrated version for optimization purposes.

The optimization measure taken was therefore to make use of this knowledge in order to manage the application buffer. The idea is to fetch the required context during changes of processing phases causing an enormous reduction in subsequent accesses to the DB as well as in transfer overhead. Additionally, this approach allows for a better DBS access optimization due to the set-oriented specification of the needed objects. To achieve this goal, it is however necessary that XPS look ahead of their work, informing the DBS about the need for new contexts. The DBS must know about XPS working units so that it can fetch the corresponding object sets into the application buffer. It should be therefore clear that such a tight cooperation is only possible in a highly integrated environment.

The measurements of DBMED in the above integrated fashion (i.e., with a controlled application buffer) showed a significant improvement of system performance (by a factor of 4.5) with regard to the previous version (see table 4.1).

	MED1 references	accesses to the KB (on sec. storage)	duration of a consultation in CPU-sec.	slow down factor with regard to main memory MED1
main memory based MED1	3574	3574	164	1
MED1 + INGRES (Coupling)	3574	3574	28105	~ 170
MED1 + INGRES + application buffer	1314	572	2946	~ 18
MED1 + INGRES + controlled application buffer	1314	93	643	~ 4

Table 4.1: Overview of measurement results of the DBMED prototype variations

4.4 Conclusions

We have been investigating a variety of approaches to undertake knowledge management tasks. As presented in this chapter, some of these approaches seem to be very appropriate to support the subtasks of knowledge maintenance. Others allow for a suitable knowledge modeling, and some other approaches appear to be optimal for knowledge manipulation.

Unfortunately, each of these approaches fails for one or more reasons when knowledge management requirements are considered in their entirety. In other words, none fulfils these demands completely.

The reason for this failure is that knowledge management support requests a combination of two technologies, AI and DBS, and demands much more than just coupling DBS as a back-end storage system to KS. To achieve the best functionality and performance, these technologies must be integrated in order to allow for a favorable combination of efforts rather than for the work of one against the other. Integration is therefore the only way to reach the necessary degree of cooperation of AI and DBS features.

To achieve such integration, *a new generation of systems specially constructed for an effective and efficient management of knowledge bases must to be designed*. In analogy to DBMS these systems are called *Knowledge Base Management Systems (KBMS)*. In developing KBMS, the experience obtained by the investigation of each of the examined approaches is extremely important. For this reason, these approaches should not be viewed as complete concepts for knowledge management but as means for research work towards KBMS.

Now, an important methodological question to be answered is how to construct such systems. DBS as well as KS already exist and are widely and successfully used. Therefore, it seems to be a very plausible idea to treat either one of them as a starting point and improve them in an evolutionary fashion towards KBMS. However, as shown in this chapter, this is a strategy only successful for research or development work with a relatively short-term outlook.

We argue that the correct approach is to start with the definition of the desirable knowledge representation framework and then develop systems on the basis of the features of this framework, just as has been done with most of the existing successful data models (e.g., relational data model). Therefore, having a long-term general purpose solution for knowledge management in mind, the development of KBMS must follow the conception of designing a new generation of systems based most certainly on the experience gained with years of DBS and AI usage, however, not restricted to their resulting concepts. Extensions of existing technologies for building DBMS or KS are constrained by their point of origin and can only be stretched so far towards yielding more intelligent DBMS or more efficient and robust KS tailored to specific applications [My86].

In this sense, KBMS should be developed on the basis of the results of the investigations described in this chapter but not restricted to them.

5. KBMS Architectural Issues

The previous chapter of this work described current and future needs of a new technology integrating features of the AI and DB fields as well as the motivation for its development . This new technology, called *Knowledge Base Management Systems*, translates a new generation of *systems aimed at the effective and efficient management of knowledge bases.*

KBMS, as the answer to existing KS limitations regarding knowledge management tasks, should be in analogy to DBMS viewed as independent systems, where these tasks are achieved in a very appropriate way. It is therefore clear that the fulfillment of the previously described KS knowledge management requirements is the goal of KBMS. As such, features to be provided by KBMS are dictated by these requirements.

The design of an architecture for KBMS demands, however, much more than just realizing what to fulfil. For an exact specification of a system architecture, it is necessary to investigate, above all, the application environment of KBMS in order to understand the importance, the use, as well as the purposes of these systems' features. In doing so, essential design issues will become evident, allowing for an accurate architecture specification.

In this chapter, we specify an architecture for KBMS, defining exactly the features to be provided by each of the system's components and showing how such features are influenced by the requirements of the KBMS application environment. We begin with a general overview of our KBMS architecture proposal. Then, we provide the motivation for the most important issue of our approach (i.e., knowledge independence) followed by a detailed description of each proposed system component.

5.1 Overall Architecture

In examining the KBMS application environment, one observes that there are three more or less orthogonal ways of looking at KBMS. These dominant and distinct viewpoints determine distinct facets of KBMS, corresponding in some sense to the three different aspects which play important roles when constructing and employing KS: user need, knowledge engineering support, and available resources.

In the same way, KBMS should first of all satisfy the needs of their applications (i.e., KS or end-users). Secondly, they must support knowledge engineering tasks. And thirdly, some resources or implementation aspects should be taken into account in order to manage the knowledge efficiently. Thus, KBMS should provide features seen from these three different points of view:

- application,
- engineering, and
- implementation

as expressed in figure 5.1.

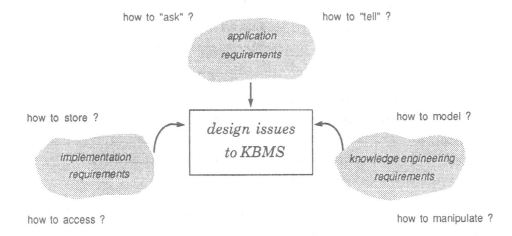

how to "ask" ?

how to "tell" ?

application requirements

how to store ?

how to model ?

design issues to KBMS

implementation requirements

knowledge engineering requirements

how to access ?

how to manipulate ?

Figure 5.1: KBMS architectural issues

These distinct viewpoints lead to a natural division of KBMS architecture into three different layers: implementation layer, engineering layer, and application layer, where the corresponding KBMS features are in particular considered (figure 5.2).

At the implementation layer, adequate data structures, efficient algorithms, and other suitable constructs necessary to process and to supply the knowledge maintained in some storage device to the upper layers are to be supported. The engineering layer focuses on a KBMS from the viewpoint of the knowledge engineer or KB designer. Here the KBMS is seen in terms of how the knowledge of an application can be modeled and manipulated. In other words, this layer deals with descriptive, operational, and organizational aspects of the desirable knowledge representation framework. The application layer treats knowledge in an abstract way, independent of the implementation layer's task of efficiency and the engineering layer's task of modeling. Here it is seen functionally in terms of what KBMS know about the KS application domain.

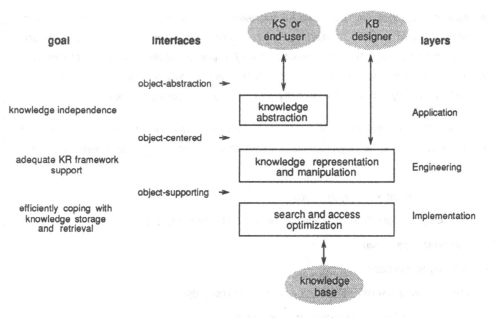

Figure 5.2: Overall KBMS architecture

As such, the application layer looks at the information content of a KB, the engineering layer considers the modeling aspects of the application world expressed as KB contents, and the implementation layer views the KB in terms of its internal representation and access algorithms. For these reasons, whenever we talk about KB in terms of data structures actually manipulated by some algorithms, we are referring to the implementation layer. In discussing about the ways the knowledge of an application may be expressed, manipulated, and changed by the KB designer, we are dealing with the things which concern the engineering layer. Finally, if our discussion of a KB is in terms of what the KS may ask or tell the KBMS about the application world, we are talking about the application layer.

5.2 Knowledge Independence

Traditionally, KR systems or KS components responsible for the knowledge management have been designed just to support what we called the engineering layer, i.e., the layer whose competence comprises providing flexible ways of modeling and manipulating the symbolic structures that together form the KB. Since the way in which knowledge is organized and the way in which it can be accessed are seen at the external interface of those systems, KS have information about the knowledge organization and retrieval possibilities built into their logic (i.e., embedded in their programs). Any modification in the structures of the knowledge therefore requires program modifications. Changing the kind of the KR framework used, for example from frames to semantic networks, would even be impossible since this would mean throwing the entire KS away and implementing a new one. This dependence on the KR framework applies even to the semantics of some of the most important elements found in these systems (see, for example, the many different existing meanings for the IS-A relationship [Br83]; see also sections 3.3.2 and 3.3.4).

However, with the employment of KBMS, this issue of allowing KS to "understand" the KR framework promises to be very problematic. KBMS should be continuously ameliorated by means of

- extending provided modeling constructs,
- introducing new operations more appropriate for the KB design process,
- adapting storage structures,
- modifying access paths,
- bringing forward new data structures better suited to knowledge maintenance, or
- applying new techniques for accessing the KB more efficiently,

however without affecting their application programs.

Knowledge independence defined as *the immunity of KS against changes in the KBMS* is therefore the key answer to this problem. KBMS must, analogously to DBMS and in opposition to existing KR systems, be characterized not in terms of the representational framework they use but functionally in terms of what they know about the KS domain. Hence, they must be strictly designed on the foundation of the knowledge representation hiding principle, which guarantees the local confinement of all kinds of modifications as well as improvements throughout the system lifetime, therefore isolating KS from the representation of knowledge.

This idea of abstraction aimed at the independence of knowledge was what motivated us to introduce another layer (the application layer) above the engineering layer in the architecture of KBMS. At the object-abstraction interface, KS can, therefore, work independently from the representational specification of the KR framework supported by the engineering layer. In fact, KS are not interested in the realization of things like the complexity of frame structures, the variety of links in a semantic network, the properties of inheritance mechanisms, or the power of reasoning facilities. They are really interested in what they can ask or tell the KBMS about the knowledge of their domain, which is stored in the KB managed by the KBMS. This motivated us also to believe that the KS interface is the one supported by the application layer (object-abstraction interface). The interface for the KB designer is, however, a different one. He (in opposition to the KS) is concerned with the aspects of the KR framework. He decides whether a specific information is to be represented as a frame, a slot, or an aspect, or even in form of a rule or a fact.

Therefore, we argue that the KB designer interface is the one supported by the engineering layer (object-centered interface).

5.3 The Application Layer

Aimed at knowledge independence, the application layer treats knowledge in an abstract manner, independent of the internal aspects involved with the engineering and implementation layer. Knowledge is seen at the application layer interface functionally, in terms of what the KS can ask or tell the KBMS about their application domains. Therefore, at the object-abstraction interface the KB can be compared with an abstract data type that interacts with the end users or KS through a set of manipulation operations. These operations should enable KS to ask questions about the stored knowledge and to tell the KBMS something about their application domain to be introduced into the KB. Thus, they correspond to the functions necessary to fulfil knowledge manipulation requirements.

However, the realization of such functions differs from that of traditional KR systems. Since knowledge is treated as an abstract data type, the way it is acquired or changed by the application layer is completely hidden from the KS. Because of this, no distinction can be made between knowledge that is extensionally stored and that which has to be implied (intensionally) at the object-abstraction interface. The decision as to whether just simple retrieval capabilities or inference of some kind is required to answer a question is not to be made by the KS, but in this layer. As a consequence, the object-abstraction interface is only characterized by knowledge manipulation requirements associated with storage and retrieval operations since deduction requirements are fulfilled internally. In other words, it is the responsibility of the application layer to select the appropriate symbolic structures to represent knowledge, as well as to select the appropriate retrieval mechanisms and reasoning operations whenever necessary, both to answer questions and to assimilate new knowledge, expressed in the form of a language provided at the object-abstraction interface. (Note that the engineering and implementation layers play a supporting role in this context). In fact, the details as to which symbolic structures are being manipulated and with which mechanisms is of little use to the KS. They are really interested in what can be known and how what is known can be retrieved or changed at any given time.

We consider, therefore, the existence of only two basic types of operations at this level: one to enable the KS to ask the KBMS questions to be answered on the basis of the knowledge kept in the KB and another one to permit the KS to tell the KBMS new knowledge to be maintained in the KB. The first operation of the query language allows, for example, the KS to ask whether a particular vehicle (e.g., auto1) is an instance of automobiles or what causes the excessive consumption of gas when running a car. The second operation of the query language, that is able to cause changes in the knowledge, allows the KS to tell the KBMS, for example, that auto1 is an instance of automobiles, without having to worry about how this is represented in the used knowledge representation model. In the same way, it would be able to tell the KBMS that a malfunction of fuel injection causes the injection of surplus amounts of gas into the motor and this, in turn, causes wastage of gasoline, without having to worry about the fact that this knowledge has to be presented in the form of rules to be evaluated backwards as the KBMS is asked about the cause for the excessive consumption of gas.

It is therefore clear that knowledge manipulation requirements are fulfilled by the application layer, which, however, conceals from the KS whether or not the application of inference mechanisms was necessary to answer their questions. In the same sense, those inference processes which have been initiated as consequence of changes on the KB are also concealed. Therefore, the application layer interface reflects the aspects of the KR model supported by the engineering layer, concealing, however, every aspect that translates the way the knowledge has been represented and manipulated. In other words, the application layer supports the knowledge concealing principle, guaranteeing knowledge independence.

The discussed functional view of the KB was originally introduced in KRYPTON [BFL83,LB86], where ask and tell operations were split in two different interfaces: a terminological Tbox and an assertional Abox. However, the issues supported by KRYPTON do not meet the idea of knowledge independence. By having two different interfaces, before making changes in a KB, a KRYPTON user has to decide, for example, whether the KB's theory of the world should imply these changes (tell operation at the Abox) or the KB's vocabulary should include them (tell operation in the Tbox). In other words, he has to decide whether these changes should be intensionally or extensionally represented. We argue that such a decision should not be made by the user but in the application layer so that the way knowledge is represented can be concealed from the system's users. We believe that this is the only possible way to view a KB as an abstract data type. Furthermore, KRYPTON's interface has not been developed for a KBMS context and consequently is neither flexible nor powerful enough to meet the requirements of KBMS applications. (For example, ask statements are restricted to yes/no questions and tell operations do not allow for updates of the KB contents, i.e., they are restricted to insertions [BM86, pp. 57]).

The object-abstraction interface must certainly permit adequate and flexible ways to select the application's domain knowledge and to cause changes in the KB, corresponding to the many ways knowledge can be accessed and changed. The most important issues, that should be supported by the query language, although only very seldom found in existing KS, are the following:

- completeness

    The query language supported by the application layer must be complete. That is, it must allow for a flexible retrieval as well as storage of all kinds of knowledge expressed by the KR model (i.e., the whole KB contents).

- extensibility

    The qualification of "pieces of" knowledge should not be restricted to the qualification predicates offered by the query language. An extension of the language by means of user-defined qualification predicates must be supported.

- projection

    In addition to very flexible qualification constructs, the user should have facilities for specifying the form of his retrieval results. These facilities should permit the user defining his own projections in order to suppress unnecessary information of the qualified knowledge. Clearly, KRYPTON's ask statements, restricted to yes/no questions, do not satisfy such requirement.

- set orientation

    Set orientation permits the KS to obtain as well as to change several "pieces of" knowledge with just one operation. This reduces communication overhead between KS and KBMS and offers an enormous optimization potential for the lower layers.

- recursion

    The query language must support recursive processing, otherwise knowledge independence cannot be guaranteed. By delegating the evaluation of recursive queries to the KS, the aspects of how knowledge is represented and manipulated cannot be concealed from the KS since this information is needed to process the recursion. Moreover, the evaluation of recursive queries, when done within the KBMS, offers optimization potentials [DS86].

- state-oriented changes

    When specifying changes in the KB, the user should only describe the new state of the KB, corresponding to the new circumstances of his application world. Without having to worry about the way to reach this new state, the decision as to how to represent it can be taken by the application layer so that the way knowledge has been represented can be concealed from the system's users. This is particularly important when concealing whether knowledge has been stored extensionally or intensionally. Therefore, a tell statement embodies all existing change operations of DBS (i.e., insert, delete, and update), strengthening the idea of abstraction associated with the application layer.

5.4 The Engineering Layer

A computer system, and with it a KS too, constitutes a model of the real world, about which it contains specific information pertinent to a particular application [Ab74,BC75]. Based on this assertion, the process of software specification can be viewed as the process of building an accurate model of some enterprise [BMW84]. This view underlines the focus of the engineering layer. At this level, a KBMS is seen from the point of view of the KB designer, i.e., the knowledge engineer, who considers the KBMS in terms of how the knowledge of an application can be modeled.

Therefore, the starting point in designing this layer is to choose the KR framework to be supplied to the knowledge engineer at the layer's interface (object-centered interface). Such a framework, defined by means of a KR model, or Knowledge Model (KM) for short, allows for an accurate representation of the model of expertise (see chapter 3), reflecting directly the user's natural conceptualization of the universe of discourse. To design such KM, it is therefore necessary to identify the constructs people apply during the process of describing the real world.

This appears to underline also the work being done on data modeling in the area of DBS as well as knowledge representation in the area of AI. Both fields accept the above observation, working, for that reason, on the development of models that also reflect such user's natural conceptualization. The main difference between the engineering layer's KM and these other representational schemes lies in the emphasis which they give to the different kinds of knowledge to be modeled. Rather than being declarative, procedural, or structural with respect to the emphasis on such kinds, the KM must remain neutral, equally focusing on all of them. It must mix various concepts, thereby integrating all different aspects of knowledge in order to obtain the powerful framework necessary to allow a natural modeling of all aspects of every application world.

As discussed in the previous chapters, there are basically three distinct kinds of knowledge that are involved in a KS application. The first kind, i.e., the declarative knowledge, refers to that knowledge about the passive parts of the application domain. Considered by almost every data model and KR scheme, it defines information about the existing objects, their attributes, important constraints, etc. The second kind defines the procedural characteristics of the application domain as well as of the human experts solving problems in this domain and is therefore called procedural knowledge. Finally, the third kind, i.e., the structural knowledge, defines the ways for organizing the first two. Clearly, these three kinds of knowledge are to be reflected in different constructs of the KM. They define three different aspects of it, which we denote descriptive, operational, and organizational.

In this section, these different aspects to be provided by the KM are discussed from a neutral point of view: we consider them not from the realization in a particular KR scheme or data model as done previously (see section 3.3 and 4.2.1) but from the conceptualization of the real world viewed by human observers, in our context the knowledge engineers.

5.4.1 Descriptive Aspects

Descriptive aspects of the KM focus on the declarative characteristics of the application world. For this reason, they are suitable for describing the passive parts of the domain knowledge because of its inactive nature.

Other approaches which have the same purpose are, for example, data models. Expressed rough-ly, they are based on the notion of "record" (with numeric or string fields) and some "links" between them. However, these primitives are more appropriate for modeling the way in which the data is stored and accessed in the computer than for representing the real world concepts underlying them and their relationships [Bo86].

In contrast to data models, the KM provided by the engineering layer should represent the world not in a form that might be optimal for a program work, but reflecting exactly what this world looks like.

As such, the engineering layer views the declarative parts of the application world comprehended in terms of conceptual *objects*, also called entities, which have descriptions (i.e., attributes or *properties*) associated with them and have *relationships* with each other in meaningful ways. Fur-thermore, activities (i.e., *operations* on these objects) occur with time, resulting in changes in the objects and in their inter-relationships. Both object (including properties and relationships) and activity descriptions are subject to *constraints* which define the concepts and distinguish "reality" from other possible worlds [Bo86].

The term object is used here to refer to a data structure in the KB that is intended to denote an entity in the world. For example, a KB might contain an object to represent the person Mary. Objects are also used to represent abstract concepts such as person, car, etc.

This observation provides the motivation for the first important axiom of the KM: *everything existing in the real world, even those entities used to describe other entities, are objects of the mod-el.* By viewing the world like this, it becomes clear that object types (i.e., classes) are also objects of the model, corresponding to the abstract concepts of the real world mentioned above. Thus, there should not be any difference between so-called object types and object instances. Both are treated as objects of the model. Hence, the difference made by DBS between object types incor-porated in the DB-schema and instances incorporated in the DB is eliminated here. Both types and instances are to be treated as objects of the model so that definitions of static structures as meta-information should not exist. Semantically, there can be objects representing types or objects representing instances. There can even exist objects which represent both a type in one context and an instance in another. Nevertheless, the model must treat all objects in the same way although it knows exactly the semantic meaning of each one in each particular context. For the knowledge engineer, it is therefore possible to apply the same operations to manipulate object types as he does to instances.

It is also important that *entities in the application's world should correspond to objects in the KM*. More stringently, a one-to-one correspondence between the entities in the world and the objects in the model must exist, thus preventing, for example, the knowledge about an entity (e.g., a person) being spread out among several objects of the model. This corresponds to our second important axiom.

In the world, and consequently in the KM too, *an object can exist without having a "key" (i.e., a unique external identifier) and yet be distinct from other objects*. In other words, it is clear that an object is not the same thing as a name for it. As a consequence, relationships should exist between objects and not between their names, identifiers, or descriptions.

Each object is composed of attributes expressing the properties of the entities. For example, the object auto1 (see figure 5.3) possesses the attributes color, owner, location, and price, denoting the particular real world entity owned by Mary, that has a white color, a price of US$1000, and is, at the moment, located on the 5th avenue.

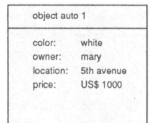

Figure 5.3: Example of a description of objects' properties

Attributes may be further described. This allows expressing constraints over the attributes as well as incorporating more semantics into the KM (figure 5.4). Typical descriptions to be supported are the data type of the attribute value (possible_values), minimum and maximum number of values allowed (cardinality), and default specifications. For example, by defining that the owner of a car must be either a person or an institution, a KBMS "knows" some more details about the application world rather than just interpreting owners as a heap of characters. Such a specification allows the model to infer that owners of cars are always persons or institutions when asked about it. Note that the semantics of the KM is therefore closely related to a form of reasoning capability. (Such reasoning capabilities are stressed in the section about the organizational aspects, see 5.4.3).

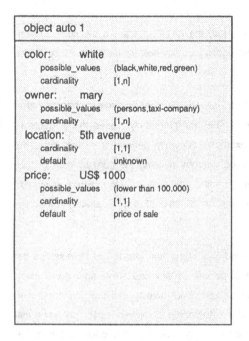

Figure 5.4: Example of attributes' descriptions

Object attributes are multiple-valued (for example, the property color in figure 5.3). Moreover, beyond traditional data types (integer, string, and boolean) others like lists, tables, and texts should be also supported since they are typical in KS application domains.

Our last axiom says that *relationships between real world entities are properties of them and should, for that reason, be expressed as attributes of the objects.* This makes it easier to locate related objects by just following chains of properties without having to explicitly introduce intermediate objects, as done by a lot of data models [Bo86]. For example, the property owner of the entity auto1 just expresses the relationship between it and the person Mary (see figure 5.3).

5.4.2 Operational Aspects

Operational aspects are involved with the representation of procedural characteristics of the application domain as well as of the solving expertise of the human experts.

Behaviors

In the previous section, we have viewed the passive side of the application domain. We defined it as a collection of inactive objects having only declarative characteristics associated to them. However, real world entities also have procedural characteristics so that the application domain should, in truth, be defined as a collection of active objects, or actors. The first important procedural characteristics of the entities is their behavior, i.e., the knowledge about the comportment of the entities in general. For example, the knowledge about the actions that take place when moving a car defines a particular aspect of its behavior.

When modeling the application domain, such behaviors as well as other procedural characteristics of the real world entities are very important because they are intrinsically related to the declarative properties of these entities. Behaviors, for example, generally perform transformations on the declarative properties of an entity when activated, thereby defining the comportment of this entity in a particular situation. For example, the "running" behavior of cars, when activated, changes the amount of gasoline kept in the tank as well as the amount of miles already run up by the car, just as it occurs in the real world.

Behaviors are therefore also properties of entities and should, for this reason, be represented as attributes of the objects and treated exactly in the same way as any descriptive attribute. Consequently, most of the axioms made in the previous section about objects and their attributes are also valid here. Therefore, an integrated view of the automobiles described earlier still presents the discussed structure except for some new attributes expressing the procedural properties of these cars (figure 5.5).

The activation of behaviors occurs, as in the real world, by interactions between objects. For example, when John wants to make his taxi go, he interacts with it by means of starting its motor and driving it. The activated component of the interaction, i.e., the receptor, specifies the kind of operations to be taken. As a property of itself, the receptor "knows" the actions associated with its behavior. Observe that John does not have to know anything about the actions underlying the running process when driving his taxi. The only thing he has to know is how to interact with it in order to set it into motion. Once having been activated to move, his taxi works by its own as long as John drives it accordingly.

Behaviors usually provoke not only changes on some properties of the objects but also activate behaviors of other objects. For example, running will certainly activate a lot of other behaviors of the components (i.e., motor, wheels, etc.) of the car.

```
┌─────────────────────────────────────────────────────┐
│ object auto 2                                        │
├─────────────────────────────────────────────────────┤
│ color:       black,white                             │
│   possible_values   (black,white,red,green)          │
│   cardinality       [1,n]                            │
│ owner:       taxi-company                            │
│   possible_values   (persons,taxi-company)           │
│   cardinality       [1,n]                            │
│ location:    4th avenue                              │
│   cardinality       [1,1]                            │
│   default           unknown                          │
│ price:       US$ 2500                                │
│   possible_values   (lower than 100.000)             │
│   cardinality       [1,1]                            │
│   default           price of sale                    │
│ number_of_passengers: 3                              │
│   possible_values   (between 0 and 5)                │
│   cardinality       [1,1]                            │
│   default           3                                │
│ driver:      john                                    │
│   possible_values   (persons)                        │
│   cardinality       [1,1]                            │
│ amount_of_gasoline:32                                │
│   possible_values   (between 0 and 40)               │
│   cardinality       [1,1]                            │
│   unit              liters                           │
│ amount_of_miles:42575                                │
│   possible_values   (greater than 0)                 │
│   cardinality       [1,1]                            │
│ running ( change location, increase amount_of_miles, │
│             decrease amount_of_gasoline)             │
│   unit              miles                            │
└─────────────────────────────────────────────────────┘
```

Figure 5.5: Example of a description of behavioral attributes

Reactions

The second very important procedural knowledge found in the application domain are the reactions of the real world entities when particular situations occur: for example, the reaction of John when a car in front of his taxi suddenly brakes impetuously. When describing such knowledge, one is not interested in characterizing comportments of the objects but the consequences of real world events.

It is clear, however, that such consequences can only have effects on the real world entities. Therefore, they are translated to either activations of object's behaviors or modifications of its declarative knowledge. In the above example, a possible consequence of the described event might be the activation of the "braking" behavior of John's car so that nothing else occurs. Another consequence might be the accident itself which will cause a lot of changes in the descriptions of each object involved (both cars, John, the other driver, etc.).

Another example of such kind of knowledge is the reaction of John when the tank of his taxi is almost empty. In this case, the action of filling the tank of the car (i.e., a behavior of John) will be carried out.

It is important to observe that the description of the real world situations is declarative knowledge. For this reason, the corresponding reactions are closely related to the descriptive aspects of the KM and should be consequently linked to objects and/or object properties. Reactions are therefore further descriptions of the objects and their attributes and should be treated just as other descriptions. Hence, the above reaction of an empty tank is found under the attribute descriptions of the property "amount_of_gasoline" in John's taxi (figure 5.6).

```
object auto 2

color :        black,white
    possible_values    (black,white,red,green)
    cardinality        [1,n]
owner :        taxi-company
    possible_values    (persons,taxi-company)
    cardinality        [1,n]
location :  4th avenue
    cardinality        [1,1]
    default            unknown
price :        US$ 2500
    possible_values    (lower than 100.000)
    cardinality        [1,1]
    default            price of sale
number_of_passengers : 3
    possible_values    (between 0 and 5)
    cardinality        [1,1]
    default            3
driver :     john
    possible_values    (persons)
    cardinality        [1,1]
amount_of_gasoline : 32
    possible_values    (between 0 and 40)
    cardinality        [1,1]
    unit               liters
    reaction : on empty tank, activate driver to fuel
amount_of_miles : 42575
    possible_values    (greater than 0)
    cardinality        [1,1]
running (   change location, increase amount_of_miles,
            decrease amount_of_gasoline)
    unit               miles
```

Figure 5.6: Example of a description of a reaction

Situation-action Rules

Up till this point, the constructs which we have been analyzing were involved with the description of the domain knowledge expressed by means of objects, attributes, actions, relationships, and constraints. The KM should, however, also have constructs to represent the problem solving knowledge of the human experts about this application domain.

Empirically, it seems that experts express most of their problem solving know-how simply as a set of situation-action rules. Situations are usually associated with the description of some real world state and actions mostly determine some kind of conclusions of the expert about this state. As such, situations as well as actions are of a passive nature. They define descriptive aspects of the application domain and are, for this reason, a kind of declarative knowledge. Nevertheless, the most important aspect of such situations and actions are not their declarative contents but the procedural effect resulting by the combination of both, i.e., "when situation X occurs then action Y will succeed". This procedural aspect is closely related to the reasoning process and should be supported by the KM. This means that the KM should firstly offer constructs to allow the representation of such situation-action rules and secondly mechanisms to interpret them (i.e., to make deductions).

Another important aspect of such rules is that they are a kind of meta knowledge since they define information about the domain knowledge. Both domain and expert knowledge are therefore connected but are not dependent on each other. Note, for example, that the domain knowledge may be expressed without the representation of any expert knowledge about it. For this reason, they should be modeled independently from each other, allowing for modifications as well as an incremental expansion of anyone of them without affecting the other. The KM should, however, offer ways to refer to the domain objects, their attributes, and descriptions when specifying situation-action rules.

5.4.3 Organizational Aspects

People rarely describe the real world as we discussed in the previous sections, i.e., in terms of specific "factual" information about the application domain. Not surprisingly, they usually use constructs which have their roots in epistemological methods for organizing knowledge (i.e., the structural knowledge about a domain). In other words, in trying to model the application world people generally involuntarily apply some abstractions in order to organize their knowledge in some desired form. Abstraction permits someone to suppress specific details of particular objects, emphasizing those pertinent to the problem or view of information at hand. It is therefore the fundamental modeling tool used for describing knowledge and is, for this reason, the most important construct to be supported by the KM [Ma88a]. Hence, it is fruitful to focus, in fullest detail, on each of the existing abstraction concepts and to formalize them, characterizing their meaning, examining their applicability, and studying their usefulness in order to differentiate them from one another.

Numerous papers [BMW84,Br81,SS77b] have tried to describe one or another concept and many models [BS85,Co79,STW84,HM78] have been developed following some of these descriptions. Nevertheless, precise definitions of the semantics and of the applicability of these concepts do not exist. Additionally, approaches towards an integration of all concepts into one model are rarely found. Most models developed concentrate on the support of one or two abstraction concepts, not taking the existence of the other ones into account.

In this section, we concentrate on a neutral view of the semantics and constructs existing behind such abstraction concepts. Firstly, these concepts will be precisely defined by characterizing their meaning. Following this, we discuss their applicability by examining the reasoning facilities built into them and show an approach towards an integration of these abstraction concepts. While reading the section, the reader should keep in mind that the points discussed previously, that is, the descriptive and operational aspects of knowledge, are still valid. Nevertheless, for sake of simplicity, we use examples based only on the descriptive aspects of the real world objects.

5.4.3.1 The Abstraction Concepts

From the viewpoint of the abstraction concepts, each real world object is either simple (i.e., defined on its own) or composite (i.e., defined as an abstraction of other objects) [Br84]. Abstractions are therefore expressed as relationships between objects, having as their purpose the organization of these objects in some form.

Two types of abstraction relationships can be found in the real world: one involving simple objects in order to build a composite object and another involving composite objects in order to build other more complex composite objects. Abstractions of the first type are, therefore, one-level relationships since they are applied only once to build the least complex composite objects. Abstractions of the second type are, in turn, n-level relationships since they can be applied n times, allowing the composite objects to be represented, in some sense, recursively by less complex ones. The differentiation of these two relationship types is quite important because of the special semantics that they embody.

5.4.3.1.1 Classification and Generalization

Modeling Purpose

Classification

Found in almost every existing data model or KR scheme, classification is the most important and the best understood form of abstraction. It is achieved by grouping objects that have common properties into a new object for which uniform conditions hold. In other words, classification is a form of abstraction in which a composite object, in this context called object type or *class*, is defined as a set of simple objects, which have the same properties and are called *instances*. This establishes an *instance-of relationship* between some simple objects (the instances) and a composite one (the class). Classification is therefore a *one-level abstraction relationship*.

For example, if there exist three objects in the real world, all of them having the properties color, owner, location, and price, (figure 5.7) someone could describe each one independently by specifying the particular values of each of their properties.

object auto 1	
color:	white
owner:	mary
location:	5th avenue
price:	US$ 1000

object auto 2	
color:	black,white
owner:	taxi-company
location:	4th avenue
price:	US$ 2500

object auto 3	
color:	white,red,green
owner:	transport-company
location:	unknown
price:	US$ 5200

a) factual description

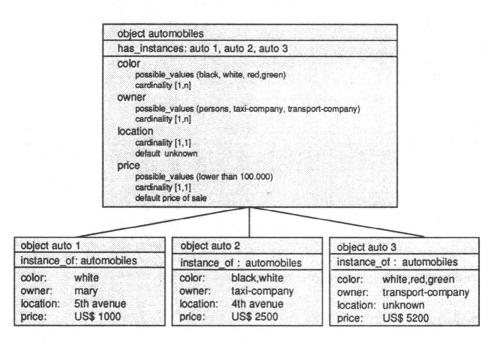

b) description by classification

Figure 5.7: Example of classification

Clearly, describing a model in terms of specific "factual" information is, however, hardly satisfactory. Frequently, it is important to abstract the details of each object and to treat them in a more generic form, without having to worry about the specific values of each property. In fact, the information required is of a generic nature, i.e., a way of referring to all those objects abstracting the details of each one. Classification provides an important means for introducing such generic information by allowing the modeler to refer to the class as a representative or prototype of its instances, into which both properties and constraints applicable to all instances are presented.

The inverse of classification, being *instantiation*, can be used, on the other hand, to obtain objects that conform to the constraints associated with the properties specified by the class. Since an object can be an instance of more than one class, instantiation can be applied to create objects that possess the properties of both classes (e.g., object auto2 in figure 5.8).

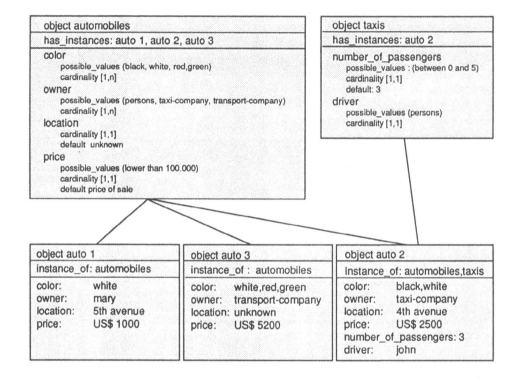

Figure 5.8: Example of a description of instances of multiple classes

Generalization

Generalization is the complementary concept of classification.

Let us say that in addition to the three automobiles described in the last example (figure 5.8), our real world also has trucks (truck1, truck2) and boats (boat1). Classification would then provide the description shown in figure 5.9. However, as well as in the case of classification, it might be important to have a way of referring to all these three classes, or even to all its instances, abstracting the details of each one. In other words, we look for a way of extracting from one or more given classes the description of a more general class that captures the commonalities but suppresses some of the detailed differences in the descriptions of the given classes. Generaliza-

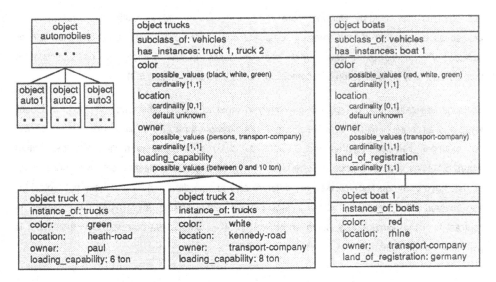

a) description by classification

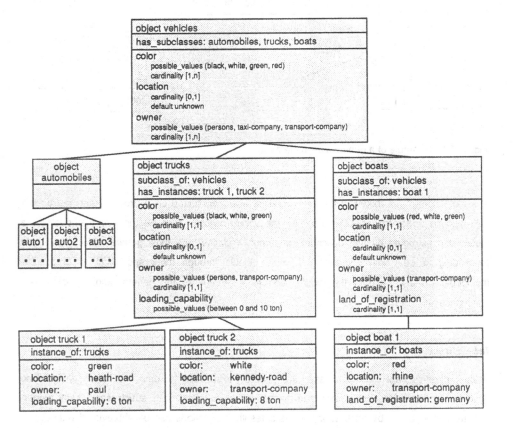

b) description by generalization and classification

Figure 5.9: Example of generalization

tion provides this way, by allowing more complex composite objects called *superclasses* to be defined as a collection of less complex composite ones called *subclasses*, establishing an *is-a* or *subclass-of relationship* between super- and subclasses. In this example, the class vehicles is then defined as a generalization of automobiles, trucks, and boats (figure 5.9).

Since generalization can be applied recursively in order to specify other superclasses of a higher level, it is an *n-level relationship* which organizes classes into a *generalization or is-a hierarchy*. For example, vehicles together with aircrafts could be generalized to means_of_transportation (figure 5.10). As a consequence, a large homogeneity among certain classes is derived since classes that have common superclasses are different only in little details. This is usually not typical for conventional DB applications, where a large inhomogeneity among object types (i.e., classes) in contrast to a big homogeneity within an object type (i.e., among the corresponding instances) is generally the rule (see section 4.2.1.1).

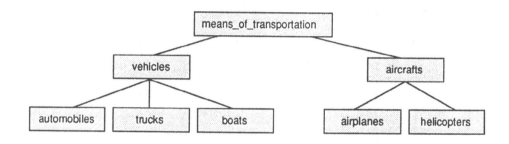

Figure 5.10: Example of a generalization hierarchy

The methodology for modeling the real world is, however, based on a process that has exactly the opposite effect to generalization, i.e., the *specialization*. According to this methodology, a model is constructed by first describing in terms of classes the most general objects and then proceeding to deal with sub-cases of these objects through more specialized classes. This methodology makes use of the most important advantage of the generalization concept, i.e., inheritance.

Inheritance

Since properties kept by superclasses are generally also valid for their subclasses, there is no need to repeat the description stored in the superclass for each of its subclasses. These properties are just inherited by each subclass. As a result, descriptions can be abbreviated without losing the necessary flexibility to describe the properties of the objects, and some classical errors can be avoided by reducing the amount of repetition in descriptions.

There are two basic ways to view the description associated with a class and consequently to treat inheritance [BMW84]. The first one, which is the way KR schemes usually view classes, is that classes simply characterize prototypical instances. As a consequence, inherited properties might be contradicted by subclasses of a class or even by particular instances of them. The second one, which represents the approach followed by semantic data models, views the description associated with a class as necessary conditions (i.e., properties and constraints) that each instance or subclass must satisfy. The consequences of these two views follow immediately:

- If classes are treated in a prototypical sense, inheritance is done by default (default inheritance), i.e., inherited properties are valid only if they are not overridden in the definition of a subclass or instance. For example, even if there is a property in the description of the class birds which says that all birds fly, and penguins is a subclass of birds, penguins do not necessarily fly.

- If classes are treated as templates, inheritance is now strict (strict inheritance), i.e., all inherited properties must exist and be valid for each subclass and consequently for each instance. In this case, it would not be possible to define a property which says that all birds fly, in the class birds, since this property is not satisfied by all subclasses of birds.

At a first glance, the prototype sense of classes seems to be the most appropriate one since it allows a direct representation of exceptions. However, it weakens the assertional force associated with class definitions. By allowing inherited properties to be overridden at a subclass, classification cannot hold between the subclass' instances and its superclasses. For example, it is not possible to assert that the instances of penguin (e.g., tweety) are also instances of birds since they cannot satisfy all properties' constraints specified by birds (see definition of classification). By analyzing the semantics of the template sense thoroughly, one may realize that it not only supports ways to represent exceptions but also fortifies the semantics of the classification concept. Here, exceptions can be expressed by refining the definition of a property as a class is specialized. For example, at the superclass birds the motion property would express that birds either fly, swim, or both and at the subclass penguins, this property would be refined so that the motion of penguins is restricted to "swim". Consequently, all constraints associated with superclasses are valid for the subclasses since they are either the same or even more restrictive (e.g., the property color in figure 5.9b). Naturally, all instances of subclasses are then also instances of the superclasses, fortifying therefore the classification concept.

For all these reasons, we adopt the second view of what a class might be. Thus, we can assert that the only possible changes to inherited properties (i.e., from a class to its specializations) are those that restrict the constraints associated with them.

Resume

Summarizing the idea of classification, we can say that an object becomes an instance of a class by adding values that satisfy the constraints of the properties of the class. In other words, the instance-of relationship is restricted to changes of the properties' values, requiring that everything else is kept constant.

Generalization is an n-level relationship between composite objects (superclass and subclasses), which (together with classification) builds an is-a hierarchy. Subclasses have either exactly the same properties of its superclasses, in this case with more restrictive constraints (e.g., color), or new properties in addition to the inherited ones (e.g., price). In other words, the is-a relationship is restricted to addition of new properties or to restriction of constraints, requiring that everything else is kept constant. For this reason, classification also holds between superclasses and instances of subclasses so that generalization can be viewed as complementary to classification.

5.4.3.1.2   Element- and Set-Association

Modeling Purpose

Element-Association

Frequently, it is necessary to group objects together not because they have the same properties (classification) but because it is important to describe properties of the group of objects as a whole.

Let us say that in our transportation example each vehicle (i.e., automobiles, boats and trucks) has an additional property to express its upkeep costs. Let us also assume that someone is interested in representing the set of vehicles owned by some particular transport company in order to express properties of its fleet like, for example, the average of upkeep costs. Since such properties can only exist in association with objects (see first and forth axiom in section 5.4.1), it is necessary to define a new object possessing this property.

The first idea one could apply is to define a new class having the vehicles owned by this company as instances. However, if one analyzes the definition of classification once again, one will realize that this model is not consistent. A class holds the definition of properties and associated constraints, that each of its instances respectively own and satisfy. Consequently, each instance of vehicles_of_transport_company (i.e., auto3, boat1, truck2) would have to have the property average_of_upkeep_costs. This is, however, a property that neither these objects possess nor can they satisfy it on their own. It is, therefore, not a property of each object but of the group as a whole.

To eliminate this problem one has to use the element-association concept. According to it, another type of object, called *set* object, is introduced to represent these types of properties. In other words, element-association is a form of abstraction in which some objects, called *elements*, are considered as a higher level object, called set. The details of the element objects are suppressed and the properties of the group are emphasized in the set object, establishing an *element-of relationship* between elements and set.

Set-Association

As one can see, the element-association concept, also called grouping, partitioning [He75], or cover aggregation [HM78], corresponds to a part of the set theory of mathematics. Therefore, in addition to the one-level relationship described above, which builds composite objects (sets) based on simple ones (elements), it is also necessary to have a way to express relationships between composite objects (sets) in order to support the set theory completely. These relationships are embodied in the so-called set-association concept, where they are denoted *subset-of relationships*. This would correspond to say that the set vehicles_of_transport_company is a subset of the set means_of_transportation_of_transport_company, which unifies not only the vehicles of the company but also its aircrafts. In this manner, the element-association relationship corresponds to the mathematical relation "$\in$" (belongs to) while the set-association one to the relation "$\subset$" (is contained in). Thus, the subset-of relationship is a *n-level* one since it can be applied recursively, defining (together with the element-of relationship) a hierarchy of objects, called *association hierarchy* (figure 5.11).

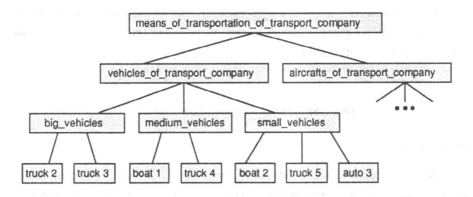

Figure 5.11: Example of an association hierarchy

Similar to the assertion made in the is-a hierarchy, that every instance of a class is also an instance of the class' superclasses, elements of a set are here also elements of the set's supersets. In the same way, objects may be elements of many sets, and sets may be subsets of many other ones.

Set Properties and Membership Stipulations

Clearly, there is no inheritance in the association since the properties described in the sets are not characteristics of the elements themselves. Indeed, they express properties of the set as a whole, which are determined based on properties of the elements, for example: average, maximum, and minimum of values.

In addition to these set properties, set descriptions contain other properties which are valid for each element of the set. For example: every element of the set vehicles_of_transport_company has the company as value of the property owner. We denote these properties membership stipulations.

A set object can become a subset of another by restricting some of the membership stipulations. For example, elements of the set vehicles_of_transport_company have as value of the property loading_capability either high, medium, or low, while the value of the elements of the subset big_vehicles is restricted to high (figure 5.11). By restricting the membership stipulations, the calculation of the set properties will be consequently restricted to a subgroup of the elements of the superset, determining different values for these properties. For example, the calculation of the property average_of_upkeep_costs of the set big_vehicles will be restricted only to the large trucks and not to those of the whole fleet.

Resume

Association relates objects by element-of and subset-of relationships building an association hierarchy. An object becomes a subset of another object by restricting the membership stipulations, which, in turn, restrict the elements used to calculate set properties. Objects are elements of sets when they satisfy the sets' membership stipulations.

5.4.3.1.3 Element- and Component-Aggregation

Modeling Purpose

Frequently, it is necessary to treat objects not as atomic entities, as classification, generalization, and association do, but as a composition of other objects. Let us examine, for example, the object automobiles. It might be important for a particular application to express that automobiles consist of a motor, wheels, and a body, suppressing, however, at a first moment, the specific details of the constituent objects (i.e., that these objects own also properties and also consist of other objects). This conforms to the abstraction concept of aggregation, according to which a collection of objects is viewed as a single higher-level object. Automobiles are treated, therefore, as an aggregation of the objects motor, wheels, and body.

Like the other concepts, aggregation involves two types of objects: simple and composite. Simple objects, called *elements*, express atomic ones in the aggregation, i.e., those objects which can not be further decomposed. Together they comprise the lowest-level composite objects or simplest *components*. These can, in turn, be used to build more complex higher-level components so that an *aggregation or part-of hierarchy* is formed (figure 5.12). Between component objects there is an *subcomponent-of relationship*, whereas between component and elements a *part-element-of relationship* exists. Subcomponent-of relationships establish the elementary concept that we denote component-aggregation in accordance with set-association and generalization, whereas part-element-of relationships establish the element-aggregation concept in accordance with element-association and classification. Naturally, the subcomponent-of relationship is a continuation of the part-element-of one. Thus, elements of subcomponents are also elements of the subcomponents' supercomponents.

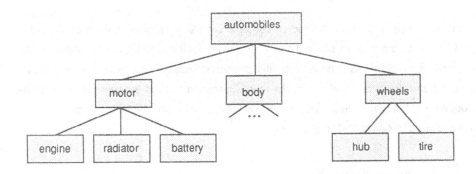

Figure 5.12: Example of an aggregation hierarchy

Aggregation Properties

The aggregation concept corresponds to the notion of property in the sense of composition since it expresses the idea that automobiles "consist-of" a motor, wheels, and a body. More stringently, we can say that the aggregation concept describes necessary properties that an object must own in order to exist consistently. In other words, component objects cannot exist without their part elements. Clearly, it is hard to imagine an automobile without a motor. Note that this requirement makes the aggregation concept quite different from the others. Classes may exist without their instances, and empty sets may occur in the association. Properties of aggregation objects are, therefore, unlike the other concepts, not to be interpreted as characteristics of them but as other objects representing their parts. Usually, these properties do not change with time since objects hardly change their parts. Note that automobiles are always built from the same components. Moreover, objects with different components are probably different objects. If one says, for example, that his object is not an aggregation of motor, wheels, and body but an aggregation of motor, wings, and body, one might not be describing automobiles any more but air-planes.

Resume

The aggregation concept treats a collection of element objects as properties of a single higher-level (component) object. These properties, also called part-of properties, express relationships which usually do not change with time and must have a non-null value in order to characterize objects completely. Applying aggregation recursively over the objects, an aggregation hierarchy is built, having the atomic objects (elements) as its leaves.

5.4.3.2 Built-in Reasoning Facilities

As seen in section 5.4.3.1, the abstraction concepts provide three different ways of organizing objects: the is-a, the association, and the aggregation hierarchy. Although this organizational character is a significant issue provided by the abstraction concepts, the most important advantage of the abstraction relationships are the built-in reasoning facilities they provide. By organizing objects in abstraction hierarchies, special "automatic" reasoning facilities are supported as part of each modification and retrieval operation.

Classification/Generalization Reasoning

The most usual and important of these reasoning facilities is the one built into the is-a hierarchy, i.e., inheritance. It enables descriptive information to be shared among multiple objects, determining the internal structure of instances and providing the means for an automatic maintenance of semantic integrity constraints.

This reasoning facility is based on the structure of classes (see section 5.4.3.1.2). In this manner, by inserting objects in the model and expressing the belief of the modeler that they are instances of any classes, the system has the capability to exactly reason the internal structure of these objects. For example, by expressing that a particular object is an instance of automobiles, the KM can retrieve the "belief", that this object has a color, an owner, a location, and a price. In the same way, if the class means_of_transportation has the subclass vehicles, for example, and vehicles has the subclass automobiles, the KM can reason that automobiles is a subclass of means_of_transportation although this information is not explicitly represented in the KM. Consequently, the system will also reason that all instances of automobiles have the properties specified in means_of _transportation and satisfy the associated constraints.

It might be important to point out here that this view of classification and instantiation does not correspond to the one supported by conventional DB models. In DBS, the belief that an object is an instance of a class (e.g., a tupel of a relation) is not explicitly represented in the model and cannot, for that reason, be queried. Indeed, the insertion of an object is conditioned to the specification of the object type (i.e., to the specification of exactly one instance-of relationship). In other words, an object can only exist if it has an object type (i.e., class) implicitly associated with it. Additionally, it is not possible to change the type of an object. For example, it is not possible to express in the relational model the belief that the object auto1 is not an instance of automobiles but of trucks. The only way to do this is by deleting the object auto1 from the automobiles relation and inserting a new one in the trucks relation, which however will not be interpreted as the same auto1 object. Thus, the instance-of relationship is static in conventional DBS (see section 4.2.1.1).

According to the above observations, before inserting an instance object into the model, a conventional DB-user must firstly reflect upon the structure of this object. By determining exactly what it looks like, the type (i.e., relation) to which it belongs is also determined and the corresponding insert operation may be now issued. As a consequence of this whole process, which terminates with the insertion of the object, an instance-of relationship between inserted object and its specified type will be then implicitly created. Because of this, class descriptions (i.e., properties with associated constraints) cannot be used in the DB world to dynamically reason "beliefs" about the instances' structures, but as helpful conditions (in the sense of type description) to avoid errors by the insertion (or more general by the modification) of objects.

In the KM, objects may exist on their own. It is important, therefore, to allow the modeler to insert a particular object, even when he does not know its object type (for example, he is not sure at insertion time, whether auto1 is an automobile, a truck, or even something else). Consequently, objects may exist in the model independent of the existence of instance-of relationships. Frequently, an object is firstly inserted into the model without any instance-of specification. After this, the modeler might reflect upon the type of this object or he might want to see how the object would look if it were an instance of a particular class (e.g., he "believes" at first that auto1 is an automobile) and defines an instance-of relationship. (Note that in the second case the modeler would be using the KBMS in order to determine the structure of the objects, defining dynamically instance-of relationships). The KM will then deduce the object structure, generating a more detailed description of this object. Based on this new description, the modeler might now realize that it does not correspond to the real world, starting the determination of the object type once again. Therefore, instance-of relationships correspond, in truth, to the actual beliefs of the modeler, which may change at any time without affecting the existence of the objects. For that reason, these relationships must be explicitly represented in the model so that they may be queried at any time. Thus, instance-of specifications here are, in contrast to the conventional DB world, the cause and not the consequence of the whole process. Because of this, class descriptions cannot be used to avoid errors by the insertion of objects as done in conventional DBS. They are to be used to deduce the structure of these objects in conformity to the actual beliefs of the modeler.

Another reasoning facility can use the (already given) structure of objects to determine the position of an object within the is-a hierarchy. Based on the characteristics of the subclass-of and instance-of relationships, the KBMS can reason by analyzing the structure of a given object which objects can be superclasses, subclasses, and instances of it. Additionally, by using the constraint specifications, the KM can determine whether a given item could be a value of a given property so that the existing generalization and/or classification relationships are not violated. For example, when a value is being added to an instance object property which already contains the maximum number of permitted values, the value must be either rejected, otherwise the instance-of relationship between the instance and the class where this constraint is specified do not hold anymore, or this relationship must be dissolved. The decision as to what action should be taken must be made by the modeler. The only thing the KBMS may do is to report the inconsistent state, which would be provoked if it accepts the change. (Note the difference to conventional DBS here, too).

Association Reasoning

As in the generalization/classification, the power of the association concept lies in the "beliefs" the model can reason when two objects are related by the corresponding abstraction relationship. For example, by expressing that truck2 is an instance-of trucks (figure 5.9), the system can reason that it is also a vehicle, has a color, an owner, a location and, a loading_capability. Association works in the same way. For example, if there is a set fast_vehicles in our model with the membership stipulation that every element of this set is a vehicle and moves fast, by expressing that truck truck2 is an element-of this set, the system can reason that truck2 is a fast vehicle.

The difference between generalization/classification and association is that class properties (i.e., those specified by the classes defining the structure of the instances) form the structure of the objects, while membership stipulations do not. Indeed, by restricting the membership stipulations to be expressed only by the structure of the element objects, the power of the association concept would be almost completely lost.

Let us first examine the meaning of the membership stipulations. The consequence of expressing that truck2 is an element of fast_vehicles, i.e., that it moves fast, could also be obtained by defining a property directly in truck2, which describes this characteristic of it. If fast_vehicles has many elements, the same could be accomplished by defining a new class, where the speed property (i.e., fast) would be specified, which would then be inherited by each instance of it (in this case by the elements of fast_vehicles). Thus, membership stipulations correspond to common properties with common values, heterogeneous objects (i.e., objects which do not have common super-classes) possess. Association has, therefore, in some sense a built-in inheritance in its concept. However, the power of the association concept lies exactly in the not-inheritance of these properties.

Let us assume that it is necessary to model the beliefs of another user who wants to group the slow_vehicles together. Let us also assume that this second user is of the opinion that truck2 is a slow vehicle and asserts that truck2 is an element-of slow_vehicles. Although at a first glance our model seems to be inconsistent since truck2 is at the same time element-of fast_vehicles and slow_vehicles, this is not at all inconsistent since each of these sets represent beliefs of two different people. The model would, however, be in an inconsistent state if these two properties were described by the generalization/classification concept and consequently inherited to truck2 since they would define two different structural descriptions for truck2. Note that, in this case, truck2 would have two different descriptions: one with value fast and another with value slow by the same property. (In the AI world this problem is known by the name multiple inheritance conflict).

However, the meaning of association is another. By not applying inheritance, it does not define different structural descriptions of truck2 but different "views" of it. That is, truck2 is a fast vehicle (which is the same as saying that truck2 has an additional property expressing that it is fast) viewed from the set fast_vehicles. However, viewed from the set slow_vehicles, truck2 is a slow one. (Note that membership stipulations are properties that every element must satisfy in order to be an element of the set (see section 5.4.3.1.2). They are, in other words, indeed properties of the elements.)

Association, unlike generalization/classification, therefore allows the system to reason beliefs which are neither bound nor restricted to the structure of the objects. As a consequence, very different "worlds", which can even contradict each other, can be easily modeled. Because of this, association has been found very useful in modeling planning and design activities since it is very appropriate in representing hypothetical worlds and belief spaces [Co78].

Naturally, by specifying the membership stipulations based on the structure of the element objects (e.g., elements of the set vehicles_of_transport_company must have the company as value of the property owner), the system could determine whether a change in an element object might be allowed in order not to violate the element-of and/or subset-of relationship. Clearly, the system could either reject such a change or accept it. In this case, the violated element-of and/or subset-of relationship would be dissolved and new ones, now satisfied by the "new" object, would be created. Nevertheless, reasoning based on the structure of the objects is not the goal of the association concept but of the generalization/classification.

In addition to this reasoning facility, association provides another one which, however, works just in the other way that inheritance does. That is, while generalization/classification reasoning facilities depend on the structure of classes (i.e., they flow downwards just like inheritance), this reasoning facility provided by the association concept is independent of the structure of the sets. Rather set properties are determined by the properties of the elements (i.e., they flow upwards). Thus, while changes in the classes (e.g., the deletion of a property) imply downward changes in the model, changes in the set properties do not cause any modification in the objects which are covered by this set. However, by modifying the elements, upward changes in the set properties are caused. For example, by changing the value of the property upkeep_costs of a vehicle of the transport_company, the KBMS must correspondingly reason the new value of the set property average_of_upkeep_costs of the sets vehicles_of_transport_company and means_of_transportation_of_transport_company. In the same manner, reasoning is necessary when new objects become elements of a set in order to maintain a consistent view of the modeled world.

Aggregation Reasoning

Like the association, the aggregation relationships are not dependent on the structure of the objects. They support the notion of complex objects, which allows a user at any particular moment to view an object as a single unit (i.e., together with all its parts) and at a subsequent time to view only parts of it as independent objects. By the aggregation, objects are therefore viewed in one context as objects of their own and in another as components of other objects.

However, unlike the association, the reasoning facilities provided by the aggregation concept are based on the structures of the objects and, furthermore, on properties common to components, subcomponents, and elements. These reasoning facilities are supported by predicates which are specified over the aggregation hierarchy and are based on these common properties [RHMD87]. A property whose value decreases while going downwards over the aggregation hierarchy, for example, weight (the weight of a subcomponent is always either the same or smaller than the weight of its supercomponents) is said to be monotonically decreasing. Properties whose value increases going downwards in the aggregation hierarchy are denoted monotone increasing.

Based on these properties, predicates are defined so that reasoning can be carried out. A predicate is upward implied if its satisfaction for an object implies that all its supercomponents satisfy it. For example, the predicate "weight > 1 ton" is upward implied since all supercomponents have a weight bigger than one ton if any of their subcomponents or elements does. A predicate is downward implied when satisfying it at a component implies satisfying it at descendents. For example, "scheduled_completion_time < June" is downward implied since all subcomponents and elements have a scheduled_completion_time smaller than the one of their supercomponents.

Reasoning facilities of the aggregation concept corresponds to the conclusions the KM can make based on these implied predicates when two objects are related by the subcomponent-of or element-of relationship. For example, conclusions about the weight of a component can be made based on the corresponding upward implied predicate. In the same manner, the KM can use these implied predicates as constraint specifications to determine whether a given value could be the value of an object's property so that the monotony of this property is not violated.

A last reasoning facility of aggregation is related to the axiom that objects may not exist without their subcomponents and elements. Because of this, by deleting objects, the KM can reason that all subparts of these objects should also be deleted. For example, when a particular automobile is removed from a KB, the KM reasons that its motor, its body, and its wheels are removed together with it.

5.4.3.3   Integration of Abstraction Concepts

Up till now, we have isolated the discussion about each abstraction concept from the others. We have seen, for example, that association builds a hierarchy of objects which, however, up to this point, was constructed independently of the is-a hierarchy. The same has been done with the aggregation. Hence, the three existing abstraction hierarchies could be summarily sketched as shown in figure 5.13.

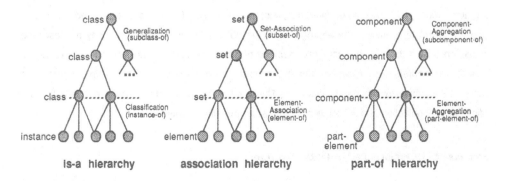

Figure 5.13: Summarizing sketch of the abstraction concepts

Naturally, in the real world, this independence does not exist. Objects are obviously instances of classes, elements of sets, and components of aggregations at the same time. For example, the elements of the set vehicles_of_transport_company are respectively instances of automobiles, boats, and trucks (see figure 5.9 and 5.11). The same occurs with the component of an aggregation, for example, a particular motor, which can be an instance of the class motors and an element of the set powerful_engines.

We realize, therefore, that the first assertion made about the entities of the real world in section 5.4.1, i.e., that every one is an object of the model, has still been satisfied in spite of our independent consideration of the abstraction concepts (see section 5.4.1). However, the second one can only be satisfied if all abstraction concepts are considered together so that all information about an entity are concentrated into one object of the model. This has an additional advantage. By considering all abstraction concepts together, descriptions of one concept can use the descriptions of the others. This will allow much richer and more precise descriptions of world entities which are to be obtained following the development of models that reflect even more directly and naturally the user's conceptualization of the real world. A final advantage is that objects can be concisely described without losing the necessary flexibility, and some classical errors provoked by the introduction of redundancy can be avoided by reducing the amount of repetition in the descriptions.

Hence, objects of the KM may now have six types of relationships to other objects (instance-of, subclass-of, element-of, subset-of, part-element-of, subcomponent-of) corresponding to the different roles they play in each abstraction hierarchy. Consequently, the semantic meaning of the objects can be very different from context to context in which they are found. There are objects expressing instances in one context and elements in another, and even objects representing classes, sets, and components in different contexts. For example, the object automobiles may be the subclass of vehicles in a context, where structural properties which are to be inherited to the instances are described. In another context, it might be the set where properties like cheapest_auto, most_expensive_auto, average_price, and number_of_autos are expressed. And in a final one, it might represent the aggregation of the objects motor, wheels, and body as described in section 5.4.3.1.3. Thus, the semantic meaning of an object can only be determined in regard to a particular context (i.e., together with the corresponding abstraction relationship). Figure 5.14 shows a schematic explanation of this idea. The whole object descriptions now embody both classification/generalization and association as well as aggregation properties.

Stepwise Enrichment of Objects' Description

Let us first consider the properties of the classification/generalization concept together with association.

By concentrating both class properties and set properties into just one object (e.g., automobiles), set properties will be inherited together with the class properties by all instance objects. This is, clearly, not desirable.

To avoid this problem, it is important to differentiate set and class properties in order to restrict inheritance to class properties. This is achieved by including a property type (instance or own) associated with each property. In this way, instance-properties are those concerned with classification/generalization and own-properties those with the association. Instance-properties are therefore inherited since they describe characteristics of the instances of a class, while own-properties are not inherited since they describe characteristics of the set objects themselves.

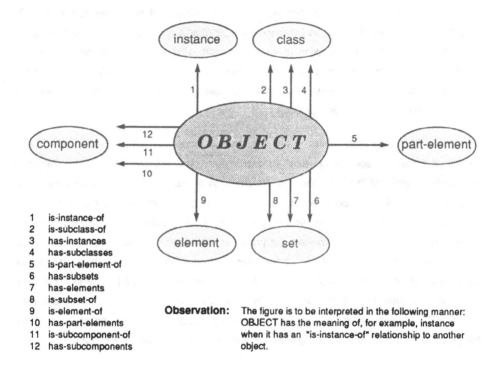

1   is-instance-of
2   is-subclass-of
3   has-instances
4   has-subclasses
5   is-part-element-of
6   has-subsets
7   has-elements
8   is-subset-of
9   is-element-of
10 has-part-elements
11 is-subcomponent-of
12 has-subcomponents

Observation: The figure is to be interpreted in the following manner: OBJECT has the meaning of, for example, instance when it has an "is-instance-of" relationship to another object.

Figure 5.14: Schematic summary of the abstractions' semantics

Naturally, in the case that an object plays the role of a class in one context and of an instance in another, it is also important to avoid inheritance of instance-properties. Clearly, properties which are inherited by the object in the second context because it is an instance should not be further inherited in the first context where it is a class since they describe characteristics of the object related only to its existence as an instance. Because of this, we generalize the meaning of the own-properties by not restricting them to the association concept. Therefore, own-properties express properties of any object itself (e.g., an instance or a set). Hence, inheritance occurs over the generalization/classification relationships according to the following rules:

- instance-properties are inherited as instance-properties by the subclasses of a class and as own-properties by its instances, and

- own-properties are not inherited at all.

By combining aggregation with the other concepts, it is also important to differentiate the aggregation properties from the other properties of the objects (as it was done in the case of association and generalization/classification) since values of aggregation properties are to be interpreted as other objects of the model. Note that the semantics of aggregation properties is very different from the semantics of class and set properties. While aggregation properties represent parts of the objects, class and set properties represent characteristics of them (see section 5.4.3.2). As a consequence, we introduce an indication as to whether a property describes an aggregation relationship or not in the description of each object property, additionally to the type own or instance. We indicate part-of properties as non-terminal ones since their values correspond to other objects of the model, whereas the other ones (generalization/classification and association properties) are denoted as terminal properties.

Considering the object automobiles, it has the terminal properties color, owner, location, price, number_of_autos, cheapest_auto, most_expensive_auto, and average_price, which represent characteristics either of the instances or of the set of all automobiles, and the non-terminal properties motor, wheels, and body, which represent the parts of automobiles (figure 5.15). Since each instance of automobiles also has the parts motor, wheels, and body, we use the classification concept and define these non-terminal properties additionally as instance-properties so that they are passed on as non-terminal own-properties to each instance of automobiles. In this way, we integrate all abstraction concepts and use the facilities of some of them (in the example inheritance) for the description of the others (in this case aggregation). The result, as already mentioned, is an abbreviated description. By not using classification, the definition of the aggregation properties motor, wheels, and body must be repeated at each instance of automobiles.

As discussed in section 5.4.3.2, the abstraction relationships must be explicitly represented in the model. Since class and set properties do not contain the necessary information to represent the corresponding abstraction relationships, we introduce some pre-defined properties in each object in order to directly express these relationships. Additionally, we combine these properties in pairs so that a symmetric modeling is obtained. Classification is represented by the properties has-instances, specified at a class, and its "back reference" instance-of, specified at the corresponding instances. The has-subclasses property defined for a superclass corresponds to the subclass-of property defined for a subclass. Together they represent the generalization concept. In the same manner, element-association is represented by the properties has-elements and element-of, whereas the set-association concept is supported by has-subsets and subset-of (see figure 5.14).

To represent the relationships of the aggregation concept, we could also use pre-defined properties (e.g., subcomponent-of, has-subcomponents, part-element-of, and has-part-elements). However, this is not necessary since aggregation properties already exactly specify the meaning of such relationships. Furthermore, by expressing each aggregation relationship in a property, aggregation can be better combined with other concepts, allowing specific constraints to be assigned to each particular relationship, as shown in figure 5.15. Note that it would not be possible to have a possible_value and cardinality specification for each subcomponent of automobiles if these subcomponents were represented together by only one pre-defined property (has-subcomponents) as done in the other abstraction concepts. Clearly, a symmetric modeling is also desired here. Because of this, the specification of a property representing a "back reference" to be maintained at the subcomponent or element is required as a non-terminal property is defined.

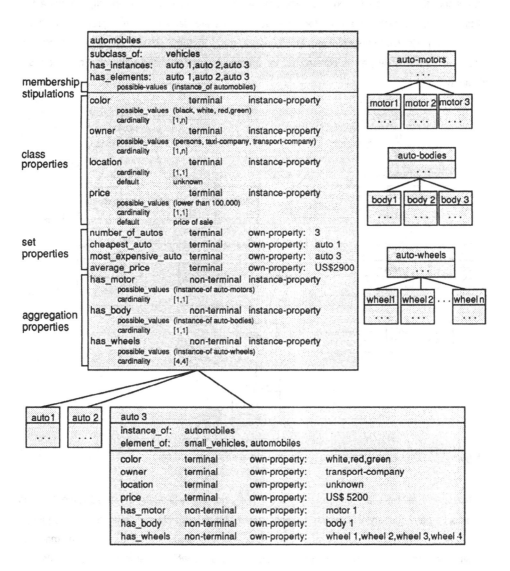

Figure 5.15: An integrated view of the object automobiles

Before finishing our discussion, we would like to briefly consider a final example of a model integrating all abstraction concepts. The example, shown in figure 5.16, describes the production of a hypothetical automobile factory. It produces different automobile models (model x, model y...) each of which have different variants (standards, luxurious...). Automobiles, models, and variants are related by the generalization concept so that general characteristics of automobiles are inherited by each automobile model, where they are correspondingly specialized and complemented with other characteristics specific to this model. The models' properties are then inherited by its variants, where they are specialized and complemented once again, expressing exactly the characteristics of each automobile variant. Moreover, automobiles are defined as an aggregation of many automobile parts (batteries, motors, etc...), which may, in turn, consist of other components. Since each automobile part is constructed for a particular model, these parts also build an is-a hierarchy.

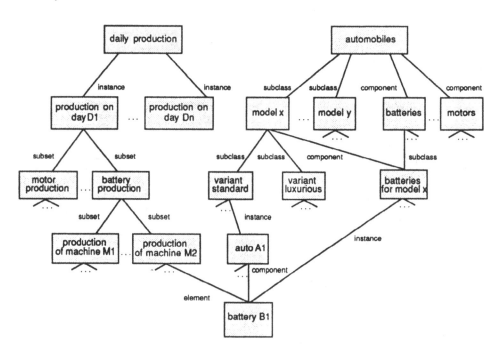

Figure 5.16: Exemplary application integrating the abstraction concepts

At the leaves of the is-a hierarchies there are the automobiles actually produced (auto A1) and automobile parts (battery B1), which are once again, like its superclasses, related by the aggregation concept. With the necessity of a daily control of the production of each factory machine, automobile parts (battery B1) are grouped together in sets, whose elements are the parts produced by a particular machine on one day. This will allow the comparison of the performance of different machines as well as the frequency with which they produce defective parts. Machine productions are grouped together in part production sets (battery production, motor production...) and these, in turn, in a daily production set (production on day D1). Each daily production has set properties such as total number of produced parts, number of machines involved, etc. In order to avoid defining these properties at each daily production set, we use the classification concept and describe them as instance-properties at the class daily production. Over the instance-of relationship, they are then inherited as own-properties, defining the structure (i.e., the set properties) of each daily production set.

5.4.3.4 Conclusions

In this section, we have discussed the abstraction concepts: the most important constructs to be supported by the KM provided by the engineering layer. We preferred to consider them from a neutral point of view, treating them in the same way human observers consider the conceptualization of the real world, instead of providing a detailed description of the realization in a particular model. The focus of the section has, for this reason, primarily been on defining the semantics of them, on showing their applicability, and on presenting a way to integrate them into the KM.

We have argued that object descriptions should embody all abstraction concepts so that objects can play different roles (i.e., class, set, component, etc.) at the same time depending on the relationships they have to other objects. Based on the existence of these relationships, the most important advantage of the abstraction concepts (their built-in reasoning facilities) is used to make deductions about objects:

- Inheritance is used to reason the internal structure of instances,

- Membership Stipulations are used to reason beliefs about elements defining different "views" of them, and

- Implied Predicates are used to make conclusions about aggregation objects based on the monotony of properties.

5.5 The Implementation Layer

The goal of this layer is to efficiently cope with storage of knowledge and the supply of it to the engineering and application layers. For this reason, many of the issues of this level are related to traditional database problems applied to large knowledge bases possibly shared by multiple users: storage structures, search techniques, efficiency, control of concurrent access, logging and recovery mechanisms, etc.

Based on the storage of the entire KB in virtual memory and, therefore, neglecting the existence of access problems, time has not, traditionally, been a criterion to measure the effectiveness of existing KS (see chapter 4). Usually, this measurement was made by only considering the power of the features offered by the engineering layer. In fact, both the engineering and the application layer ignore the issues of how the knowledge is stored and accessed, by relegating this to the implementation layer. Nevertheless, with the use of secondary storage devices, efficiency, particularly time efficiency, by accessing the knowledge and making it available to the other layers became the major problem of concern in this layer.

A prerequisite in identifying the specific requirements to be supported here is, therefore, the investigation of the behavior of KS running on secondary storage environments. It is important to have great depth in the characteristics of KS accesses to the KB as well as in the necessary structures to map knowledge in order to define adequate mechanisms to increase the KBMS performance. Such an investigation is certainly quite a difficult task since this kind of KS does not exist (as already mentioned, almost every existing KS keeps its knowledge totally in virtual memory). Because of this, we have adapted some available KS to work on secondary storage environments, in order to pursue this investigation [HMP87].

Some of our observations were already briefly discussed in chapter 4, in which we presented some of the experiences gained by the construction of some coupling prototypes as well as by the mapping investigation with the MAD model. In this section, we abstract the particular conclusions of each of these concrete investigations, putting together those results which will dictate the specific requirements to be supported by the implementation layer. Further requirements which are closely related to traditional DBS features will not be discussed but are, however, equally as relevant as the following.

Access characteristics

The accesses made at the implementation layer interface (object-supporting interface) are mainly to tiny granules. In the frame-based KR scheme environment, for example, they refer to individual attributes of objects rather than to the objects as a whole. Sequences of accesses to attributes of the same object are also typical. This occurs because inference engines can only process one "piece of" knowledge at a time so that accesses to very small amounts of information result. It is, therefore, important to have mechanisms in the implementation layer that enable the reduction of the path length when accessing KB contents, allowing the application (i.e., KS) to reference KB objects almost directly. In other words, we propose the design of an implementation layer aimed at high locality of references to the KB contents.

Access types

In general, during a KS consultation accesses to the KB are mostly referred to read and write operations. Insert and delete operations may also occur, however, with very low frequency since these operations are associated with some kind of structural change of the KB. In other words, during a consultation, modifications in the structures of the KB (e.g., changing object types or adding new instances to a type) are very seldom. Clearly, during the KB construction process, this situation is just the inverse.

This strong stability should be exploited at this layer when choosing the storage structures for the KB. Since KB construction is an iterative and incremental process and consequently does not require a performance as high as KS consultation, the implementation layer should give more priority to the optimization of the retrieval operations.

Access frequencies

The frequency of accesses to object attributes also differ very much. Dynamic attributes (i.e., the ones that represent the knowledge inferred during a consultation or some specific information about the case being analyzed) are accessed with very high frequency; static attributes (i.e., the ones that represent the expert knowledge of the KS), on the other hand, are accessed with very low frequency (see section 4.3.3.2 for further comments on static and dynamic knowledge). This is a consequence of the way reasoning mechanisms of KS use knowledge. Typically, each "piece of" static knowledge, for example the action of a rule, is used just once during the reasoning process when the KS needs to infer a particular knowledge, i.e., the dynamic knowledge that this rule infers. However, each "piece of" dynamic knowledge, for example the information that the patient has fever, is needed on several occasions. Since it is applied to infer several other "pieces of" dynamic knowledge, i.e., the fever information can occur in the conditions of several rules, it is used and therefore accessed very frequently.

Figure 5.17 serves as an example of such KS access behavior. It presents the distribution of MED1's accesses (see section 4.3.3.2) to static and dynamic attributes of its object types.

In order to make use of this KS access characteristic, when storing KB objects, this layer should split them, keeping dynamic and static attributes separate. By exploiting this kind of clustering in the storage structures, the locality of the KS accesses will be surely better supported. Furthermore, when the KS refers to dynamic attributes (what occurs in most cases), the implementation layer may access only these. As a consequence, I/O operations as well as transfer overhead will be strongly reduced since the dynamic attributes are much smaller than the static ones. In the case of MED1, for example, they just represent about ten percent of the KB contents.

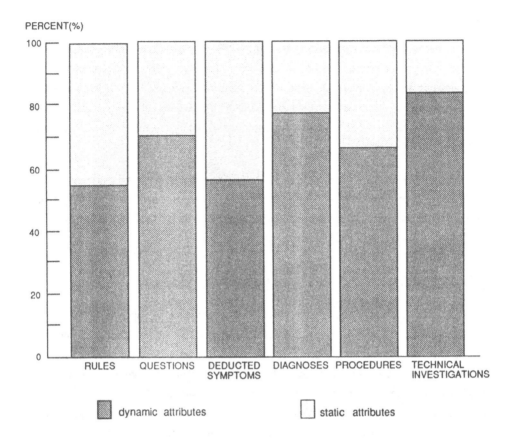

PERCENT(%)

Figure 5.17: Distribution of MED1 accesses between static and dynamic attributes

Processing contexts

It has been observed that in each phase of the problem solving process, KS accesses concentrate on the contents of just some objects of the KB. The reason for this is that KS needs different parts of the KB to work on different problems. The accessed objects represent, therefore, the knowledge needed to infer the specific goal of that phase. As discussed previously in section 4.3.3.2.4, these objects together build what we have called context. (In [MW84], Missikoff and Wiederhold come to similar conclusions by observing the presence of problem and context related clusters in the KB). The existence of such processing contexts depends, therefore, on the problem solving strategy being used. For example, KS exploiting constraint-propagation have contexts corresponding to the several constraints defined in the KB. In the same manner, a problem-reduction strategy determines contexts for processing each partitioned subproblem, and generate-and-test organizes KB contents according to the KS pruning activity (see section 3.5).

Although processing contexts are known just after the definition of the problem solving strategy and the construction of the KB, during a KS consultation, the context needed in each phase can be neither static nor determined at the beginning of this consultation. Usually, it is dynamically established by some information that the KS deduces during the preceding phases (i.e., dynamic knowledge) so that it is possible to determine the next context needed only at the end of a phase. For example, in a hypothesize-and-test environment contexts needed in test phases depend directly on the suspicions generated in the foregoing hypothesize phases. This knowledge about the behavior of KS accesses disables therefore a static but enables a dynamic preplanning of the accesses to the KB that should be used at this layer for optimization purposes. The implementation layer should exploit the existence of such processing contexts building further clusters in the storage structures as well as applying more appropriate access paths. Such measures will then improve the implementation layer support of the locality of KS accesses, increasing KBMS performance as a whole.

Temporary maintenance of dynamic knowledge

Since the values of the dynamic knowledge are derived during a consultation and will be, of course, different from case to case being analyzed by a KS, they generally lose their significance at the end of a consultation. The static knowledge on the other hand represents the expertise of the human experts and is, for this reason, relevant for each KS consultation. Because of this, the values of the dynamic attributes are to be kept only temporarily by the KBMS, whereas the static ones are to be stored permanently.

Multi-user environments

One can imagine that in multi-user environments, the static attributes are accessed concurrently by each user in order to infer the values of the dynamic ones corresponding to the case which the KS is analyzing for each one. Thus, keeping just one copy of the static knowledge would be sufficient since it will be accessed by multiple users. However, the KBMS must maintain for the dynamic knowledge as many versions (i.e., some kind of private data) as the number of users working with KB (figure 5.18). These versions are then accessed individually since the values of the dynamic attributes of one user have no meaning to the other ones. Thus, in multi-user environments synchronization should be controlled only for static knowledge.

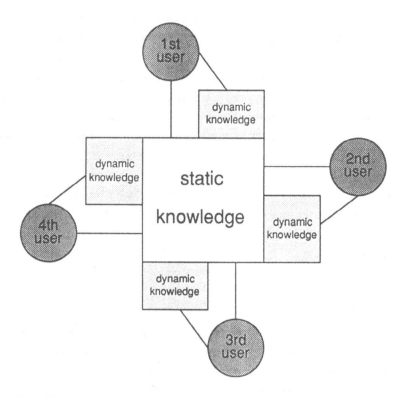

Figure 5.18: Knowledge management in a multi-user environment

Knowledge structures

Knowledge structures of KS are usually very complex. Often, KB contents are defined as a composition of other KB contents so that the implementation layer must cope with the handling of complex objects. Furthermore, most KS present not only the usual single-valued attribute types. Frequently, attributes are multiple-valued and present data types (lists, texts, and procedure) whose length may vary extremely. In general, it is not possible to fix the length of an attribute, since it may change dynamically during the consultation, and even not its maximal length. Consequently, KBMS should make use of more sophisticated storage structures and access paths as those normally provided by DBS.

5.6 KBMS Features Reviewed

In this chapter, we discussed architectural issues of KBMS, i.e., systems whose goal is the effective and efficient management of KB. We have advocated the division of KBMS into three different layers, which support the requirements of the application, the needs of the KB designer, and the requirements of an efficient knowledge management. The main philosophy of such systems is the idea of abstraction aimed at the independence of knowledge. At the system interface, knowledge should be seen not in terms of the flexible representational framework supported by the engineering layer for the KB designer but functionally in terms of the application's beliefs about its domain. In order to achieve this functional view of the KB, it is necessary to restrict the communication between application and KBMS to some kind of ask and tell operations, however, providing:

- multiple ways to select as well as to store all kinds of knowledge found in the application's world,

- user-defined qualification predicates,

- user-defined projection clauses,

- flexible forms to cause changes in the KB,

- set-oriented queries, and

- recursive processing.

A second very important philosophy is the effective support of the needs of the knowledge engineer. Clearly, this philosophy has also been the goal of most existing KR systems [FK85, BS83, FWA85, Wi84b, GWCRM86], which try to support these needs by focusing on the improvement of the expressiveness (i.e., descriptive aspects) of their representation model. However, in a KBMS context, expressiveness is just one of the three aspects to be considered at the engineering layer. Here, organizational and operational aspects are equally as important as descriptive ones. Because of this, an effective support of the needs of the KB designer is to be achieved by a mixed knowledge representation framework defined by the KM. It should offer constructs to represent the procedural characteristics of the application world, i.e.:

- behaviors of the objects of the application domain,

- reactions of these objects to particular real world events, and

- situation-action rules expressing the expert solving know-how.

Additionally, mechanisms for knowledge organization should be embodied by the KM since they are the fundamental modeling tools applied for describing knowledge. The engineering layer should therefore support all abstraction concepts, enriching the semantics of the KM with their several built-in reasoning facilities.

Finally, both operational and organizational aspects should be uniformly integrated with a very rich descriptive part of the KM, allowing for an accurate representation of the whole declarative characteristics of the application domain, i.e., objects, their properties, relationships, and constraints.

As one may see, the KM integrates the three different aspects of knowledge in the concept of object, thereby defining the so-called object-centered representation.

A third and final significant philosophy of KBMS should pay attention to performance requirements. Most important is the framework to be provided by the implementation layer for the exploitation of the application locality. Therefore, it is desirable to have mechanisms that

- enable the reduction of the path length,

- offer fast access to stored objects,

- reduce I/O operations as well as transfer overhead,

- efficiently cope with multi-user access, and

- allow for an adequate mapping of the knowledge structures

when referring to KB contents. Further features of the implementation layer should reflect traditional DBS characteristics in order to

- guarantee the maintenance of the KB semantic integrity,

- allow for KBMS exhibiting high reliability as well as availability, and

- permit the distribution of the KB.

It may be now important to investigate whether the discussed KBMS approach fulfils knowledge management requirements of KS (see section 4.1).

Considering at first the functions for knowledge maintenance, we argue that the several concepts supported by the implementation layer fulfil not only the efficiency requirements but also the other growing KS demands on managing the KB adequately.

Knowledge manipulation functions are considered by both the application and the engineering layer. Whereas the first cares for the isolation of representational aspects from the application, supporting, however, an appropriate set of retrieve and store operations, the latter provides flexible and appropriate ways for deriving new knowledge.

Knowledge modeling requirements are certainly fulfilled by the issues supported at the engineering layer. Its framework, defined by means of the KM, allows for an accurate representation of the model of expertise, reflecting directly the user's natural conceptualization of the universe of discourse.

In closing, we argue that our KBMS approach also provides the necessary means for supporting the incremental KS construction process. Firstly, it permits the knowledge engineer to use the KM as a tool for dynamically defining the structure of the KB contents. Thus, it supports the necessary design issues. Secondly, KB contents (e.g., object types, behaviors, reactions, constraints, situation-action rules, etc.) may be created and modified without losing any of the previously existing information. It allows therefore KB contents to be incrementally specified, thereby supporting knowledge reformulations. Finally, it permits an easy validation of KB contents since almost the whole knowledge of the application world is explicitly represented, thereby providing means for design refinements.

6. The KBMS Prototype KRISYS

In the previous chapter, we have described an architecture for KBMS, thereby defining the features to be provided by the system components and showing how they may fulfil the requirements of KS. Following this architectural approach, we have designed and implemented a multi-layered prototypical KBMS, called KRISYS (Knowledge Representation and Inference SYStem), in which these features have been incorporated [Ma88b].

In this chapter, we describe our prototypical architecture for KBMS in order to illustrate how to apply the issues discussed in chapter 5 to build realistic KBMS. We begin with a general overview of the system architecture followed by a detailed description of the knowledge model supported by KRISYS and of each of its components.

6.1 Overview of the System Architecture

KRISYS is architecturally divided in different modules reflecting the aspects of the multi-layered KBMS approach previously described (figure 6.1) [Ma88b]. The application layer corresponds to the KOALA processing system. It is responsible for the realization of the application interface of KRISYS which is defined by the language KOALA (KRISYS Object-Abstraction LAnguage) [De88,HS88b]. This language provides the user or KS with an abstract, functional view of the KB thereby restricting all interactions with KRISYS to two types of operations: TELL and ASK, to respectively assert that (pieces of) knowledge should be true in the KB and to retrieve information. In a TELL-statement, the user specifies only the information to be asserted. The processing system decides what kind of operation is needed (e.g., create, modify, delete, etc.) to achieve the specified state and takes the appropriate actions. In an ASK-statement, the specified condition is either proved by the system (yielding 'true' or 'false') or used for retrieval of knowledge from the KB. However, the user is totally unaware of the way in which the requested information has been retrieved, i.e., if it has been directly accessed, deduced, or computed in some way [DM89].

Assertions and conditions are both expressed as formulas constructed according to a first order predicate calculus which is based on predefined predicates and functions that embody the semantics of the underlying knowledge model of KRISYS [DM89]. The terms of this knowledge model, called KOBRA (KRISYS OBject-centered RepresentAtion Model), are defined by a mixed knowledge representation framework that is provided by the Object-centered REpresentation System (ORES) [Mo88,Kn88,Le88] for the KB designer. Thus, this module corresponds to the previously described engineering layer and its interface to the object-centered interface. ORES supports an *object-centered representation* of the application world by means of its basic concept, i.e., the schema which is an object having attributes to describe its characteristics. For the structuring of the KB, it provides the *abstraction concepts* of classification, generalization, association, and aggregation together with their corresponding *built-in reasoning facilities*. ORES and, accordingly, the knowledge model of KRISYS support an *integrated view of KB objects*: a schema may describe an object having several abstraction relationships to many others. As a consequence, KRISYS eliminates the difference between data and meta-data *integrating meta-information into the KB*. Finally, to represent procedural characteristics of the application world, ORES provides methods, demons, and rules, with which behavior of domain objects, reactions to real world events, and the problem solving know-how may be respectively represented [Kn88].

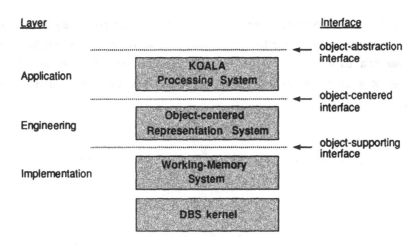

Figure 6.1: Overall system architecture of KRISYS

The requirements of the implementation layer are fulfilled by two distinct modules. The DBS kernel is responsible for the storage and management of the KB. The Working-Memory System embodies the *"nearby application locality"* concept, thereby reducing DBS calls as well as the path length when accessing the objects of the KB [LM89]. This component manages a special main memory structure, called working-memory, which acts as an application buffer, in which requested KB objects are temporarily stored. The replacement of these objects is carried out in accordance with the processing contexts of the KS (section 5.5) so that DBS calls, accesses to secondary storage, as well as transfer overhead are substantially reduced.

6.2 The Knowledge Model of KRISYS

6.2.1 Survey of the KOBRA Constructs

The knowledge model of KRISYS (KOBRA) provides the KB designer with a mixed representation framework integrating several concepts originating from the fields of knowledge representation and data models. Special emphasis is put on a complete support of all the aspects of knowledge (i.e., descriptive, operational, and organizational) so that a powerful framework is obtained, allowing a natural and accurate modeling of all aspects of the application world.

The structure of the objects

In the KOBRA model, the three knowledge aspects mentioned above are equally incorporated in its basic concept: the *schema* (not to be confused with a DB-schema!). A schema is the symbolic representation of a real world entity. It is always clearly identifiable by a unique schema name and is composed of a set of attributes describing the properties of the corresponding real world object (figure 6.2).

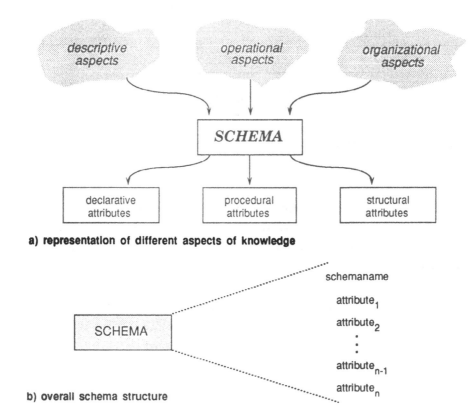

a) representation of different aspects of knowledge

b) overall schema structure

Figure 6.2: The schema concept

Since properties may be either of a declarative, procedural, or structural nature (see chapter 5), attributes are used to express descriptive characteristics of the real world entities as well as their behavior or abstraction relationships to other schemas. KRISYS supports, therefore, an *object-centered representation* of the application world since every entity existing in the application domain is expressed as an object of the KOBRA model represented by the schema concept (figure 6.3).

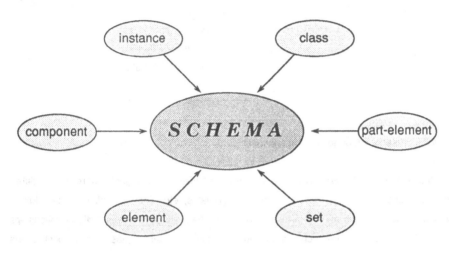

Figure 6.3: Object-centered representation

The organization of the KB

In order to enable the knowledge engineer to structure the KB adequately, KOBRA supports the *abstraction concepts* of classification, generalization, association, and aggregation. These concepts are seen as special relationships between schemas, defining the overall organization of a KB as a kind of complex network of objects.

The abstraction relationships are specified either in predefined attributes occurring in each schema (classification, generalization, and association) or by user-defined attributes (aggregation). They are combined in pairs allowing for a symmetric modeling of the application world. So, to the attribute representing the classification concept (INSTANCE_OF) there corresponds another one representing the instantiation concept (HAS_INSTANCES). In the same way, generalization is represented by the attribute SUBCLASS_OF, whereas specialization is expressed with HAS_SUBCLASSES. The abstraction concept of element-association is represented by the attributes ELEMENT_OF and HAS_ELEMENTS and set-association by SUBSET_OF and HAS_SUBSETS (figure 6.4). Aggregation is only partially provided. That is, KOBRA allows the representation of complex objects by using user-defined attributes, but the actual version of KRISYS does not support the corresponding built-in reasoning facilities.

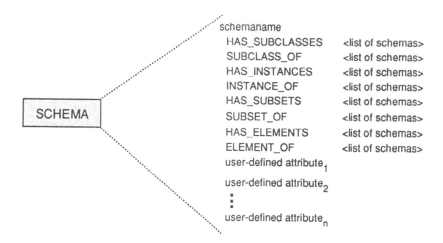

Figure 6.4: Representation of abstraction relationships

The knowledge model of KRISYS supports an *integrated view of KB objects*: there are no different representations for classes, sets, instances, aggregates, etc. They are all integrated into a schema which may describe an object related to many others via several abstraction relationships (figure 6.3). Therefore, the same schema can, for example, represent a class with respect to one object and a set or even an instance with respect to another. As a consequence, the difference between data and meta-data, which is usually apparent in existing data models (see section 4.2.1), is eliminated in KRISYS so that *meta-information is integrated into the KB*.

The structure of attributes

Attributes can be of two kinds:

- *slots*, used to describe descriptive aspects of the schema (i.e., characteristics, relationships to other schemas, etc.), and

- *methods*, used to describe its operational aspects (i.e., the behavior of the real world entity).

Hence, KOBRA supports an *object-oriented representation*. It allows both attributive characteristics and procedural properties of the real world entities to be integrated into a schema.

Slots and methods have the same structure (figure 6.5). Both possess an attribute name, value, type, and a schema name that specifies where the attribute was defined (origin). The type indicates whether an attribute represents characteristics of the schema itself or of its instances. Characteristics of a schema are described by the type OWNSLOT and OWNMETHOD whereas the characteristics of an instance by INSTANCESLOT and INSTANCEMETHOD respectively.

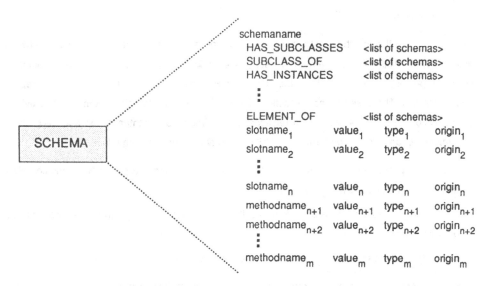

Figure 6.5: Structure of slots and methods

Figure 6.6 shows the representation of the object auto2 (see chapter 5) together with its superclasses (automobiles and taxis) in the KRISYS notation. Since all attributes of auto2 describe characteristics of itself, they have type OWNSLOT or OWNMETHOD. Note that there is no difference in the representation of behavior (running), attributive properties (color, price, etc.), and relationships to other schemas (owner and driver).

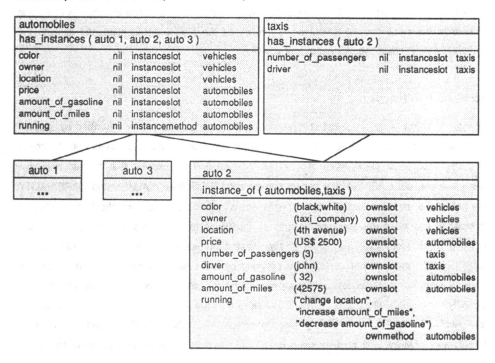

Figure 6.6: Example description of auto 2

Built-in reasoning facilities

As already mentioned, the abstraction concepts are seen as special relationships between objects. What distinguishes them from user-defined relationships (e.g., driver relating automobiles with persons) and substantiates their use in conceptual modeling is their application-independent semantics. These semantics are defined by built-in reasoning facilities automatically provided by the system as soon as abstraction relationships are specified. Inheritance, the reasoning about the structure of an object, is performed in KRISYS according to the following rules:

- A schema passes on its instanceslots and its instancemethods respectively as instanceslots and instancemethods to its subclasses.

- A schema passes on its instanceslots and its instancemethods respectively as ownslots and ownmethods to its instances.

- Ownslots as well as ownmethods are not passed on at all.

Since ownslots and ownmethods represent characteristics of their schemas, they are used not only to express class properties but also set properties, thereby also supporting the reasoning facilities of the association concept.

KRISYS treats class descriptions as necessary conditions that each instance or subclass must satisfy in order to be related to it. Thus, inheritance is carried out in a strict manner (*strict inheritance*) fortifying the assertional semantics of such class definitions. Additionally, *multi-inheritance* is also supported. The KOBRA model allows a schema to be instance or subclass of several classes at the same time, therefore directly reflecting the real world situation and defining the structure of the KB as a complex network of schemas.

Attribute descriptions

In order to characterize an object in more detail, attributes can be further described by *aspects*. For example, the POSSIBLE_VALUES aspect of the color slot of auto2 specifies that the colors of it should be either black, white, red, or green (figure 6.7). To express that the car may have several colors, the CARDINALITY aspect can be used. POSSIBLE_VALUES and CARDINALITY are predefined aspects used to specify restrictions on attributes, which are checked by KRISYS in order to guarantee the semantic integrity of the KB. In this way, changes of attribute values violating these restrictions are automatically rejected. In addition to POSSIBLE_VALUES and CARDINALITY, three further aspects are provided by the system for slots: COMMENT can be used to store an optional textual description. DEFAULT contains default values for the slot. DEMONS is used to attach procedures to the slot which are activated when the slot is accessed (see section 6.4.3). There are three predefined aspects for methods: DEFAULT_METHOD, COMMENT, and DEMON, and their meaning is just the same as for slots. In addition to the above mentioned predefined aspects, KOBRA enables the knowledge engineer to define his own aspects for a more detailed description of the application domain (e.g., unit for the slot amount_of_gasoline, currency for the slot price, etc.). Figure 6.7 presents the complete schema structure of the real world entity auto2, i.e., including slots, methods, aspects, etc.

auto 2			
instance_of (automobiles,taxis)			
color	(black,white)	ownslot	vehicles
possible_values	(black,white,red,green)		
cardinality	[1,n]		
owner	(taxi_company)	ownslot	vehicles
possible_values	(or (instance_of persons) taxi_company)		
cardinality	[1,n]		
location	(4th avenue)	ownslot	vehicles
cardinality	[1,1]		
default	(unknown)		
price	(US$ 2500)	ownslot	automobiles
possible_values	(and (integer) (interval <0 100000<))		
cardinality	[1,1]		
default	(price of sale)		
currency	(US$)		
number_of_passengers (3)		ownslot	taxis
possible_values	(and (integer) (interval <0 5>))		
cardinality	[1,1]		
default	(3)		
driver	(john)	ownslot	taxis
possible_values	(instance_of persons)		
cardinality	[1,1]		
amount_of_gasoline (32)		ownslot	automobiles
possible_values	(and (real) (interval <0 40>))		
cardinality	[1,1]		
unit	(liters)		
amount_of_miles (42575)		ownslot	automobiles
possible_values	(and (integer) (interval >0 ∞>))		
cardinality	[1,1]		
running	("change location",		
	" increase amount_of_miles",		
	"decrease amount_of_gasoline")		
		ownmethod	automobiles
unit	(miles)		

Figure 6.7: Complete description of auto 2

By now, the schema structure supported by KOBRA can be fully understood: each schema is com- posed of its name, some abstraction relationships to other schemas (specified in predefined slots), and user-defined attributes; each attribute is represented by its name, its value, its attribute type (i.e., ownslot, instanceslot, ownmethod, or instancemethod), its origin, and its aspects; aspects are, in turn, composed of their name and their value (figure 6.8).

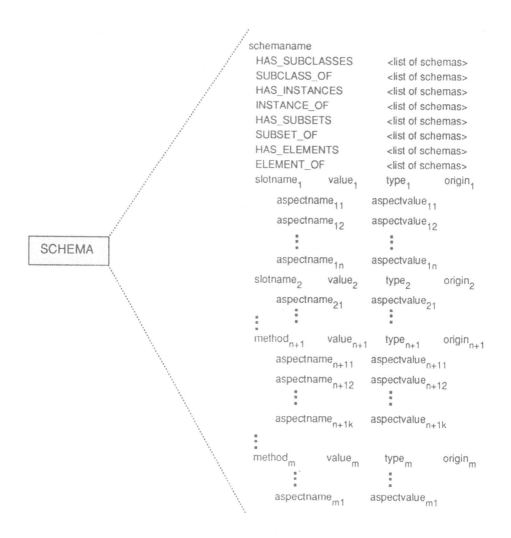

Figure 6.8: The complete schema structure

Data-orientation and general reasoning facilities

Sometimes, it is necessary to specify reactions to certain kinds of events occurring in the application world. For example, to ensure the semantic integrity of a transportation KB, it is necessary to guarantee that updates of the amount_of_miles slot of a vehicle are only allowed to increase the millage. It may also be desirable to remind the driver to fuel the car every time the amount_of_gasoline drops below a certain value. Clearly, these reactions should not be implemented in the application programs but explicitly represented in the KB. In KRISYS, this is supported by the concept of *demons*, i.e., procedures attached to the attributes which are automatically activated when the attributes are accessed. Demons can be used to compute attribute values or to check and ensure semantic integrity constraints, triggered by changes in the KB.

General reasoning facilities are provided by *rules*. The knowledge engineer may, for example, wish to represent diagnostic informations to find out the reason for the break-down of an automobile, which are to be activated during the problem solving process in order to deduce the required information.

In KOBRA, rules and demons are viewed as any other schema of the KB. Due to the object-centered representation, rules are schemas characterized by their attributes "conditions" and "actions", whereas demons are schemas described by their behavior. Thus, there is no further construct in KOBRA necessary to support data-orientation or to support reasoning. So, the specification of rules and demons is straightforward in KOBRA: the KB designer only needs to create the appropriate schemas and fill in the attribute values. However, the activation of demons and the interpretation of rules is totally controlled by internal components of KRISYS (carried out in ORES, see section 6.4) and therefore not visible to the user. For this reason, derivation of new information as well as checks of semantic integrity constraints are not explicitly started by the user in KRISYS but performed implicitly by the system. As a consequence, when querying the system, the user is unaware of the way in which the requested knowledge has been retrieved from the KB (i.e., if it has been accessed, deduced by the interpretation of some rules, computed by some demons, etc.), thereby enforcing the knowledge representation concealing principle to be supported by KBMS (i.e., knowledge independence).

6.2.2 KOBRA Features Emphasized

After this detailed presentation of the knowledge model of KRISYS, we would like to summarize its features thereby making a comparison with the concepts provided by some other existing systems (DBS and XPS tools like ART [Cl85,In87a,Wi84b], BABYLON [GMD87,GWCRM86], KEE [FK85,In84,Fi88], KNOWLEDGE CRAFT [Ca87,FWA85], and LOOPS [BS83,SB86]), as well as with the way these concepts may be applied.

Network of objects

In KRISYS, the organization of the KB need not to be strictly hierarchical (LOOPS). KOBRA allows for the definition of a network of objects in which, for example, a class can have several superclasses. A schema can even act as an instance of several classes at the same time (e.g., auto1 may be also an instance of boats representing a kind of amphibious vehicles), thereby avoiding the introduction of "artificial" classes into the KB (KNOWLEDGE CRAFT, LOOPS, and BABYLON).

Symmetric modeling

KRISYS supports a symmetric modeling of the abstraction relationships. For each specified relation from one schema to another, KRISYS automatically maintains the correctness of the "back reference". This is particularly important during changes in the KB. For example, by not keeping the relationship between a class and its instances when modeling the classification concept, the system cannot guarantee the semantic integrity of the KB after changing the class description (ART, BABYLON, and LOOPS).

Dynamic built-in reasoning

KRISYS treats the abstraction concepts as dynamic relations, which may be changed by the KB designer or the application at any time. The corresponding built-in reasoning is, in such cases, automatically applied, keeping the KB in a semantically consistent state. Inheritance, for example, is in some systems (ART, LOOPS, and BABYLON) not more than a means to save some typing during the modeling process. Changes in the structure of a class (deletion, creation of attributes, etc.) are either not allowed or not reflected in the structure of the existing instances, leading to severe inconsistencies. By not propagating changes, an operation defined for a whole class of objects (e.g., method) may, in such systems, work for one instance (e.g., a new one) but fail for another. In KRISYS, every time that relevant information is changed, inheritance as well as the other built-in reasoning facilities are recalculated so that the system can guarantee the structural and semantic integrity of the KB. It is, therefore, also possible to insert an object without any relationship to a class and then dynamically establish or change classification relationships. (This is neither possible in DBS nor in LOOPS and in BABYLON).

Complete support of abstraction concepts

KOBRA puts special emphasis on a complete support of the abstraction concepts in order to use their semantics as the basis for the maintenance of the integrity of a KB. By neglecting the existence of some of these concepts (generalization by DBS, association by DBS, KEE, BABYLON, and LOOPS, and aggregation by DBS, ART, BABYLON, KEE, KNOWLEDGE CRAFT, and LOOPS), a substantial amount of real world semantics has to be maintained in the application programs, thereby severely weakening the expressiveness and the semantic power of the knowledge model.

Integrated view of KB objects

KOBRA provides the same representation for classes, instances, sets, elements, components, and aggregates. They are all incorporated within a schema, which may describe any of the above abstraction objects, depending on the existing relationships to other objects. Therefore, when modeling the application world, there is no need to introduce two distinct representations in order to support both association and generalization/classification (ART and KNOWLEDGE CRAFT). It is also not necessary to make a kind of "hodgepodge" with the semantics of the generalization/classification in order to be able to support some of the built-in reasoning facilities of the association (KEE).

Following the lines of its object-centered representation, KOBRA enables the KB designer to define different roles for the same KB object. This feature of KRISYS avoids the introduction of redundancy into the KB when, for example, a schema represents a set with respect to one object and a class or even an element with respect to another. (Such a feature is not provided by any of the systems mentioned above.)

Integration of meta-information into the KB

As a consequence of the previously discussed feature, KOBRA does not differentiate between data and meta-data. Such a differentiation (DBS) does not reflect the situation in the real world since changes affecting the application model may also occur.

Uniform representation of all kinds of knowledge

KOBRA provides the knowledge engineer with a powerful representational framework, in which he may express all different kinds of knowledge by means of the same constructs (schema, slots, methods, and aspects). He is not forced, for example, to continually change from one environment to another and, consequently, also between distinct formalisms when expressing rules and the objects to be affected during their evaluation (ART, BABYLON, and KNOWLEDGE CRAFT).

Rich spectrum of concepts for modeling

The mixed representation framework supported by KRISYS integrates several concepts allowing for a natural and accurate modeling of all aspects of knowledge. These concepts, only partially provided by the mentioned systems, include:

- object-orientation (methods),
- data-orientation (demons),
- reasoning mechanisms (rules), and
- semantic KB organization (abstraction concepts).

6.3 The Application Interface

Reflecting the uniform treatment of objects and meta-object supported by the knowledge model of KRISYS, an appropriate application interface should provide operations for the KB design as well as for its access and manipulation. All these operations should be characterized by the term knowledge independence, defining the level of abstraction where the language ought to be situated. It should allow the user to operate independently from the internal representational aspects of the KBMS, concentrating on the information he wants to put into or retrieve from the KB and not on how this information is acquired or assured.

Following this issue, a KB of KRISYS may be seen as a kind of abstract data type with the operations

TELL : KB x information => KB
ASK : KB x information => information

The language KOALA, the application interface of KRISYS, which is defined by means of these two operations, therefore, provides an *abstract, functional view of the KB*. As already mentioned, with the TELL-statement, the user may specify true assertions, i.e., facts or pieces of knowledge in order to appropriately modify the KB to contain the asserted informations. To retrieve KB contents, the ASK-statement may be applied. The specified condition is either proved by the system or used for the selection of the required information.

Syntactically, both statements are composed of two parts (figure 6.9). In the projection clause, the user specifies what kind of information about the qualified objects should be retrieved. In the assertion part of the TELL-statement, the sentences to be asserted are specified. Finally, the selection clause is used to qualify information which is to be either retrieved by an ASK-statement or modified according to the assertions of a TELL-statement.

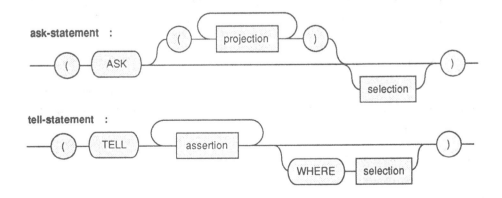

Figure 6.9: Syntax of ASK and TELL

The evaluation may be described by means of the *model-theoretic approach* [GMN84]. That is, the KB is considered from the viewpoint of logic as a model of a first-order theory expressed by KOALA. In this logical formalization, there are three basic assumptions that govern the evaluation of KOALA statements. These assumptions, which express a certain implicit representation of negative facts and define the universe of reference for KB queries, are:

- Closed World Assumption (CWA)

  This assumption, which is also called convention for negative information, states that every fact not known to be true is assumed to be false [Re78].

- Unique Name Assumption (UNA)

  It states the unequivocal identification of KB objects, e.g., schemas with different names represent distinct real world entities [GMN84].

- Domain Closure Assumption (DCA)

  It defines the universe of reference as being the KB contents. As such, there are no other objects, attributes, aspects, etc. in the world than the ones appearing in the KB [GMN84].

In view of these assumptions, the semantics of the logical operators are defined as

- FORALL   -   "for all objects in the KB",
- EXIST   -   "there is an object in the KB", and
- NOT   -   "NOT (formula) is true, if (formula) cannot be deduced from the KB contents".

In the following, we give a detailed presentation of the language, illustrated with examples based on a KB for transportation (the same used in chapter 5). First, the selection clause will be described, thereby giving the semantics of the elements of KOALA (formulas, predicates, and terms). After this, we show the structure as well as the characteristics of the ASK- and TELL-statement.

6.3.1 The Constructs of KOALA

The selection clause specifies an expression structured in accordance to the first-order predicate calculus. That is, the selection is built by formulas combined with the usual logical operators: not, and, or, there exist, and for all. The logical formulas are built with predicates. These use either constants, variables, or functions as their terms. The last one can, in turn, use variables or constants as terms again in order to address the objects of the KB. KOALA supports functions and predicates to be applied to objects (schemas), attributes (slots and methods), attribute values, and attribute descriptions (aspects).

In each of the following sections, we present the structure of formulas, predicates, and terms. Because KOALA was developed not only for interactive use but also as an interface for applications written in LISP, its structures are specified in a LISP-like functional notation: e.g., a term is given as a list of elements (enclosed by brackets) containing the name of the function as its first and the operands as the remaining elements. An operand of a term can always be a constant or a variable but also a term with an appropriate result type, therefore enforcing the orthogonality of the language [Da84]. The structures are illustrated with some examples in which KOALA constructs are written in capital letters. Additionally, we give an overview of the syntax of the described construct in the form of diagrams. These diagrams do give a complete presentation of the constructs of the language, but sometimes, they neglect some syntactical elements. A complete specification of KOALA is presented in the appendix as well as in [De88,HS88b].

6.3.1.1   Formulas

Formulas may be built in KOALA according to the following rules (figure 6.10):

- a predicate is a formula,

- if f is a formula, then (NOT f) is also a formula,

- if f1, f2, ..., fn are all formulas, then (AND f1 f2 ... fn) is a formula too,

- if f1, f2, ..., fn are all formulas, then (OR f1 f2 ... fn) is also a formula,

- if f is a formula, then (EXIST variable-list f) and (FORALL variable-list WITH selection f) are also formulas, and

- further formulas do not exist.

The semantics of the above components of the syntax are illustrated by some examples in the course of the following sections.

6.3.1.2   Predicates

The simplest elements of the formulas are predefined predicates that embody the semantics of the underlying KOBRA model (figure 6.11).

Type of KB content

In KOALA, constants and variables may express different contents of the KB: schemas, slots, methods, values, slot- and method types, or aspects. For example, to express the existence of a particular object (auto2 in the following example) in the KB, one should specify

(IS_SCHEMA auto2).

Analogously, to assert the existence of other kinds of KB contents (i.e., slots, methods, and aspects), further predicates (i.e., IS_SLOT, IS_METHOD, and IS_ASPECT) are provided. For example, the expression

    (IS_SLOT owner)

specifies that owner is a slot in the KB.

formula :

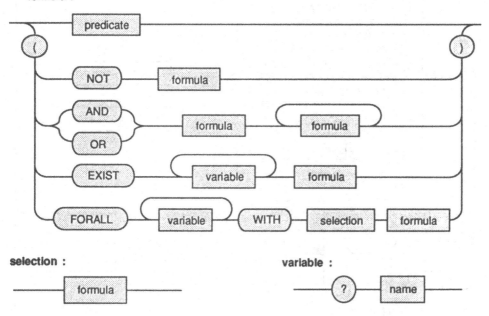

Figure 6.10: Syntax of formulas

Abstraction relationships

Schemas may be related to each other either directly or indirectly because of their abstraction relationships to further objects. So, KOALA provides two different predicates to express direct or indirect relationships between schemas for each abstraction concept. The next example shows an expression asserting that auto1 is an instance of automobiles and boats (but not necessarily a direct instance of them):

    (AND (IS_INSTANCE auto1 automobiles)
        (IS_INSTANCE auto1 boats)).

predicate :

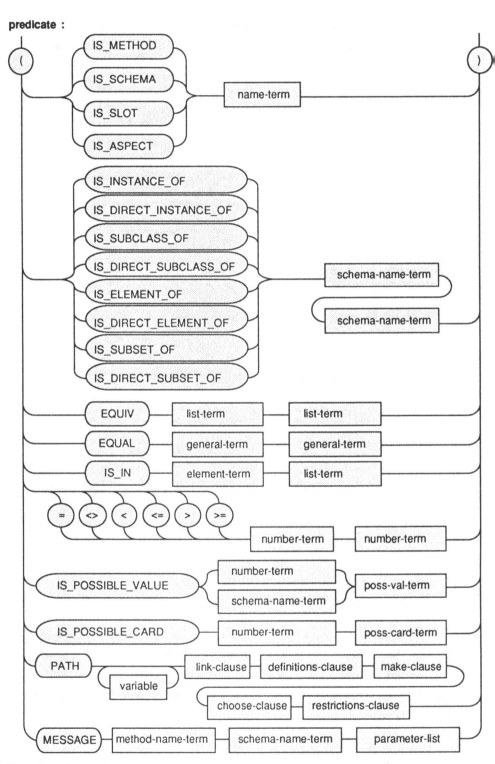

Figure 6.11: Syntax of predicates

The following formula specifies that truck1 is a direct element of the set paul's_things, whereas the next one expresses that truck1 is an element of the set paul's_family's_things either because it is a direct element of this set or because it is an element of some of the subsets of this set:

(IS_DIRECT_ELEMENT truck1 paul's_things)

(IS_ELEMENT truck1 paul's_family's_things).

Comparisons

KOALA provides comparison predicates to work with names, lists, sets, and numbers:

- EQUAL checks the equality of two elements (names, numbers, variables, lists, etc.).

- IS_IN specifies the membership of an element in a list.

- EQUIV expresses the equivalence of two sets.

- =, <>, <, <=, >, and >= allow numerical comparisons.

For example,

(EQUIV (a b) (b a))

yields the logical value true.

Integrity constraints

Attribute description predicates allow the user to formulate questions about slot value restrictions and cardinality specifications. For example, an expression to check whether transport-company is an allowed value for the slot owner of automobiles would look like

(IS_POSSIBLE_VALUE   transport_company

(ASPECTVALUE possible_values owner automobiles)).

In this example, the function ASPECTVALUE has been used to yield the possible_values specification of the owner slot.

Generalized transitive closure (GTC)

Recursive queries may be expressed in KOALA by using the PATH predicate, with which a special class of recursion equations, i.e., generalized transitive closure [DS86], can be specified. Different clauses (LINK, RESTRICTION, etc.) are used in the PATH predicate for a detailed description of the GTC-problem. The LINK-clause, for example, may contain a complex condition which speci-fies the relation used as the basis for the closure computation. Additional information may be carried along with the retrieved transitive relations (e.g., the total distance between two cities) which may be used to qualify an optimal path (e.g., the route with the shortest distance). The specification of additional information is made in the DEFINITION-clause, whereas the criterion for the qualification of paths is defined in the CHOOSE-clause. The MAKE-clause allows for the grouping of several paths in order to generate further information (e.g., average of the distance between two cities). Finally, the RESTRICTION-clause permits the specification of further qualification criteria for the paths (e.g., only those paths starting in a particular city). (We refer to [De88] for a detailed description of the PATH predicate. Examples will be presented in the forthcoming sections.)

Behavior

Finally, KOALA provides the MESSAGE predicate to formulate questions about the behavior of KB objects. For example, if the KB designer has defined a method "fast" for the automobiles of our KB which returns true if the maximum speed of the vehicle exceeds a certain limit, one can use the MESSAGE predicate to express that auto2 moves fast:

(MESSAGE fast auto2)

6.3.1.3 Terms

As already mentioned, predicates are built with terms (figure 6.12) which may, in turn, be either a

- constant,
- query-variable, or just variable for short, or
- function having further terms as arguments.

Variables (denoted by an identifier with a leading question mark) are allowed in predicates and terms in order to be instantiated during the evaluation, thereby yielding KB objects that satisfy the stated conditions. For example, to assert the existence of a fast amphibious automobile in the KB, one may express

(EXIST ?A
     (AND (IS_INSTANCE ?A automobiles)
         (IS_INSTANCE ?A boats)
         (MESSAGE fast ?A))).

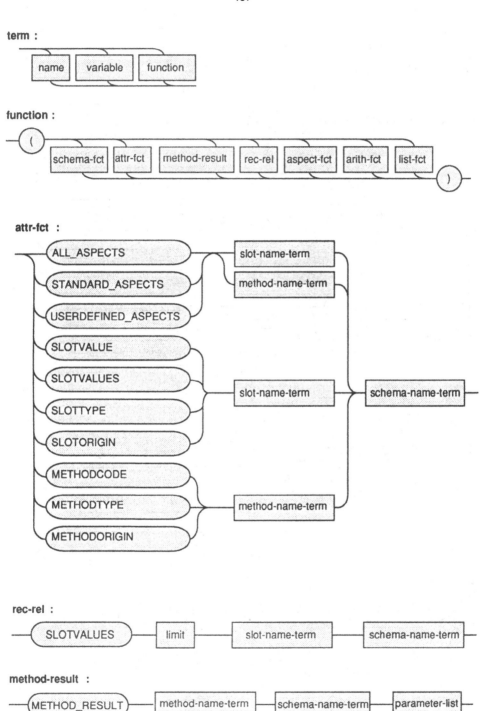

Figure 6.12: Syntax of terms

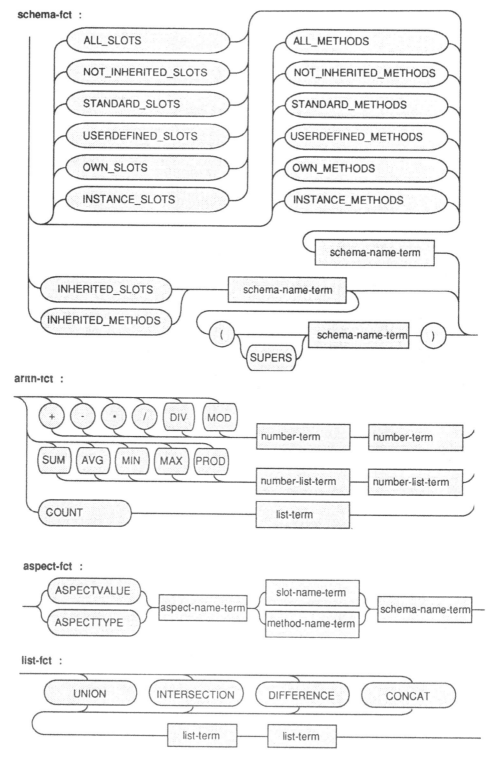

Figure 6.12: Syntax of terms (cont.)

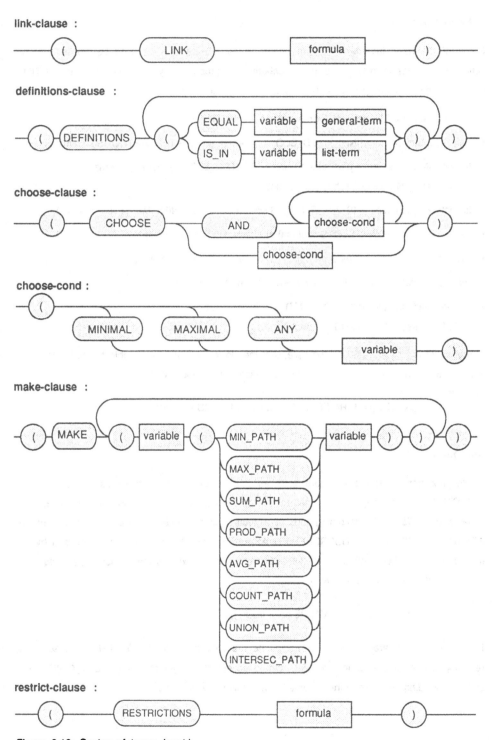

Figure 6.12: Syntax of terms (cont.)

Schema functions

Some of the most important functions provided by KOALA are those to be applied on the schemas in order to manipulate their attributes. In general, they have the form (FUNCTION schema) and yield a group of attributes. KOALA offers functions to select:

- all slots (ALL_SLOTS schema) or methods (ALL_METHODS schema) of an object,
- only the inherited ones (INHERITED_SLOTS schema), (INHERITED_METHODS schema),
- the inherited ones from a particular object (INHERITED_SLOTS schema (schema)), (INHERITED_METHODS schema (schema)),
- its instance_attributes (INSTANCE_SLOTS schema) or (INSTANCE_METHODS schema),
- its own attributes (OWN_SLOTS schema) or (OWN_METHODS schema),
- the abstraction relationships of an object (STANDARD_SLOTS schema),
- the system-defined methods (STANDARD_METHODS schema), and
- user-defined attributes (USERDEFINED_SLOTS schema), (USERDEFINED_METHODS schema).

If one would like to express, for example, that the slot color found in the object auto2 was inherited from either automobiles or its further superclasses, one would specify

(IS_IN color (INHERITED_SLOTS auto2 (SUPERS automobiles))).

Slot functions

These functions, specified in figure 6.12 as part of the attribute functions, have the form (FUNCTION slot schema) and are used to manipulate the elements of a slot (i.e., its value, type, aspects, etc.). To yield particular groups of aspects, one may use the functions ALL_ASPECTS, STANDARD_ASPECT, and USERDEFINED_ASPECTS. The slot value may be accessed by the functions SLOTVALUE and SLOTVALUES. For example, to express that a slot value is equal to a specific value, one should specify

(EQUAL green (SLOTVALUE color truck1)).

Furthermore, there are functions to manipulate the type of a slot (SLOT_TYPE slot schema), returning either ownslot or instanceslot, and to access the origin of a slot (SLOT_ORIGIN slot schema), yielding the name of the schema in which this slot was defined.

Method functions

To manipulate the elements of a method, there are functions corresponding to those provided for slots (see figure 6.12). Additionally, KOALA offers a method function to activate the behavior of the schema (METHOD_RESULT method schema parameters). For example, let us assume that the knowledge engineer has defined a method for the schema taxi-company to choose the most appropriate taxi to pick somebody up at a given place. To activate this method yielding the number of the taxi that should be sent to the World Trade Center, one may express

(METHOD_RESULT choose_taxi taxi_company world_trade_center).

Recursive relations

In KOALA, terms may be nested. For example, to retrieve the father of John's mother, one may directly express

(SLOTVALUE father (SLOTVALUE mother John)).

Therefore, by using the SLOTVALUES function continuously, one may express the transitive closure of the relation defined by the specified slot. In order to enable the user to directly formulate such recursive queries, KOALA provides a function (SLOTVALUES* slot schema) with which the computation of this transitive closure may be achieved. For example, to retrieve the ancestors of John, one can use

(SLOTVALUES* parents John).

The "*" in the slotvalues term indicates that the recursion process of the closure computation continues until no further ancestors can be found. One can use a positive integer (starting at zero) instead of the "*" to indicate that the recursion should stop at a certain depth. For example, if we are interested in the ancestors of John up to his great-grandparents, the appropriate expression would be

(SLOTVALUES2 parents John).

Aspect functions

Aspect functions have the form (FUNCTION aspect slot/method schema). They are used to access the value of a particular aspect (ASPECTVALUE) or the type of it (ASPECTTYPE). For example, to retrieve the possible_values specification of the color slot of automobiles, one should express

(ASPECTVALUE possible_values color automobiles).

Numerical functions

KOALA offers several functions to evaluate arithmetic expressions involving +, -, *, /, DIV, and MOD as well as to calculate sum, average, minimum, and maximum value of a set of numbers or even to count the number of elements of a set. For example, the expression

(<= 2 (COUNT (SLOTVALUES color auto2)))

asserts that auto2 has at least 2 different colors.

List/set functions

Finally, there are functions to manipulate sets (UNION, INTERSECTION, and DIFFERENCE) and lists (CONCAT).

6.3.2 ASK and TELL

As already mentioned, the application interface of KRISYS is completely specified by the operations ASK and TELL. ASK takes a sentence (specified in the selection clause) and checks on the basis of the current contents of the KB whether it is true or false. If it is true, the KB objects that have been qualified may be retrieved according to the specification of the projection clause (figure 6.13).

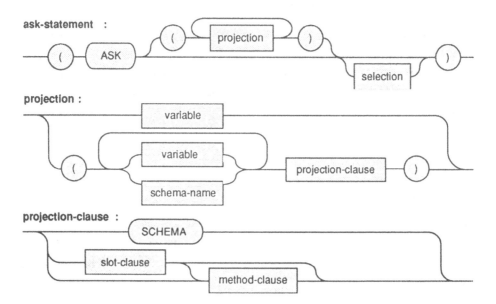

Figure 6.13: ASK-statement

slot-clause :

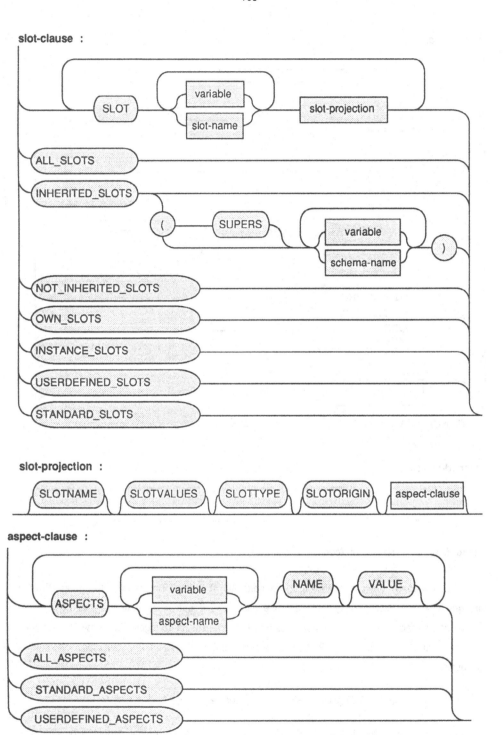

slot-projection :

aspect-clause :

Figure 6.13: ASK-statement (cont.)

method-clause :

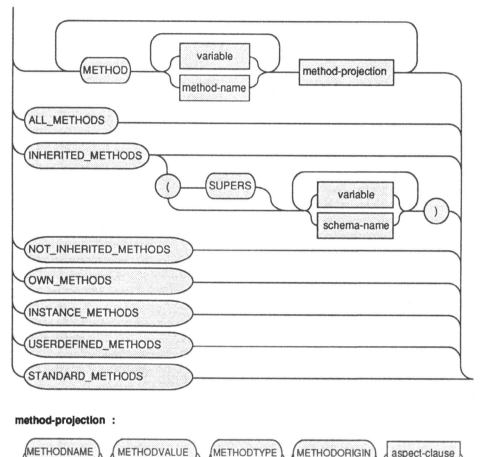

method-projection :

METHODNAME METHODVALUE METHODTYPE METHODORIGIN aspect-clause

Figure 6.13: ASK-statement (cont.)

The TELL-statement takes a sentence and asserts that it is true. The effect is to change the KB into one whose contents imply that sentence. Naturally, it can also occur that the contents of the KB can already imply the sentence asserted. In this case, no changes will be made since they are not required. For example, if the KS asserts that automobiles is a subclass of vehicles expressing

(TELL (IS_DIRECT_SUBCLASS automobiles vehicles))

two situations may occur. Either the KB already contains this information requiring no changes, or the KB does not contain it and, consequently, changes must be made. Here, many things can happen. If neither automobiles nor vehicles exist as schemas in the KB, both will be created and related to each other by the abstraction concept of generalization. If only one of them exists, the other one will then be created and related to the first one as specified above. And if both of them exist, only the generalization relationship will be built.

The sentences to be asserted are specified in the assertion clause of the TELL-statement (figure 6.14). An assertion is syntactically similar to the selection part however more restrictive. It is, for example, not possible to specify formulas combined with logical connectors in order to avoid ambiguities (note that if one asserts p v q, it is impossible to know whether p, q, or both are true).

is-in-assertion :

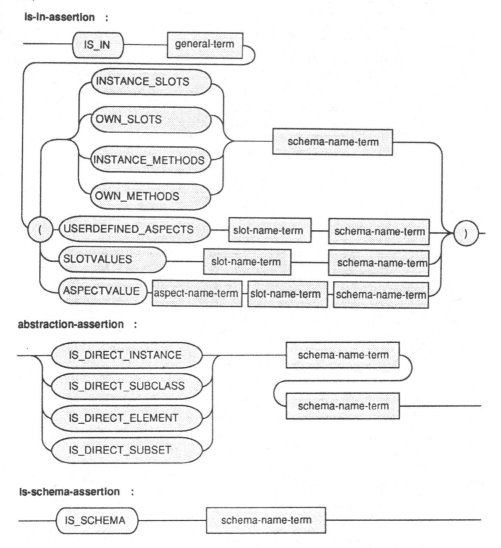

abstraction-assertion :

is-schema-assertion :

Figure 6.14: TELL-statement

is-in-assertion :

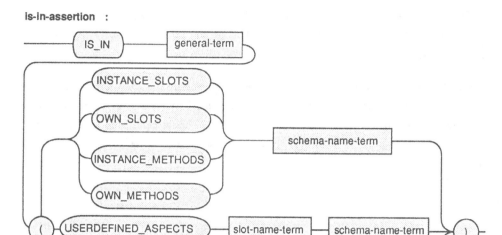

assign-assertion :

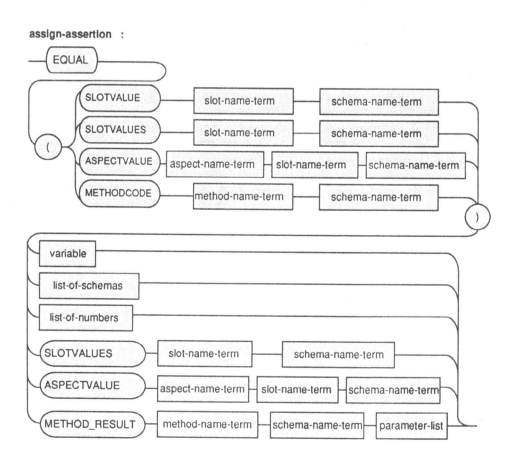

6.3.2.1 An Overview of the Evaluation

The simplest ASK-statement is the one without projection clause. For example,

(ASK (IS_SCHEMA bicycles))

describes the query "is there a schema called bicycles in the KB?" and would be evaluated to false in our example. The same predicate can be used in

(TELL (IS_SCHEMA bicycles))

to assert that the corresponding information should be represented in the KB. In this case, the system would automatically create the schema bicycles if it is not already contained in the KB.

State-oriented changes

Note that when specifying assertions, the user does not have to determine the kind of operation to be performed by the system but simply to describe a state (in the above example, "the schema bicycles exists in the KB") which he wants to be achieved. It is the responsibility of the system to determine the way in which this state can be reached. If, for example, the asserted information is already represented in the KB, the system will carry out no operation at all.

The following TELL-statement asserts that auto3 is a kind of amphibious automobile and is owned by the transport-company.

(TELL   (IS_DIRECT_INSTANCE auto3 automobiles)
           (IS_DIRECT_INSTANCE auto3 boats)
           (EQUAL   (SLOTVALUE owner auto3) transport_company))

Note again that the type of operations actually performed to achieve the described state in a TELL-statement is not specified by the user. In this example, the creation of schemas or abstraction relations, the activation of the corresponding built-in reasoning (here inheritance), etc. are only performed if the information does not already exist in the KB. In this sense, the specification of transport-company as a value for the owner slot either modifies an existing (probably inherited) slot of auto3 or creates a new slot owner with the appropriate value.

Multiple assertions

In one TELL-statement, the user may give a list of assertions (as in the last example), which are then implicitly connected by logical conjunction (and), i.e., each of the assertions is made true. In other words, all facts asserted in one TELL-statement are guaranteed to be true after the statement has been successfully performed. If the assertions contradict each other or cannot be asserted for some other reason (e.g., value class violation), the system refuses to accept the whole statement. The following assertions establish the generalization relation between taxis and means-of-transportation, create the schema auto2 as an instance of taxis and automobiles, and initialize the owner slot, automatically created by the inheritance process along the newly established abstraction relations, with the value taxi-company:

```
(TELL      (IS_DIRECT_SUBCLASSES taxis means_of_transportation)
           (IS_DIRECT_INSTANCE auto2 taxis)
           (IS_DIRECT_INSTANCE auto2 automobiles)
           (EQUAL   (SLOTVALUE owner auto2) taxi_company)).
```

Changes of the object structures

Until now, we have only used predicates and terms related to abstraction relations and values of attributes. We have not yet explicitly asserted facts about the structure of the schemas. When the structure of a KB object is modified, inheritance as well as the other built-in reasoning facilities are automatically recalculated. The following TELL-statement defines passengers as an instanceslot of the class taxis and asserts via the possible-values aspect that only persons are allowed as passengers of taxis. This attribute is, therefore, inherited by all instances of taxis (e.g., auto2) during the execution of the statement.

```
(TELL      (IS_IN passengers (INSTANCE_SLOTS taxis))
           (EQUAL   (ASPECTVALUE possible_values passengers taxis)
                    (INSTANCE_OF persons)))
```

Changes of integrity constraints

Analogously to changes of the object structures, modification of the integrity constraints may also provoke a reevaluation of the built-in reasoning. For example, the following TELL-statement changes the possible_values specification of the owner slot of automobiles to either persons or companies excluding, however, the transport-company.

```
(TELL      (EQUAL
                    (AND  (OR  (INSTANCE_OF persons)
                               (INSTANCE_OF companies))
                          (NOT_ONE_OF transport_company))
                    (ASPECTVALUE possible_values owner automobiles))).
```

Negated facts

As already mentioned, the evaluation of negated predicates is carried out according to the CWA, which allows an implicit representation of negative facts. Therefore, the assertion of a negated predicate acts as a removal of the specified information from the KB. For example, if a vehicle called vehicle1 is first represented as an automobile but then for some reason recognized to be a truck, the statement

    (TELL   (IS_DIRECT_INSTANCE vehicle1 trucks)

                (NOT (IS_DIRECT_INSTANCE vehicle1 automobiles)),

performs the corresponding corrections in our KB, thereby deriving the new structure of vehicle1. However, this does not affect those attributes of vehicle1 common to automobiles and trucks. The values of the attributes that both (automobiles and trucks) possess, such as owner and location, are preserved by the inheritance process.

Behavioral attributes

Methods (i.e., behavior of objects) may be activated either by the MESSAGE predicate or by the METHOD_RESULT term. Let us assume that a method send-taxi has been defined for the schema taxi-company having two parameters, person and location, indicating by whom and from where a taxi is being requested:

    (TELL (MESSAGE send_taxi taxi_company (Mr. Smith Empire-State-Building)))

activates this method simulating the action that Mr. Smith tells the taxi company to send a taxi to pick him up at the Empire State Building.

Complex conditions

ASK- and TELL-conditions may be arbitrarily complex formulas constructed according to the rules of predicate calculus. Variables are allowed within predicates and terms to represent schemas, slots, methods, values, or aspects which may be existentially or universally quantified. For example, to determine whether an automobile that has the color red exists in our KB, one may specify

    (ASK (EXIST ?X

                (AND (IS_INSTANCE ?X automobiles)

                    (EQUAL   (SLOTVALUE color ?X) red).

The system then determines if the specified condition is true in the KB, i.e., whether it can be deduced from its contents.

More complex conditions can be formulated with combinations of logical connections:

```
(ASK (EXIST ?X
          (AND   (IS_INSTANCE ?X automobiles)
                 (OR   (EQUAL (SLOTVALUE color ?X) red)
                       (< (SLOTVALUE price ?X) 1000)))))
```

determines whether an automobile that has either the color red or costs less than $ 1000 exists in our KB.

Set-oriented retrieval

Set-oriented retrieval of information is achieved by the use of free (i.e., unquantified) variables in the condition part. These variables, which have to be specified in the projection clause (printed in bold letters in the following examples), are then instantiated with all KB objects which satisfy the stated conditions. In other words, instead of proving the condition, the system instantiates the variables, returning objects as a result of the retrieval operation. The above query may serve as an example:

```
(ASK (?X)  (AND  (IS_INSTANCE ?X automobiles)
                 (OR  (EQUAL (SLOTVALUES color ?X) red)
                      (< (SLOTVALUE price ?X) 1000)))).
```

During the evaluation, the free variable ?X is instantiated with all automobiles satisfying the condition "color = red or price < $ 1000".

Projection of retrieved information

In a projection clause, the user specifies what kind of information he is interested in. In the above example, the projection clause contains only the variable, indicating that only the names of the qualified objects should be retrieved. A projection clause as in

```
(ASK     (?X SCHEMA)      (AND . . .))
```

would lead to the retrieval of the whole schema description of the qualified objects. The user may also specify (groups of) attributes and aspects which he is interested in:

```
(ASK     (?X SLOT owner) . . .)
```

restricts the result to the name of qualified objects together with their owner slot whereas

```
(ASK     (?X   INHERITED_SLOTS ASPECTS possible_values cardinality) . . .)
```

defines a projection yielding the name of the schema and all its inherited slots together with the aspects possible_values and cardinality.

Set-oriented assertions

Variables may also be used in a TELL-statement to perform set-oriented assertions. In such cases, the selection part of TELL is used to specify the information to be modified by the assertions. For example, a statement to select all vehicles belonging to the transport-company which are also automobiles in order to "sell" them to the taxi-company would look like the following TELL operation:

```
(TELL          (EQUAL   (SLOTVALUE owner ?X) taxi_company)
    WHERE      (AND     (IS_INSTANCE ?X automobiles))
                        (EQUAL (SLOTVALUE owner ?X) transport_company))).
```

Here, only the owner slot of the selected objects has been changed.

Joins

For the connection of information, KOALA offers a similar mechanism as the well known database join. In this case, the user formulates conditions containing several variables which are related to each other:

```
(ASK)      (?A ?B)
           (AND   (IS_INSTANCE ?A automobiles)
                  (IS_INSTANCE ?B boats)
                  (EQUAL (SLOTVALUE owner ?A) (SLOTVALUE owner ?B))))
```

selects pairs of automobiles and boats having the same owner.

```
(ASK       ((?A SCHEMA) (?P SLOT address SLOTVALUES))
           (AND   (IS_INSTANCE ?A automobiles)
                  (EQUAL (SLOTVALUE color ?A) red)
                  (IS_IN ?P (SLOTVALUE owner ?A))))
```

selects all red automobiles and their owners. The result of the query is a list of pairs where the first element of each pair is the schema description of a car and the second is a list of the name and the address of the related owner.

User-defined predicates

The next query demonstrates the use of methods as user-defined predicates. We assume for this example that the KB designer has defined the method fast as an instancemethod for vehicles. The code of this method may also be different for the subclasses of vehicles, reflecting the fact that the criterion for distinct kinds of vehicles may not always be the same (e.g., 70 miles/hour may be fast for a truck but slow for a car). The query

```
(ASK      (?V SCHEMA)
          (AND   (IS_INSTANCE ?V vehicles)
                 (MESSAGE fast ?V)))
```

selects all fast vehicles in the KB. The MESSAGE-predicate in our ASK-statement activates the method fast for all instances of vehicles (i.e., cars, trucks, etc.) and keeps only those for which the method returns the value true.

Nested terms

In KOALA, it is very easy to reference objects via relations between schemas across several stages since terms may be nested. Using the aggregation hierarchy, we may, for example, select all automobiles with six-cylinder engines with the query

```
(ASK      (?X)
          (AND   (IS_INSTANCE ?X automobiles)
                 (EQUAL   (SLOTVALUE number_of_cylinders
                                 (SLOTVALUE engine
                                       (SLOTVALUE motor ?X)))
          6))).
```

For every automobile, the innermost SLOTVALUE-term uses the motor slot to determine its motor-component, which is again an object of the KB. The appropriate subcomponent is then accessed via the engine slot. If the number-of-cylinders slot of the engine has the right value, the automobile containing this engine will be qualified as a result of the query.

6.3.2.2   The Expressive Power of KOALA

One of the most important requirements for a knowledge language is the support of flexible ways to qualify and search the contents of the KB [Hä88b]. In the following, we give a few examples of queries demonstrating the expressive power of KOALA.

Retrieving objects of different (undefined) types

Usually, DB languages require an exact specification of the type of qualified objects (for example, in the FROM-clause of an SQL-query). In KOALA, predicates may be used to dynamically (i.e., during evaluation) determine the types (i.e., classes) of the qualified objects. KOALA also allows queries without any type specification. For example, the query

```
(ASK    (?X SCHEMA)
        (AND    (IS-SCHEMA ?X)
                (IS-IN owner (OWN_SLOTS ?X))
                (IS-IN Mr. Smith (SLOTVALUES owner ?X))))
```

does not restrict objects to any type but qualifies all schemas having Mr. Smith as value of the property owner. To restrict the types of resulting objects to vehicles and houses, one may specify

```
(ASK    (?X SCHEMA)
        (EXIST ?T
                (AND    (OR (IS_SUBCLASS ?T vehicles)
                            (EQUAL ?T houses))
                        (IS_INSTANCE ?X ?T)
                        (IS_IN owner (OWN_SLOTS ?X))
                        (IS_IN Mr. Smith (SLOTVALUES owner ?X))))).
```

If translated into SQL-like notation, the last two queries would correspond to a query of the type

```
SELECT      *
FROM        *   (or tables qualified by a predicate)
WHERE       attribute = value
```

Retrieving objects via different (undefined) attributes

If one wants to find out which objects are in some way related to Mr. Smith, a query of the type

```
SELECT      *
FROM        *   (or qualified tables)
WHERE       *   = value
```

would be necessary where even the name of the attribute used for qualification is not specified. In KOALA, this query may be expressed in the following way:

```
(ASK    (?X SCHEMA)
        (AND    (IS_SCHEMA ?X)
                (EXIST ?S (AND   (IS_IN ?S (OWN_SLOTS ?X))
                                 (IS_IN Mr. Smith (SLOTVALUES ?S ?X))))))).
```

Since variables can also be used for names of attributes, it is easy to formulate a condition to select all objects containing Mr. Smith as a value of one or more of their attributes. As the result of the query, all objects having any kind of "relation" to Mr. Smith are returned.

Qualified projection

In analogy to their use for the specification of object types and the retrieval of objects, conditions can be introduced to dynamically select attributes, aspects, etc. for the projection clause. Thus, KOALA supports qualified projection which can be described in SQL-like notation as

```
SELECT    (attributes qualified by predicates)
FROM      * (or qualified relation)
WHERE     * = value.
```

Our last KOALA-query may be slightly modified to serve as an example:

```
(ASK    (?X SLOT ?S)
        (AND    (IS_SCHEMA ?X)
                (IS_IN ?S (OWN_SLOTS ?X))
                (IS_IN Mr. Smith (SLOTVALUES ?S ?X))))
```

gives for each qualified object its name and a description of the attributes representing relationships to Mr. Smith. This might, for example, be the owner slot for one object, the driver slot for another, both owner and driver slot for further ones, etc.

Recursive queries

In addition to the features presented so far, KOALA allows the formulation of recursive queries, particularly the computation of transitive closure (TC) and generalized transitive closure (GTC) [DS86]. Let us assume, for example, that the class persons has the instanceslot parents representing the relation between a person and his (or her) parents. To retrieve the automobiles of all ancestors of a particular person, which involves computing the TC of the parent-relation, we can use the query

```
(ASK    (?P ?A)
        (AND    (IS_IN ?P (SLOTVALUES* parents Mr. Smith)))
                (IS_INSTANCE ?A automobiles)
                (IS_IN ?P (SLOTVALUES owner ?A))).
```

For the retrieval of information requiring the computation of a GTC, the PATH-predicate may be used. For example, if one wants to know how long it will at least take to go from Paris to Vienna by train, it is necessary to build the closure of all the ways of traveling between these two cities and then to choose the time of the fastest route. (For simplicity, we do not consider the departure and the arriving times of the trains at each intermediary station in order to compute possible changes).

```
(ASK    (?time)
        (PATH ?time
            (LINK
                (EQUAL   (SLOTVALUE end_station ?train_line)
                            (SLOTVALUE start_station ?NEXT_train_line)))
            (RESTRICTIONS
                (EQUAL paris (SLOTVALUE start_station ?FIRST_train_line)
                (EQUAL vienna (SLOTVALUE end_station ?LAST_train_line))
            (DEFINITIONS
                (?time (SUM(ALL(SLOTVALUE time ?train_line)))))
            (CHOOSE
                (MINIMAL ?time))).
```

The closure of all train lines is expressed at the LINK clause. Since we are not interested in all train connections in Europe, it is necessary to restrict them in the RESTRICTION clause to those leaving from Paris and arriving in Vienna. In the DEFINITIONS clause, the concatenation operator (in this case, the sum of the time) is expressed, whereas the aggregation operator (here the shortest time) has been specified in the CHOOSE clause.

A similar example may be built with the taxi-company. Let us consider the following problem: taxi1 has been chosen by the taxi-company to pick up Mr. Smith. We need to know the length of the shortest route for taxi1 to get to the Empire State Building from its current location in order to give this route as parameter for its running method. Let us assume that all connections between certain places are represented as instances of the class connection having the attributes start, end, and distance to describe the places which are connected and the distance between them. We could then achieve the requested action with

```
(TELL    (MESSAGE running taxi1 ?route)
    WHERE (PATH ?route
                (LINK   (EQUAL   (SLOTVALUE end ?connection)
                                    (SLOTVALUE start ?NEXT_connection)))
                (RESTRICTIONS
                    (EQUAL    (SLOTVALUE start ?FIRST_connection)
```

```
                        (SLOTVALUE location taxi 1))
            (EQUAL    (SLOTVALUE end ?LAST_connection)
                        empire_state_building)))
    (DEFINITIONS
            (EQUAL ?route (ALL(?connection)))
            (EQUAL ?dist (SUM (ALL(SLOTVALUE distance ?connection)))))
    (CHOOSE (MINIMAL ?dist))))).
```

Rules and demons

Up to this point, we have not mentioned the definition and activation of rules and demons. The reason for this is that no additional constructs are necessary for this task. As already mentioned in section 6.2.1, the activation of demons is automatically performed when attributes are accessed and is therefore hidden from the user. A deductive process involving the activation of rules is initiated in quite a similar way. KOALA formulas are used as conditions and actions of rules. For this reason, a TELL-statement asserting certain facts may automatically cause the activation of rules whose conditions match the specified assertions initiating a forward reasoning process. In the same way, a condition in an ASK-statement may be derived in a backward reasoning process because it matches the goal of an appropriate rule. The derivation of new information is therefore not necessarily explicitly started by the user but performed implicitly by the system.

In KRISYS, rules are schemas of the KB characterized by the attributes condition and action. In the same way, demons are represented as objects described by their behavior. Therefore, the definition of rules and demons with KOALA is straightforward: the user only has to create the corresponding schemas and fill in the attribute values by means of a TELL-statement.

6.4 Object-Centered Representation System

The engineering layer of KRISYS corresponds to the Object-centered REpresentation System (ORES) which is responsible for the implementation of the KOBRA knowledge model. This component supports the needs of the KB designer by means of a rich mixed knowledge representation framework uniformly integrated into the schema concept.

6.4.1 Overall Internal Organization

In the ORES module, every schema of a KB is treated as an instance of a system predefined schema called GLOBAL. When introducing objects into a KB, GLOBAL acts as a template for the schemas, thereby defining their internal structure. In GLOBAL, the abstraction relationships are defined as instanceslots which are then automatically inherited by every schema when it is inserted into the KB. For this reason, abstraction relationships are viewed by ORES as ownslots of the schemas with slotorigin equal to GLOBAL. So, an object defined at the application interface presents the same structure defined by the KOBRA model except for the type and origin of the abstraction attributes (figure 6.15).

auto 2			
instance_of (automobiles,taxis)		ownslot	global
color (black,white)		ownslot	vehicles
possible_values	(black,white,red,green)		
cardinality	[1,n]		
owner (taxi_company)		ownslot	vehicles
possible_values	(or (instance_of persons) taxi_company)		
cardinality	[1,n]		
location (4th avenue)		ownslot	vehicles
cardinality	[1,1]		
default	(unknown)		
price (US$ 2500)		ownslot	automobiles
possible_values	(and (integer) (interval <0 100000<))		
cardinality	[1,1]		
default	(price of sale)		
currency	(US$)		
number_of_passengers (3)		ownslot	taxis
possible_values	(and (integer) (interval <0 5>))		
cardinality	[1,1]		
default	(3)		
driver (john)		ownslot	taxis
possible_values	(instance_of persons)		
cardinality	[1,1]		
amount_of_gasoline (32)		ownslot	automobiles
possible_values	(and (real) (interval <0 40>))		
cardinality	[1,1]		
unit	(liters)		
amount_of_miles (42575)		ownslot	automobiles
possible_values	(and (integer) (interval >0 ∞>))		
cardinality	[1,1]		
running ("change location",			
" increase amount_of_miles",			
"decrease amount_of_gasoline")			
		ownmethod	automobiles
unit	(miles)		

Figure 6.15: Complete description of auto 2 at the ORES component

Internally, each user-defined schema is stored together with its name and attributes (slots and methods) which are, in turn, kept with their values, type, and origin. The maintenance of the origin specification allows an easy distinction between inherited and not inherited attributes, which is used not only by the inheritance mechanism but also for the internal management of aspects. The aspects of an attribute are always stored only once together with the schema at which they were defined, eliminating any kind of redundancy in the internal representation. Hence, the origin specification also serves as a kind of link to directly access the aspects when they are needed.

In addition to GLOBAL, ORES provides several other predefined schemas which are internally used to control the top of the different "hierarchies" (in reality, they are networks) existing in a KB (figure 6.16). In this sense, CLASSES represents the top of the generalization hierarchies, whereas SETS the top of the association hierarchies (the meaning of RULES, DEMONS, and other predefined schemas will be explained later on).

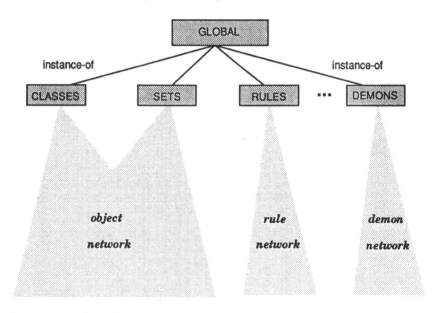

Figure 6.16: Overall organization of ORES

Following the lines of this issue, whenever a schema plays the role of a class in some context and does not have any superclass, it is connected to CLASSES by the generalization concept. The same occurs in the case of the predefined schema SETS, however, involving the association concept. The connection and disconnection of schemas with CLASSES and SETS is automatically redefined when the roles of the schemas have been changed as a consequence of an operation. An example for such a situation is illustrated in figure 6.17, in which the schema vehicles has been introduced into the KB. Since the schema automobiles has now a user-defined superclass, it is not the top of a user-defined generalization hierarchy anymore and has, for this reason, to be disconnected from CLASSES. (The cause for the connection of vehicles is certainly clear).

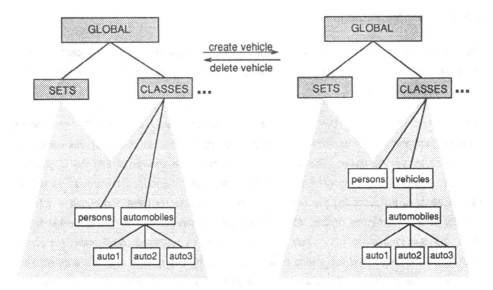

Figure 6.17: Management of a generalization/classification hierarchy

When schemas have been introduced into the KB without any relationship to other schemas, they cannot be connected with CLASSES or SETS and are then kept only as instances of GLOBAL (paul's_things and book1 in figure 6.18). However, as soon as the KB designer specifies, for example, that book1 is an element of the schema paul's_things, the organization of the object's hierarchies will be correspondingly modified.

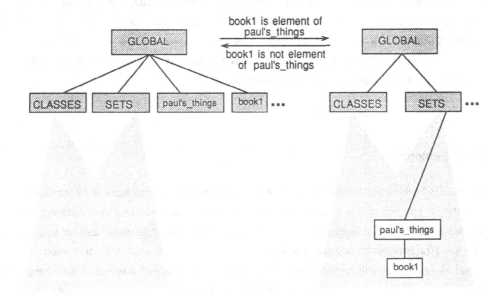

Figure 6.18: Management of an association hierarchy

6.4.2 Object Manipulation

The manipulation of KB contents occurs at the external interface of ORES (object-centered interface). This interface is composed of LISP-similar functions with which the knowledge engineer may construct a particular KB.

The functions provided by ORES may be either directly called from a LISP environment (program, interpreter, etc.) or accessed from the graphic interface supported by this component of KRISYS for the KB design. This last environment offers the knowledge engineer a graphical representation of the existing generalization/classification and association hierarchies as well as several windows for accessing the LISP interpreter, for editing, for input and output of information, for error and warning reports, etc. (figure 6.19). By navigating over the presented hierarchies, the searching within KB contents may be significantly facilitated. Additionally, the access to the LISP interpreter and the editing facilities provided by this graphic interface accelerate the definition of the structure of KB objects as well as the correction of methods, aspect specifications, etc.

ORES supports functions to create, delete, and change schemas, slots, methods, and aspect specifications. It allows both the connection and disconnection of schemas related by abstraction relationships as well as their access. It also enables the KB designer to access different groups of attributes of a schema, a particular attribute, groups of aspects, or a single aspect. Finally, it supports the activation of methods by means of the function SEND_MESSAGE.

For the specification of methods, the whole functionality of the LISP language is provided. Moreover, a method may contain calls to ORES functions including, of course, further SEND_MESSAGES. Hence, when activated, a method may access the whole KB, provoke changes on schemas, attributes, and aspects, cause the activation of other methods, as well as use the power of LISP to perform some kind of computation.

6.4.3 Demons

As described previously, ORES allows the KB designer to define procedures to be attached to attributes of schemas that are automatically activated when these attributes are accessed. This concept of *data-oriented computation* is very useful to represent intensional data or to check very complex integrity constraints. For example, if one wants to represent some information whose value changes with respect to other data (e.g., the exact age of a person, which changes every day), one needs a mechanism that generates the extensional value of this information automatically each time this information is accessed. This can be realized in ORES by using *demons*.

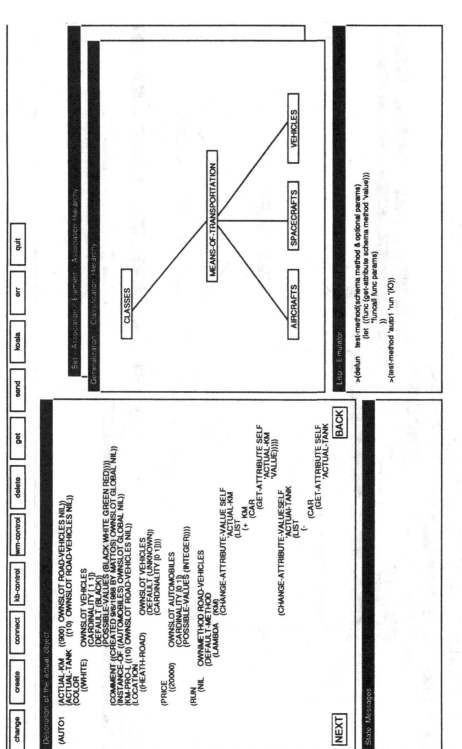

Figure 6.19a: Example of the graphic interface of KRISYS

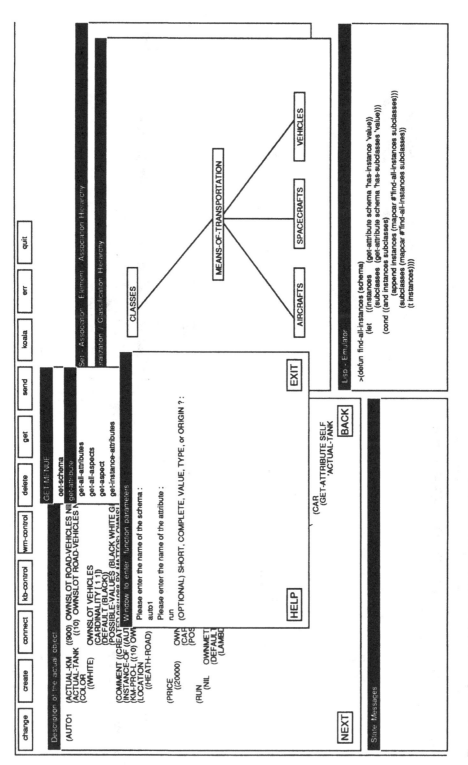

Figure 6.19b: Example of the graphic interface of KRISYS

Similar to all other objects in a KRISYS KB, demons are represented as schemas which are orga-nized in a hierarchy having the predefined schema DEMONS at the top. This schema has five subclasses: GET, PUT, ADD, RETRACT, and SEND, each containing two predefined instancemethods: <subclass name>-BEFORE and <subclass name>-AFTER. As an instance of one of these subclasses of DEMONS, a user-defined demon inherits the corresponding method attributes (GET-BEFORE, GET-AFTER, PUT-BEFORE, PUT-AFTER, ... SEND-BEFORE, SEND-AFTER), in which the code for the respective attached procedure is stored (figure 6.20). Thus, ORES enables the KB designer to specify the time of demon activation. For example, a proce-dure stored in a GET-BEFORE method will be always activated before the actual access to the corresponding attribute occurs. The same happens in the case of a PUT-AFTER demon which will be activated after the execution of the update operation on the corresponding attribute. This flexibility allows the use of demons for many different purposes. For example, demons applied to check integrity constraints should be activated before updating the value of an attribute, whereas those used to trigger actions when particular slots are modified should be activated after the access. Since the attached procedures are implemented as methods of the demons, they may use the whole functionality of LISP and of KRISYS to achieve their goals.

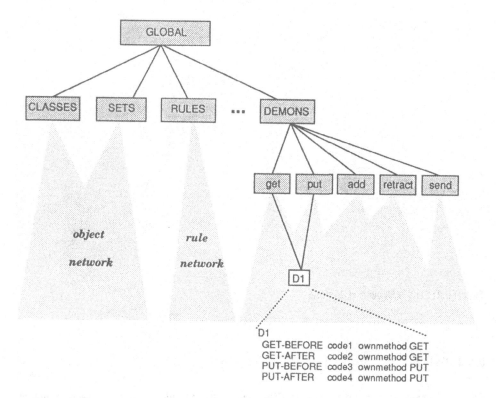

Figure 6.20: Organization of the demons hierarchy

The linkage between an attribute (S1 of schema-x in figure 6.21) and the corresponding demon is done by the specification of the demon's schemaname (d1 in figure 6.21) as value of the aspect DEMON of this attribute. Whenever an access to the attribute is made, ORES checks whether there is a DEMON aspect defined for this attribute, activating the corresponding attached procedure by sending a message to the schema specified there. Remember that the kind of access (get, put, etc.) determines the attached procedure to be evaluated. That is, a procedure specified in a GET method (either before or after) will be invoked if a get-access has been issued to the attribute, a PUT procedure is invoked by issuing a put-access, etc. By not storing the code of the attached procedure directly in the aspect of the attribute, ORES allows many attributes to use the same demons without having to introduce redundancy in the representation.

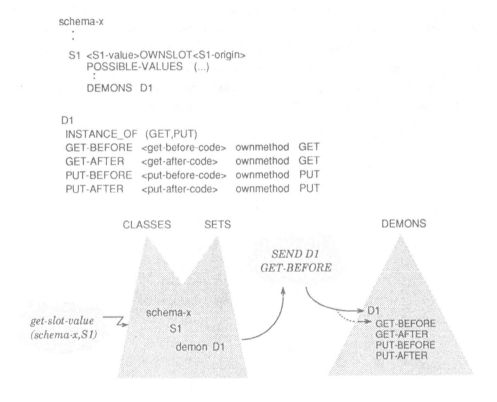

Figure 6.21: The activation of demons

6.4.4 Rules

KRISYS supports *general reasoning facilities* by means of *rules*. These are represented as schemas which are also organized in special hierarchies in the KB, having predefined schemas as superclasses.

The structure of rules

One of these predefined schemas is used to define the structure of the rules, i.e., this schema (RULES) contains some instanceslots which are inherited by each rule when it is introduced into the KB (figure 6.22). Externally, each rule has the well known form "if <condition> then <assertion>" which is specified according to the syntax and semantics of KOALA. That is, a rule can be viewed as a TELL-statement whose selection-clause corresponds to the rule condition. For this reason, rules may be built with very complex conditions and assertions (involving variables to represent any element of a KRISYS KB) since they can make use of the whole functionality of KOALA.

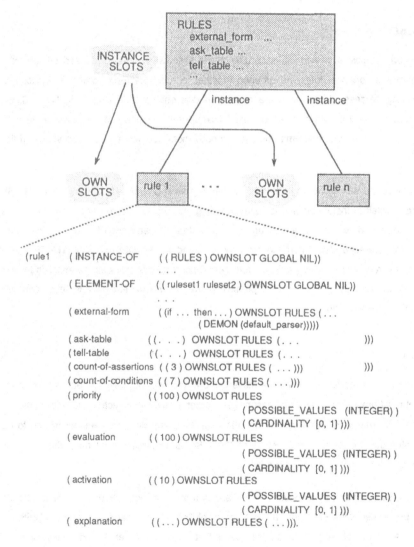

Figure 6.22: The structure of rules

During specification, the external representation of a rule is stored in the slot EXTERNAL_FORM which, by means of a demon, is used to automatically compile the rule thereby generating its internal representation (slots TELL_TABLE and ASK_TABLE in figure 6.22). Additionally, some information for conflict solving (slots COUNT_OF_ASSERTIONS and COUNT_OF_CONDITIONS) and auxiliary structures used for the realization of an efficient chaining of rules during the evaluation are produced (for details see [Le88]). Finally, the KB designer may specify some information to influence the reasoning process, such as how many times a rule may be evaluated (EVALUATION) or activated (ACTIVATION), a kind of priority to be exploited by the conflict solver (PRIORITY), etc.

The organization of rules

The organization of rules is carried out according to the association concept. Based on the existence of processing contexts, rules are grouped together in rule sets representing a kind of unit for the reasoning process. When rules are needed in different contexts (rule 3 in figure 6.23), they are related to several sets of rules by just following the semantics of the association concept. In the same way, sets of rules may be used to build more complex rule sets as shown in figure 6.23.

Every rule set has the same structure defined by their top level predefined schema (RULESETS). This schema contains instancemethods corresponding to the standard inference strategies (forward and backward reasoning) which are then inherited by each set of rules (figure 6.23). The code of the corresponding inference strategy is stored in the DEFAULT_METHOD aspect so that it may be redefined at any particular rule set. Thus, KRISYS provides the most important general reasoning strategies, however, not prohibiting the knowledge engineer to implement his own special inference algorithms.

Rule evaluation

A reasoning process is started by sending a message to a rule set. This will then activate its corresponding method (forward or backward reasoning) in order to evaluate each of its rule elements. Hence, a particular rule in KRISYS can be used in both reasoning directions without having to be redundantly stored. The reasoning direction of the rules is dynamically defined when the KS requests the activation of an inference strategy.

By the activation of a reasoning process, ORES allows the knowledge engineer either to choose one of the predefined strategies for the conflict resolution or to specify his own algorithms. KRISYS provides several search strategies (depth-first, breath-first, etc.) and many different algorithms for conflict solving (by_priority, by_number_of_conditions, etc.). All these predefined strategies are maintained in instances of the schemas SEARCH_STRATEGIES and CON-

FLICT_SOLVING_STRATEGIES and represented as methods so that the definition of further special purpose algorithms by the knowledge engineer is straightforward.

Finally, ORES allows the specification of facts to be used as the basis for the forward reasoning, the definition of break conditions to stop either a forward or a backward chaining, as well as the simulation of a reasoning process (i.e., without provoking changes in the KB). (For further details about the rule component of ORES see [Le88]).

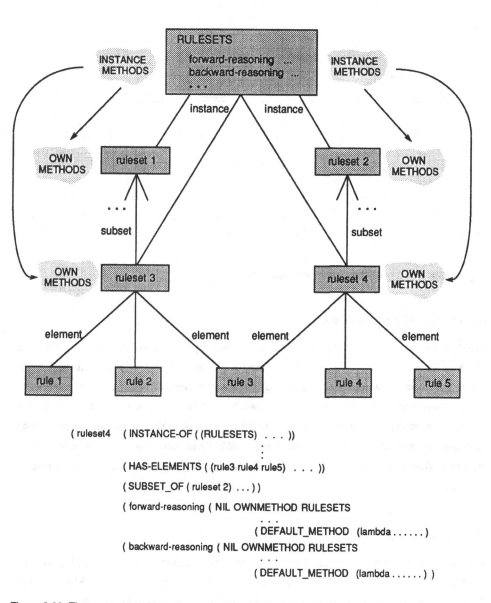

```
( ruleset4  ( INSTANCE-OF ( (RULESETS) . . . ))
                .
                :
            ( HAS-ELEMENTS ( (rule3 rule4 rule5) . . . ))
            ( SUBSET_OF ( ruleset 2) . . . ) )
( forward-reasoning ( NIL OWNMETHOD RULESETS
                            . . .
                        ( DEFAULT_METHOD  (lambda . . . . . . )
( backward-reasoning ( NIL OWNMETHOD RULESETS
                            . . .
                        ( DEFAULT_METHOD  (lambda . . . . . . ) )
```

Figure 6.23: The structure of rulesets

6.4.5 ORES Features Emphasized

In the previous sections, we described how the issues of the KOBRA knowledge model are supported by the ORES component of KRISYS. In this layer, every object of the KB is expressed as an instance of GLOBAL, which determines the internal structure of schemas. In addition to GLOBAL, further predefined schemas are maintained in order to define the different semantics of each hierarchy existing in a KRISYS KB as illustrated in figure 6.24.

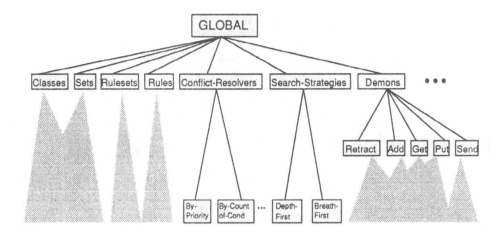

Figure 6.24: Some of the predefined schemas of ORES

Object-centered representation

ORES makes use of the object-centered concept defined by the knowledge model of KRISYS to internally represent KB contents, thereby supporting a descriptive and organizational representation of procedural knowledge. Demons and rules are also maintained as autonomous schemas in the KB being organized in networks and described by their declarative attributes and their behavior. For this reason, the major drawback presented by procedural knowledge representation schemes, i.e., lack of structural principles causing difficulty to make changes on it as well as to localize desired information (ART, BABYLON, KNOWLEDGE CRAFT, and LOOPS), is eliminated in KRISYS.

Units of reasoning

In ORES, rules are grouped in rule sets defining the units of reasoning. Therefore, during an inference process, the whole rule base does not have to be searched (ART and KNOWLEDGE CRAFT) since the knowledge engineer may specify which rule sets are to be considered. Additionally, ORES allows rules to be elements of several different sets, avoiding the introduction of redundant information when some problem solving know-how is necessary in distinct contexts (LOOPS and BABYLON).

Uniform and reasoning-independent representation

The internal representation of rules is uniform and independent of the reasoning strategy that will evaluate them. For this reason, there is no redundancy in the KB when rules are to be used both for forward and for backward chaining (ART, KNOWLEDGE CRAFT, and LOOPS).

Explicit representation of control mechanism

ORES supports an explicit representation of the control mechanism of the rule interpreter. Since neither search nor conflict solving strategies are buried in some part of the code of the interpreter, the knowledge engineer may exploit the powerful general purpose reasoning and conflict resolution strategies provided by KRISYS without, however, being restricted to them (ART, BABYLON, KNOWLEDGE CRAFT, and LOOPS). He may define new conflict solvers as well as new inference strategies to be combined either with each other or with the predefined algorithms provided by ORES so that an exact adaptation of the rule interpreter to special application tasks is possible.

Flexible and general purpose inference strategies

ORES supports the most important inference strategies. It enables the knowledge engineer to activate reasoning processes on the basis of particular assertions instead of always having to consider the whole KB (ART, LOOPS, and BABYLON). Additionally, such processes must not always reflect its deduced assertions in the KB (ART, BABYLON, KNOWLEDGE CRAFT, and LOOPS) thereby permitting, for example, the use of forward reasoning to investigate consequences of some facts without changing KB contents.

Attached procedures

The specification and the maintenance of demons is carried out independently of the objects for which they are going to be used. For this reason, ORES permits the utilization of a demon for many different schemas, allowing the specification of the time activation (i.e., before or after). Additionally, demons are provided for all kinds of attributes (slots and methods) so that the definition of attached procedures is not restricted to slots (KEE, ART, BABYLON, LOOPS, and KNOWLEDGE CRAFT).

6.5 Working-Memory System

The goal of this component of KRISYS is to efficiently cope with the two major problems of large KB management:

- long execution paths of KB accesses, and
- time consuming accesses to secondary storage.

Since KRISYS has also been designed to run in a server/workstation environment, these problems may even be aggravated by the communication as well as transfer overhead between the various machines involved in its architecture. When the KB, managed by the DBS kernel component, is maintained in a server while the other components of KRISYS together with the KS run on a workstation, knowledge has to be extracted from the server and transferred to the workstation before it can be processed. It is, therefore, desirable to have a mechanism that firstly enables the reduction of the path length and secondly minimizes the number of DBS calls when accessing the objects of the KB.

6.5.1 Processing Model

Exploitation of the application's locality

These goals are achieved by storing needed objects temporarily in a special main memory structure, called *working-memory*, rather than having to extract them from the DBS kernel every time the KS accesses them. The working-memory is a kind of application buffer which offers very fast access to the stored objects allowing the KS to reference these objects almost directly with costs comparable to a pointer-like access. Consequently, KRISYS supports a *processing model aimed at high locality of object references*, thereby drastically reducing the path length when accessing KB objects.

Knowledge transfer

During the problem solving process, objects are transferred from the KB and placed into the working-memory. Certainly, it is neither a task of the KS nor of the end-user to worry about such knowledge transfer. KBMS should support the concept of knowledge independence so that KS are unaware of the internal representation and storage of knowledge. Note that this (knowledge representation and storage) concealing principle is not provided by existing XPS tools or by the coupling approach. In a KEE environment, for example, the KS must not only know whether or not its needed objects are stored in the external DB, but also how the mapping of knowledge to DB relations is carried out in order to process a KB. Moreover, this mapping can be quite difficult because the expressiveness of the knowledge representation model is much higher than the one of the DB model. Since knowledge structures are often mapped to several DB objects, it is not always possible to guarantee that changes on the knowledge structures will be appropriately reflected in the external DB. By treating knowledge as a kind of "window" to the DB contents, KEE presents the well known problems and restrictions of updates through views [Ma83,Ke81]. Finally, when constructing a KB, the knowledge engineer has to deal with two different environments defining both knowledge structures and DB-schemas as well as the mapping from one to the other. KRISYS, on the other hand, isolates its applications from the internal representation and storage of knowledge. Therefore, it undertakes the mapping of knowledge to the structures of the underlying DBS and automatically extracts it from the server when it is not at hand in the workstation.

Exploitation of processing contexts

To replace KB objects in the working-memory, KRISYS, in general, uses a LRU-strategy. However, this may cause many calls to the DBS kernel since the unit of replacement (i.e., one object) has a very small granule. This is particularly critical just after the KS starts solving a new task at which time most of the needed objects are not found in the application buffer (see section 4.3.3.2). To minimize the number of DBS calls, the knowledge engineer should supply KRISYS with information about the KS access behavior in order to give it enough scope for optimization. As the one who knows the KS in fullest details, he knows when and which KB objects are going to be needed during KS processing. The task of the knowledge engineer is, therefore, to make known the existence of KS *processing contexts* in order to supply KRISYS with information to be utilized for performance improvement. From the modeling point of view, defining contexts means making explicit in the KB the knowledge about the KS problem solving behavior, thereby improving KB semantics [MM88].

In principle, contexts are composed of several KB objects (in general of different types) and objects may be elements of several contexts. Since contexts are not bound to constructs of the KOBRA knowledge model, they may be specified or deleted at any time during KB construction or even dynamically during KS consultation. A dynamic definition and activation of contexts is particularly important because needed contexts are often established on the basis of the results of the preceding phases of the problem solving process.

Contexts are, therefore, the most important mechanism used by KRISYS to improve access efficiency. When defined during the KB construction, KRISYS can use special storage structures or clustering mechanisms provided by the DBS kernel to optimize secondary storage accesses to these objects. But even when contexts are defined during KS consultation, our KBMS can exploit them to reduce KB accesses significantly. KRISYS exploits the existence of a context to generate a set-oriented access to the KB in order to fetch the objects of the context and store them into the working-memory as soon as it is informed that a new processing phase of the KS will begin. So, most or perhaps all objects referenced during this phase are found in the working-memory so that only a few or no references to the KB are further necessary. At the end of the processing phase, its corresponding context is then discarded from the working-memory and the context requested by the following phase is loaded into it. By means of this set-oriented fetching and discarding of KB objects, the DBS component of KRISYS can better employ its optimization potential thereby also drastically reducing I/O and transfer overhead. Finally, the KS references to individual objects will be supported very efficiently since the path length is very short when accessing working-memory objects.

In closing, one may observe that there are two orthogonal ways of looking at a context. Viewed from the knowledge engineer, a context is a collection of objects needed by a specific phase of the problem solving process of the KS, i.e., the knowledge necessary to work out a particular problem. KRISYS, on the other hand, views it as a collection of objects which are brought into the working-memory by just a single KB access. Following this approach, the knowledge engineer is still working in his framework without being involved with internal KBMS aspects although KRISYS is supplied with specific hints for performance improvement [MM88]. In other words, the processing context approach fortifies the discussed support of knowledge independence.

6.5.2 Internal Architecture

Internally, the Working-Memory System is divided in three main subcomponents as shown in figure 6.25.

The *distribution component* implements the external interface of this layer of KRISYS. It is responsible for the interpretation of the ORES calls and the resulting activation of the respective component. Access requests are satisfied by the *working-memory management* component which generates and sends simple queries (read/write accesses) to the DBS when the requested object is not found in the working-memory. (This may occur, for example, when processing contexts are not exploited.) The *context management* carries out the execution of control calls such as fetching or discarding of contexts. These operations generate set-oriented DB-operations (complex queries) to extract the contents from the KB or to discard them from the working-memory. Therefore, the working-memory manager takes care of the replacement of individual objects, whereas the context manager takes care of the replacement of object sets (contexts).

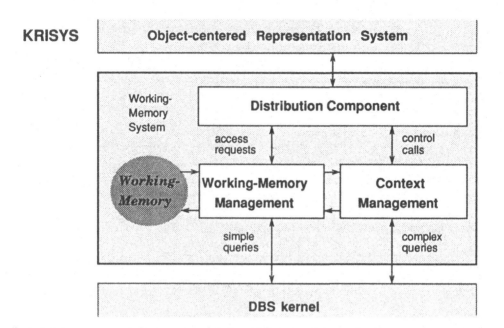

Figure 6.25: Architecture of the Working-Memory System

In order to guarantee very fast access to the working-memory contents, the working-memory management component maintains two hash-tables referring to the objects and to the attributes of the objects currently stored in the working-memory. Thus, it supports a direct access to attributes, avoiding the usual sequential search within an object, which is in some cases very inefficient (e.g., complex objects). Both, objects and their attributes, are maintained in structures with variable length containers supporting an appropriate storage of KS objects whose lengths may substantially vary [Ma86a].

6.5.3 Performance Comparison

The performance of our working-memory component has been compared with the performance of other coupling approaches between KS and DBS as shown in table 6.1. For this purpose, we have used a typical KS application in order to obtain patterns of KB accesses that characterize the working method of KS. To pursue a comparative investigation, we have adapted our application, the diagnosis XPS shell MED2 [Pu86a,Mi89], to work in different environments as shown in the table. During our consultations, MED2 has exploited a 7MB KB to diagnose fungi. Hence, we have repeatedly performed an identical application with the same performance critical parameters in each of the coupling/integration approaches. Therefore, our measurement results seem to be indicative for the quality of these investigated approaches.

	MED2 references	accesses to the KB (on secondary storage)
MED2 + DBS (direct coupling)	21303	21303
MED2 + DBS + application buffer	21303	8427
MED2 + KRISYS	23437	1105

Table 6.1: Overview of measurement results during a typical consultation

Coupling DBS and KS directly is obviously the most inefficient alternative. As already mentioned in section 4.3.3.2, every KS reference to a KB object has to be translated into a DBS call. This approach not only generates long execution paths (from application to DB-buffer) but may also provoke many accesses to the KB, depending on the DB-buffer size and on the required working sets.

To reduce the long path lengths, an application buffer may be applied in order to keep the most recently used objects close to the KS (see overall architecture in section 4.3.3.2). However, since this approach does not make use of knowledge about the KS access behavior, a large number of DBS calls is still necessary especially after changes of processing phases when most of the requested objects are not found in the buffer.

KRISYS eliminates this problem by exploiting knowledge about the KS processing model. Since the replacement of KB objects in the working-memory is carried out in accordance with the processing contexts of the KS, DBS calls as well as accesses to secondary storage and transfer overhead are strongly minimized. (Note that the number of calls increases because of the XPS control calls to inform KRISYS about the course of the problem solving process).

The improvement of performance due to the exploitation of processing contexts becomes even more evident by comparing the number of KB accesses using different sizes of the LRU-based application buffer and of the working-memory. (Figure 6.26 illustrates the number of such accesses for a typical MED2 consultation as a function of the application buffer/working-memory size.)

KB accesses

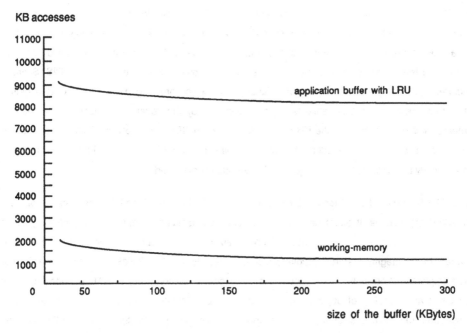

size of the buffer (KBytes)

Figure 6.26: Comparison of different replacement strategies

6.5.4 Summary

The goal of this component of KRISYS is to provide a framework for the exploitation of the application's locality guaranteeing very fast accesses to the KB objects. It takes advantage of the knowledge about the access behavior of the KS, like for example the existence of processing contexts, to maintain relevant objects close to the application, i.e., in the working-memory. The definition of such processing contexts is executed by the knowledge engineer, who however keeps working in his original framework without being involved with internal aspects of KBMS. He only has to make known the existence of contexts as well as the phases of the KS problem solving process.

6.6 DBS kernel

In chapter 4, we have shown that NDBS are able to satisfy knowledge maintenance requirements. NDBS kernels as well as their non-standard data models are much more powerful than traditional DBS and data models and can, for this reason, support maintenance tasks in a very efficient and effective manner. Moreover, the neutral NDBS kernel approach allows for an application-independent structural object representation. Especially in the case of knowledge representation, the general purpose constructs which are provided by existing non-standard data models allow for an appropriate mapping of the KS-oriented structures. For these reasons, the use of the NDBS architectural concept seems to be quite advantageous in the KRISYS architecture. Knowledge modeling and manipulation tasks, which are in general achieved at a higher level than knowledge maintenance tasks, are supported by the upper components of the system, whereas the management of the KB is undertaken by the NDBS component. Following this issue, the semantics of our knowledge structures remains outside of the NDBS kernel which views them simply as a kind of complex objects to be adequately managed.

The DBMS kernel chosen for KRISYS, named PRIMA, was developed for the support of non-standard applications. It offers neutral, yet powerful mechanisms for managing KB of all types of KS: storage techniques for a variety of object sizes, flexible representation and access techniques, basic integrity features, recovery mechanisms, etc. [HMMS87,Hä88a]. PRIMA is a PRototype Implementation of the MAD model. As discussed in section 4.2.2.1, MAD provides dynamic definition and handling of objects based on direct and symmetric management of network structures and recursiveness enabling the mapping of knowledge structures in an effective and straightforward manner.

At the time when KRISYS was implemented, PRIMA was not completely available. So, for the first version of KRISYS, we decided to implement some MAD features that are essential for knowledge management on the top of INGRES [SWKH76,Da87] in order to achieve the functionality needed by our KBMS. Therefore, our preliminary DBMS kernel is realized by an additional layer which is responsible for the mapping of schemas onto DB relations. At its external interface (i.e., the interface to the Working-Memory System), KB objects are delivered in the representational form known by the upper components of KRISYS. Internally, KB schemas are viewed as unnormalized tuples which are then mapped to a predefined DB-schema (for details about this mapping mechanism see [Gr88]).

The DBMS kernel supports functions to create and delete single schemas or a group of them. It provides operations to make modifications on the structure of KB contents including schemas, attributes, and aspects. To support the inheritance mechanism, it offers functions to insert and remove attributes in and from groups of schemas. Furthermore, it supports a set-oriented storage and retrieval of KB objects applied by the Working-Memory System for the manipulation of processing contexts. Finally, it provides the upper components of KRISYS with a transaction mechanism used to guarantee the semantic integrity of the KB when KOALA operations have not been successfully performed.

6.7 Summarizing Examples

In this section, we illustrate the control flow through the KRISYS layers by giving examples of the operations needed to solve KS queries at each of the system interfaces (we consider the working-memory as been empty and the inexistence of defined processing contexts at the beginning of an evaluation). The first example shows the execution of a simple ASK-statement to retrieve the schema auto1. The tree structure presented in figure 6.27 (where control operators, etc. are dropped for simplicity reasons) indicates the calling hierarchy needed for the evaluation of this statement, which requires the execution of exactly one operation at each system interface. Note that an operation in the DBMS kernel is necessary since the working-memory is considered as empty.

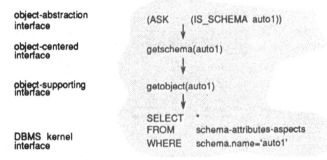

Figure 6.27: Operator tree for a simple retrieval

To illustrate the usage of the working-memory, a more complex query to retrieve all amphibious automobiles may be formulated (figure 6.28). During its evaluation, ORES dynamically specifies two different contexts (instances_of automobiles and instances_of boats) so that further (expensive) calls to the DBMS kernel (with accesses to the DBMS buffer or even to secondary storage) are avoided.

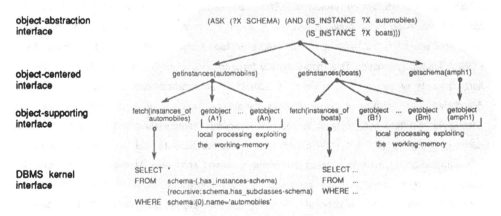

Figure 6.28: Operator tree for the evaluation of a complex ASK-statement

A last example illustrates the use of the powerful operations provided by the DBMS kernel to support TELL-operations that modify the structure of KB schemas. The operation, shown in figure 6.29, inserts the instanceslot passengers in the class vehicles thereby triggering its inheritance by all instances of vehicles. In this example, ORES exploits a processing context to retrieve and store the whole hierarchy of schemas under the class vehicles.

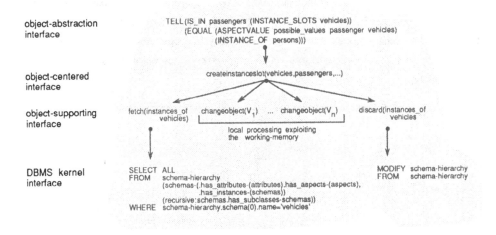

Figure 6.29: Operator tree for the evaluation of a TELL-statement

6.8 Conclusions

KRISYS is a multi-layered prototype KBMS constructed on the basis of the architectural approach described in the previous chapter. In KRISYS, the effective support of knowledge modeling requirements is achieved by a mixed representation framework defined by the means of the KOBRA knowledge model. This model equally focuses on declarative, operational, and organizational aspects of the application world. It allows for an accurate representation of the whole descriptive characteristics of the application domain, i.e., objects, properties, relationships, and constraints. It offers constructs to represent procedural characteristics of the application world such as behaviors of the domain objects (methods), reactions to real world events (demons), and situation-action rules to express the problem solving know-how. Moreover, mechanisms for knowledge organization are also integrated into the knowledge model. KOBRA supports the most significant abstraction concepts, enriching considerably its semantics with their different built-in reasoning facilities. In summary, KOBRA presents a rich spectrum of concepts for building

KB which are well integrated in its central construct: the schema, supporting an object-centered representation of the real world.

Knowledge independence is supported by means of KOALA defining a KB as a kind of abstract data type:

- The user may TELL KRISYS facts about the application world by merely specifying the "knowledge state" to be achieved.

- When ASK-ing the system, he does not have to know anything about the way the required information should be retrieved.

This approach might seem to be similar to the one described in [BFL83,LB86]. However, the approach of [BFL83,LB86] exhibits at least two crucial drawbacks: assertions may only add information to the KB in a monotonic fashion so that facts can never be removed or modified; it is not possible to retrieve KB contents in any form since the user is restricted to yes/no queries. KOALA, on the other hand, allows changes and deletions of existing knowledge as well as the selection of qualified information. It also provides

- flexible set-oriented qualification of objects,

- user-defined predicates for object qualification,

- user-defined and qualified projections of the results, and

- recursion.

The needs of the KB designer are supported by the ORES component. This module implements the knowledge model of KRISYS thereby exploiting the object-centered representation concept to support data-oriented computational features as well as flexible rule-based reasoning mechanisms.

Finally, efficiency is guaranteed by the framework provided for the exploitation of the application locality. KRISYS takes advantage of the knowledge about the access behavior of the KS in order to

- make use of the DBMS kernel mechanisms to improve access efficiency to secondary storage,

- reduce the path length when accessing KB objects, and

- minimize I/O operations as well as transfer overhead.

KRISYS accomplishes therefore fast access to the stored KB objects by exploiting the existence of processing contexts whose contents are kept close to the application in its working-memory.

7. Modeling Knowledge with KRISYS

The objective of this chapter is to show how a knowledge engineer can employ our KBMS approach in order to model some real world situations. For this reason, we focus on the design process of KS demonstrating their incremental development under a KBMS environment.

7.1 The Example

The KS incremental development will be demonstrated by using an example that will become more complex in the course of our discussion. Here, we just introduce a brief description of the situation to be modeled as well as the task of our KS.

The reader should imagine a first class restaurant in a city, let us say, like Paris or New York, where guests may select from several menus the finest and most exotic dishes and wines for their meal. The purpose of the KS is to

- advise guests in combining dishes and wines (e.g., suggesting red or white, French or Rhine wine, etc.) considering, however, known preferences since VIP guests usually frequent the restaurant regularly, and

- automatically control some conventional functions in order to supply the restaurant owner with important information such as necessity of wine ordering, stock statistics, and guests' preferences.

7.2 Incremental Development of the KS

In a KBMS environment, the development process of KS does not have the same four basic phases as described in [Ha84,Ha87] (see section 3.2.3.2). Since the knowledge model and the inference engine are already specified and implemented as part of the KBMS, the design phase becomes meaningless. The previously described refinement phase should be divided into two phases, otherwise it will be impossible to execute its tasks with large KB. Furthermore, it is necessary to extend the process to include one latter phase, called optimization, since KB are now maintained on secondary storage devices (figure 7.1). So, in KBMS environments the first step in developing a KS is to conceptualize the real world situation of its application domain (conceptualization phase). The result is expressed by means of a knowledge model (structuring phase) which is refined in a stepwise manner in order to improve it with more semantics (refinement). A validation phase is then performed causing a kind of feedback to the previous ones in order to enrich as well as to correct the KB incrementally until the KS exhibits the same level of know-how as human experts. Finally, an optimization phase is performed, aiming at the improvement of KS efficiency [MM88].

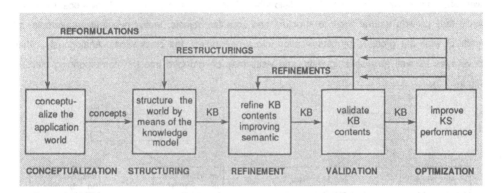

Figure 7.1: Evolutionary process of KS development

In the following, we describe the development process of our hypothetical KS, showing how the activities underlying this process are performed by means of KRISYS. For sake of clarity, knowledge about the application domain and expert knowledge (i.e., problem solving know-how) are modeled separately.

7.2.1 Modeling the Application Domain

Conceptualization

Usually, when the knowledge engineer analyses the application world, he identifies objects, also called entities, which are characterized by their properties. For instance, in our restaurant, different kinds of wine exist, and each of them has properties such as the year of vintage, site, kind of vine, number of available bottles, etc. Even events are viewed as entities: the visit of a guest has the properties guest's name, date of visit, dishes and wines enjoyed, etc. Each object is associated with some operations which may change the object's properties representing in some sense the behavior of the object as well as its interface to other objects. For example, ordering a bottle of wine is an operation associated with visits. This behavior decreases the number of available bottles of the ordered wine as well as updates the list of chosen wines of a visit.

In addition to properties and operations, objects have relationships to other objects which carry some important information. Most of these relationships are domain dependent. For example, a particular dish is related to some wines which should under all circumstances be recommended. However, there are important domain independent relationships that occur in nearly every domain and as such have well defined semantics. They are known as abstraction concepts and well understood by their underlying relationships; they play a key role in knowledge modeling since they provide natural ways to structure and organize objects. In our hypothetical example, all kinds of wine are grouped by classification into a new object, the class wines. Analogously, other beverages as well as dishes, guests, and visits may be grouped into the corresponding classes (figure 7.2).

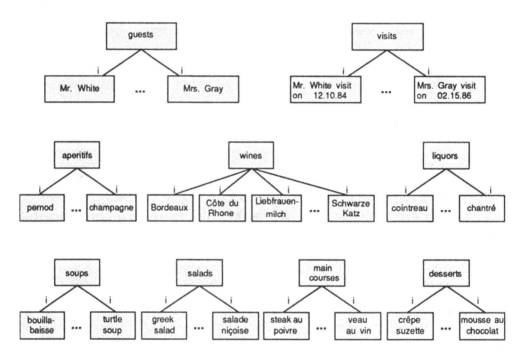

Figure 7.2: Classifying objects   (i = instance)

Classes are generalized by extracting their common attributes: soups and salads are generalized to "hors d'œuvres", and recursively, "hors d'œuvres", main courses, and desserts are generalized to dishes (figure 7.3).

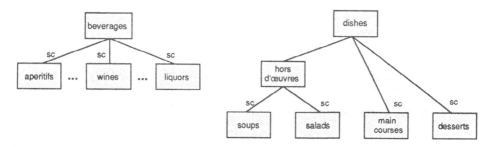

Figure 7.3: Generalization of objects   (sc = subclass)

Objects fulfilling common conditions are grouped into sets by association: all visit objects having Mrs. Gray as their value of guest's name form the set represented by the object Mrs. Gray. Recursively applied, association results in supersets: the sets French wines and Rhine wines are subsets of European wines (figure 7.4). Finally, a menu has an "hors d'œuvre", a main course, and a dessert as its parts defining a kind of aggregation relationship (figure 7.5).

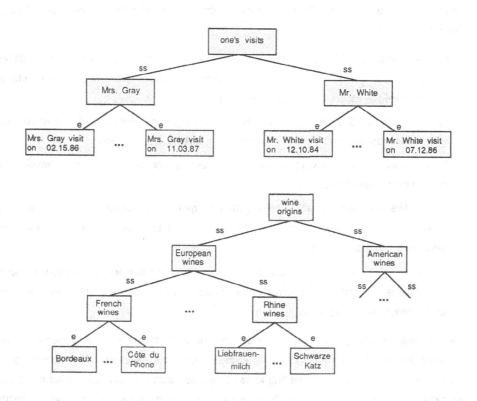

Figure 7.4: An association hierarchy   (e = element, ss = subset)

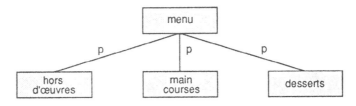

Figure 7.5: An aggregation hierarchy   (p = part)

It is important to recognize that an object does not represent a class, set, instance, etc. by itself, but only in the context of being related to other objects. The object "hors d'œuvres" is a class because it has subclasses or because it has a superclass, and the object Mrs. Gray is a set because it has elements. As any object may be related to other objects by different abstraction concepts, it may at the same time represent a set, part, instance, etc. For example, desserts is a subclass of dishes and a part of menu.

The most important aspect of abstraction concepts is that they are the basis for drawing particular conclusions about objects. There are several kinds of reasoning possible (see section 5.4.3.2). The following are some of them:

- Because "veau au vin" is an instance of main courses and this is, in turn, a subclass of dishes, it may be reasoned that "veau au vin" is an instance of dishes. (The same holds for objects that are related by association or by aggregation.)

- From the fact that Bordeaux is an instance of beverages, the conclusion that Bordeaux has, at least, the properties and operations prescribed by beverages can be drawn.

- Since elements of a set always fulfil the set membership condition, elements of French wines must be produced in France.

- The set Mrs. Gray has properties defining the average of expenses during her visits, the most frequented week day, etc. Conclusions about the values of these properties can be drawn based on the element characteristics.

- Menus are composed of "hors d'œuvres", main courses, and desserts; therefore, the calories of a menu is composed of the sum of the corresponding parts' calories. The same may occur for the menu's price, weight, etc.

By observing the above definitions, one may conclude that different kinds of properties as well as semantics exist that are involved in the abstraction concepts. Consider for example the object wines (figure 7.2), which has all existing kinds of wine as instances. This class object might have properties describing its instances such as year of vintage, site, and number of available bottles. Viewed as a set, the same object might have some properties describing the group of elements as a whole (e.g., most desired wine, most expensive wine, total number of bottles, etc.). Obviously, when an object represents both a set and a class, the set properties should not affect the instances, and the instance properties should not be used for describing the set. Additionally, instance properties do not have values because they abstractly define the structure of the instances; values are not assigned until instantiation. On the other hand, set properties possess a value because they describe characteristics of the group of elements. This even holds when instances and elements are the same as in the case of the above example.

Structuring

So far, we have described how real world objects are organized. But how can the KBMS KRISYS be employed to model such objects? In general, KRISYS provides an easy and convenient way to model real world situations according to the concepts presented above. Each entity is represented by one schema, which has attributes that describe declarative aspects of the schema (slots) and attributes that describe procedural aspects (methods). To model the abstraction concepts, standard slots occurring in each schema are used: has-instances and instance-of for classification, has-subclasses and subclass-of for generalization, has-elements, element-of, has-subsets and subset-of for association (aggregation is represented by ordinary slots).

Therefore, rather than having one schema in the model for the representation of each role played by a real world entity, a schema represents all roles of this entity at the same time. Consequently, KRISYS allows for a one-to-one correspondence between entities in the application domain and schemas in the model preventing, for example, the knowledge about an entity (e.g., a wine) to be spread out among several objects of the model. Following this approach, figure 7.6 shows the integrated representation of our application world by means of the knowledge model provided by KRISYS.

Figure 7.7 presents some entities of our restaurant application represented as KRISYS schemas. After defining the structure of KB objects, KRISYS undertakes the maintenance of the structural and semantic integrity of the KB. For example, inheritance is employed to ensure that each instance or subclass has, at least, the attributes prescribed by its superclasses. KRISYS guarantees that such integrity holds even if changes to the KB structure occur: if the attribute phone number is added to the object guests, it will be inherited immediately by all subclasses and instances of guests. In the same manner, if the property site is removed from the class wines, KRISYS automatically withdraws it from each existing wine in the KB.

Further mechanisms for the maintenance of the structural KB integrity are based on the other reasoning facilities provided by the abstraction concepts. KRISYS guarantees, for example, that every element of a set satisfies the corresponding membership conditions. As such, when one erases the value France from the slot which defines the land where a particular wine is produced, this wine is automatically removed from the set French wines.

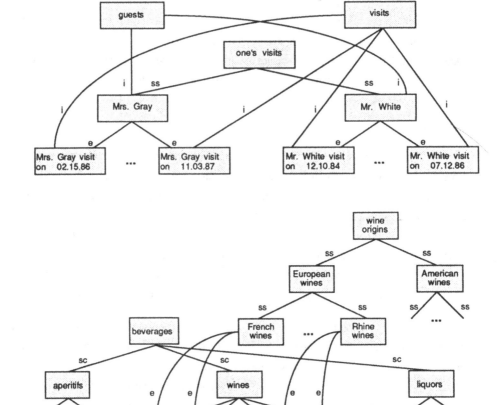

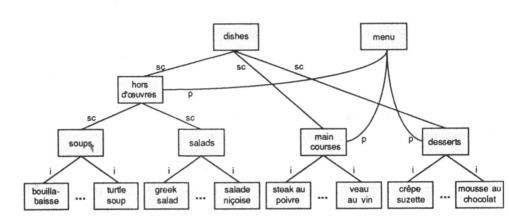

Figure 7.6: Integrated representation of objects

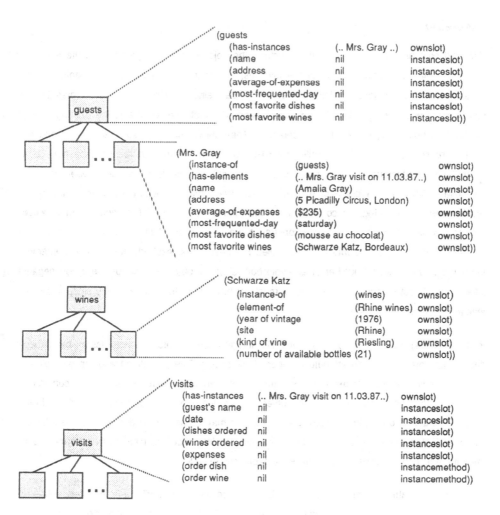

(guests
    (has-instances   (.. Mrs. Gray ..)   ownslot)
    (name   nil   instanceslot)
    (address   nil   instanceslot)
    (average-of-expenses nil   instanceslot)
    (most-frequented-day nil   instanceslot)
    (most favorite dishes nil   instanceslot)
    (most favorite wines nil   instanceslot))

(Mrs. Gray
    (instance-of   (guests)   ownslot)
    (has-elements   (.. Mrs. Gray visit on 11.03.87..) ownslot)
    (name   (Amalia Gray)   ownslot)
    (address   (5 Picadilly Circus, London) ownslot)
    (average-of-expenses ($235)   ownslot)
    (most-frequented-day (saturday)   ownslot)
    (most favorite dishes (mousse au chocolat)   ownslot)
    (most favorite wines (Schwarze Katz, Bordeaux) ownslot))

(Schwarze Katz
    (instance-of   (wines)   ownslot)
    (element-of   (Rhine wines) ownslot)
    (year of vintage   (1976)   ownslot)
    (site   (Rhine)   ownslot)
    (kind of vine   (Riesling)   ownslot)
    (number of available bottles (21)   ownslot))

(visits
    (has-instances   (.. Mrs. Gray visit on 11.03.87..) ownslot)
    (guest's name   nil   instanceslot)
    (date   nil   instanceslot)
    (dishes ordered nil   instanceslot)
    (wines ordered nil   instanceslot)
    (expenses   nil   instanceslot)
    (order dish   nil   instancemethod)
    (order wine   nil   instancemethod))

Figure 7.7: Some objects of the restaurant KB as KRISYS schemas

Finally, operations are modeled by methods and invoked by message passing: ordering a bottle of wine means sending a message to the corresponding instance of visits. This message, which is passed along with some parameter values, as for example number of bottles, will then activate the method 'order wine'. Another kind of operations representing the reactions to real world events are managed in KRISYS by so-called demons that watch for changes in the correspon- ding attributes. For example, when the number of available bottles of a wine falls short of 20, some kind of supply should be ordered. In this example, a demon is automatically invoked after modification of 'number of available bottles' to examine whether it is necessary to order or not.

Refinement

The next step after having defined the structure, the objects, and the operations of the KB is the so-called refinement phase. Such phase involves, in general, the addition of semantic integrity constraints to the previously defined KB contents. Basically, two kinds of semantic integrity constraints exist which are involved in a KS application. The first kind represents the existing reasoning facilities underlying the abstraction concepts. They always have the same semantics and are, for this reason, permanently controlled by KRISYS when abstraction relationships have been defined (see conceptualization). As such, by every visit of Mrs. Gray the set properties of the object Mrs. Gray (i.e., average of expenses, most frequented week day, etc.) are automatically recalculated guaranteeing the correctness of the inherent semantics of all abstraction concepts. The second kind of semantic integrity constraints are those dependent on the application domain at hand. They are also automatically controlled but have to be explicitly specified. For example, the value of the property 'number of available bottles' of the object wines must be a non negative integer, and 'most favorite wines' in guests must not have more than three values since it is desirable to record only the most favorite ones.

In KRISYS, application dependent semantic integrity constraints are expressed by aspects describing more exactly the attribute to whom they belong. The predefined aspects possible-values and cardinality are employed to model the above mentioned value and cardinality constraints. To assume that the number of available bottles has a value of zero when no value is stored in this slot, the default-value aspect is used. Default-method may be applied to define a standard behavior to all instances of visits. User-defined aspects are introduced to individually characterize an attribute, e.g., unit specifies that expenses are expressed in US$.

For a particular attribute, aspects are only defined once, i.e., if an attribute is inherited, it has initially the same aspects as the original attribute. KRISYS allows for modifications of aspect definitions as long as these modifications do not violate the semantics of the abstraction concepts. It is therefore possible to restrict possible-values or cardinality specifications when moving downwards in a superclass-subclass hierarchy. The extension, however, of such specifications is not permitted since the instances or subclasses having this extended specification will not be in agreement with the definition of their superclasses. KRISYS guarantees therefore that the semantics of an attribute remains the same throughout the KB. The maintenance of the attribute semantics is very proper when inheriting default values, which is especially useful for methods. (Remember that inheriting values does not make any sense). For example, the method 'order wine' in visits has the same code for each instance of visits and, consequently, can be defined just once as a default method in visits. Each instance of visits inherits 'order wine' as own-method; if no new value is assigned to the ownmethod, the default method is then automatically referenced when 'order wine' is activated.

Up to here, only integrity constraints concerning one attribute have been mentioned. Clearly, there are also integrity constraints spanning several attributes of different objects. For example, the object stock in the KB has as value of its attribute 'number of available bottles' the sum of the values of 'number of available bottles' of each instance of wines. This constraint can be controlled by demons. In this situation there are two possibilities: (a) a demon updates the sum of bottles kept by the stock object after each modification of the attribute 'number of available bottles' of any wine, or (b) every time the 'number of available bottles' of the whole stock is read, a demon first computes the sum and assigns this attribute.

Figure 7.8 presents some of the restaurant objects in more detail, i.e., including demons, value restrictions, etc.

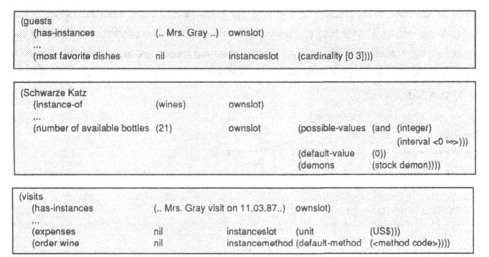

Figure 7.8: Objects of the restaurant KB in more detail

Validation

At the end of the refinement phase, a new (or a first) version of a KS prototype is ready, and the knowledge validation phase begins. Here an explicit representation of all aspects of knowledge is particularly important in order to allow for an easy localization of knowledge incorrectnesses. Generally, prototypes perform poorly at the start because of an erroneous transformation to objects of the knowledge model, an initial neglect of some refinements, or even because the knowledge engineer simply learns some more details about the application domain. By diagnosing the weakness and deficiencies of the KS, the knowledge engineer can go back to some of the developing phases either to conceptualize, structure, or refine some further aspects of the application world previously introduced into the KB, leading to an incremental, evolutionary development. Even after being constructed, KS will be continuously growing and expanding their capabilities by including new expertise into the KB so that, in reality, the described cyclic development never comes to an end.

Further refinements or changes of existing specifications are certainly the easiest modifications to be performed in the KB. These are directly achieved by using KRISYS operations to create new aspects, delete old ones, restrict them, introduce new demons, etc.

Restructuring usually generates new concepts or changes on existing ones to be modeled in the KB. The same occurs with reformulations after a new conceptualization of the real world. In our restaurant situation, the class wines exists, comprising all kinds of wine available in the restaurant. In order to supply guests with detailed information about wines, the head waiter wants to differentiate between the wines offered in the "carte" according to the several existing vines. Such information requires therefore the introduction of further subclasses of wines into the KB (e.g., white wines, red wines, rosé wines, Riesling wines, Ortega wines, etc.), where the possible-values specification of the property 'kind of vine' previously defined in the superclass wines is correspondingly restricted. After this, the instances of wines have to be connected with one of the introduced subclasses according to their kind of vine (e.g., wines produced with Riesling vines are connected with the class Riesling wines which in turn is a subclass of white wines as illustrated in figure 7.9).

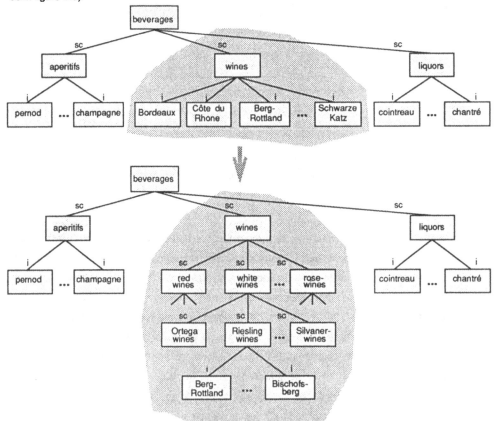

Figure 7.9: Restructuring wines

The chef is also not satisfied with the defined structure of dishes. He objects to the fact, for example, that cold dishes are not a kind of main course but a kind of "hors d'œuvre". Thus, the knowledge engineer has to introduce cold dishes as a subclass of "hors d'œuvres" and change the superclass of the corresponding dishes to that new class (figure 7.10).

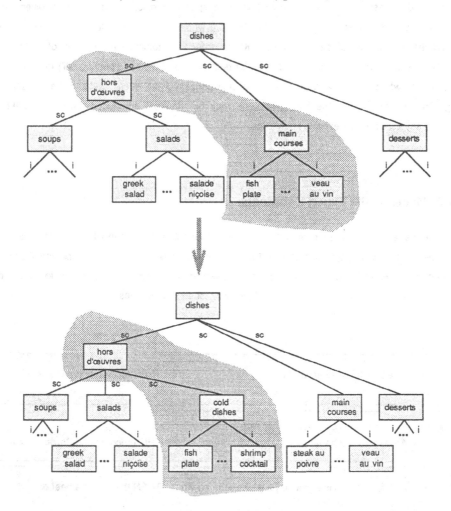

Figure 7.10: Restructuring dishes

Restructuring comprises adding new objects to the KB, inserting new classes or sets into existing hierarchies, changing the superclass of classes or instances, adding and deleting attributes, renaming objects and so on. In general, the most radical changes come from adding or deleting abstraction relationships between objects. But even in case of these radical changes, KRISYS provides direct and flexible ways to achieve such restructurings, keeping the correctness of the affected built-in reasoning facilities. Particularly, when disconnecting an instance from its class, the instance need not be deleted but may exist on its own thereby keeping its characteristics which are not dependent on its relationship to the class. This means that the knowledge engineer can restructure the KB as much as necessary without losing any of the correct information previously introduced into the KB.

A final kind of restructurings or reformulations with special significance are those involved with extensions of the kept knowledge or of the KS as a whole. For example, it may be important to extend the functionality of our hypothetical KS in order to automatize the printing of restaurant bills. Such extension may be easily achieved by defining a new method ('printing bill') for the class visits which, when activated, calculates the total expenses of the guest, updates the corresponding slot, and then prints the bill. Extensions may be therefore introduced effortlessly without affecting any aspect of the existing knowledge.

7.2.2 Modeling the Expert Knowledge

Most of the expert knowledge is difficult to be represented by traditional algorithms (i.e., by methods) as this knowledge is based on the expert's experience rather than on proven theories. Therefore, in KRISYS, expert knowledge is represented by production rules (rules for short) of the form IF <condition> THEN <action>. (Figure 7.11 shows some rules of our restaurant application.)

R1: IF a beef dish has been chosen   THEN recommend a red wine

R2: IF a red wine has been recommended
        AND there is a preference for French wines   THEN recommend Bordeaux wine

R3: IF the dish chosen is steak au poivre or veau au vin   THEN the dish is a beef dish

Figure 7.11: Some rules of the restaurant KB

In the KRISYS environment, rules that are applied to solve similar problems are grouped into one ruleset. For example, all rules that are used for determining a suitable wine for a chosen dish are grouped together. Rulesets need not be disjoint so that each rule may be an element of several rulesets which are the units of reasoning in KRISYS. If a guest preferring French wines chooses a "steak au poivre", KRISYS can provide our KS with the conclusion that a Bordeaux wine should be suggested by employing its forward reasoning mechanism. On the other hand, if the guest chooses a Bordeaux wine, the system can use just the same ruleset (that means, the same group of rules) and conclude by backward reasoning that "steak au poivre" or "veau au vin" are the most suitable dishes for this wine.

Finally, it is worth emphasizing that KRISYS allows for a separated modeling of domain and expert knowledge yielding more flexibility in the modeling process: adding or deleting rules or modifying rulesets does not affect the domain knowledge, and vice versa; changing the domain knowledge does not lead to inconsistencies in the expert knowledge.

7.2.3 Optimization

After constructing the KB, the knowledge engineer should concentrate on performance measures. The guests of our restaurant are very busy people and so cannot waste their time waiting for the suggestions of our KS.

Some of the performance difficulties of our KS result from the use of secondary storage. Our KS must deal with information about an enormous number of guests as well as dishes, wines, and other menu contents so that the whole KB cannot be kept in virtual memory. Further difficulties may result from the communications as well as transfer overhead between the various machines involved in this applications. Our restaurant has many filials that are served by several small workstations (probably one per table) on which our KS is running. Information is, however, centralized. When collecting information about a particular guest during a visit (e.g., his preferences), it is necessary to store this information in such a way that it is immediately available to every other filial. It would be a terrible situation if a VIP guest has to inform the waiter, for example, that he does not appreciate red wine, every time he visits another filial of our restaurant. For this reason, workstations are connected with a central machine (server) in which the whole KB is maintained. During KS processing, knowledge is therefore extracted from this public KB and transferred to the workstation, where it is exploited for solving problems.

Certainly, it is not a task of the knowledge engineer to worry about such knowledge transfer. Consequently, our KS does not have to explicitly inform our KBMS when knowledge is needed in some particular workstation. KRISYS undertakes this task. It analyses the references of the KS to KB objects and automatically extracts these objects from the server when they are not available in the workstation. The extracted objects are then temporarily stored in the working-memory where they can be directly referred by the KS.

The remaining difficulty is how to fetch objects from the server as well as how to replace them in the working-memory. Nevertheless, it is not a task of the knowledge engineer to find out such ways, too. He is preoccupied with the KS development and as such should not be involved with internal KBMS measures towards efficiency. He should however supply the KBMS with enough information about the KS access behavior in order to enable KRISYS to exploit its optimization potential. As the one who knows the KS in fullest details, the knowledge engineer knows which KB objects are going to be processed during each problem solving task of the KS. Since these requested objects generally represent the knowledge necessary to infer the specific goal of a solving process phase, they build together a context. For example, to suggest a wine for an ordered dish, it is necessary to have the knowledge about the dish, about available wines, about the guest's preferences, and the rules necessary to infer the most appropriate wine (i.e., the wine expert knowledge). The task of the knowledge engineer is therefore to make known the existence of such contexts, thereby explicitly representing the knowledge about the KS problem solving behavior in the KB. By doing this, KRISYS can make use of mechanisms for improving access efficiency such as clustering, special storage structures, etc. However, the most significant measure for efficiency improvement used by KRISYS are the context-oriented accesses to the KB that occur during KS consultation. KRISYS exploits the existence of these contexts generating set-oriented accesses to the KB during changes of processing phases so that none or very few calls to the DBMS component will be made during the next phase. Moreover, due to the set-oriented fetch of the required objects, the DBMS kernel can better employ its mechanisms for performance improvement reducing drastically I/O and transfer overhead.

7.3 Conclusions

In the course of this work, we have seen that KB are at the heart of any KS. As the storehouse of almost all application knowledge, its construction deserves special attention during KS development.

On the basis of this shift of viewpoint, we demonstrated in this chapter the construction of a KB for a hypothetical KS by means of our KBMS prototype KRISYS. In general, this KB construction is at first realized by a cyclic process including a conceptualization of the application world, the KB structuring, a kind of refinement to improve the KB semantics, and a validation. The process or only parts of it are then repeated until the KS performs at the expert's level of know-how. Essential in this whole process is a latter phase in which efforts are concentrated on performance measures (optimization phase).

Here, it is worth emphasizing once again the support of KRISYS for the discussed incremental KS development. Firstly, our KBMS approach permits the knowledge engineer to use its knowledge model as a tool for dynamically defining his conceptualization of the application world as KB

contents. Thus, it supports the necessary structuring issues. Secondly, the specification of the KB contents may be refined in steps, thereby improving the semantics of the whole knowledge representation. KRISYS, therefore, supports a flexible KB refinement. Thirdly, since almost the whole knowledge of the application world is explicitly represented, it permits an easy and flexible validation of KB contents, thereby providing means for feedback to any of the KS development phases. KRISYS permits the creation of the KB contents (e.g., object types, behaviors, reactions, constraints, rules, etc.) as well as its modification without losing any of the previously defined information. It therefore allows KB contents to be corrected incrementally, thereby supporting knowledge reformulations, restructurings as well as new refinements. Finally, the knowledge engineer may provide the system with enough information about the KS access behavior without becoming involved with internal KBMS aspects. KRISYS, therefore, offers a suitable framework for the exploitation of the KS locality, thereby supporting the required optimization.

8. Conclusions

Until the mid 1960's, most AI research was concerned with how to be very clever (by means of powerful general purpose problem solvers) in figuring things out: an issue that was not particularly successful in solving significant problems. A break with this naive tradition then identified the need for large volumes of special-purpose knowledge to permit programs to work effectively in real world applications. In other words, AI community realized that

*"It is better to **know** than to be able to figure out"* [Sz86, pp. 341].

This gave the impulse for the development of KS: the most successful applications of AI expertise as real world systems. Since the early 1980's, KS technology has generated a variety of products ranging from simple XPS to complex natural language understanding systems. However, the applicability of KS is still severely limited since appropriate systems for an efficient knowledge management do not exist. As shown in this work, current AI technology lacks the means to provide efficient and robust KB, whereas DBS technology lacks knowledge representation and reasoning capabilities.

These observations have motivated the development of KBMS: a new generation of systems capable of providing an efficient management of large KB. Following the lines of this issue, this work firstly investigated KS in order to exactly define the tasks to be undertaken by KBMS. We have demonstrated that KBMS functionality should integrate features for supporting

- knowledge modeling (i.e., KB construction),
- knowledge manipulation (i.e., exploiting it to solve problems), and
- knowledge maintenance (i.e., efficiently coping with knowledge storage).

We have also shown that KBMS features are directly influenced by the most important aspects of KS development and application, namely, needs of the user, knowledge engineering support, and available resources, thereby determining three more or less orthogonal ways of looking at KBMS.

A detailed investigation of these different aspects allowed us to designate KBMS design issues resulting in a natural division of KBMS architecture in three layers:

- application layer,
- engineering layer, and
- implementation layer.

According to this architectural approach, the functions for knowledge maintenance are supported by the implementation layer: the KBMS module responsible for the reliable and efficient storage of knowledge and the supply of it to the application and engineering layer.

Knowledge manipulation features are provided by both the engineering and application layer. The engineering layer supports appropriate and flexible mechanisms for reasoning. The application layer, aimed at the independence of knowledge, provides adequate retrieval and storage operations that isolates the application from representational aspects, thereby defining a functional view of the KB. That is, at the external interface of the KBMS, knowledge is viewed in an abstract manner, in terms of what the KS can ask or tell the KBMS about its application domain.

Finally, knowledge modeling requirements are supported by the engineering layer: the system component that focuses on a KBMS from the viewpoint of the KB designer. This layer implements a powerful knowledge model with which the application world can be accurately represented, directly reflecting the user's conceptualization of this application universe.

KRISYS, our multi-layered prototypical KBMS, was then described in order to demonstrate how to apply our architectural specification to build practical KBMS. We have then illustrated how a knowledge engineer can employ KRISYS to construct KS for real world application, thereby presenting the KS development process in KBMS environments.

After reading this work, one should conclude that KBMS, in some sense, integrate the expressive, accurate, and flexible representation provided by knowledge engineering tools and the reliable and efficient management supported by DBS. However, one must be convinced of the fact that KBMS, and especially KRISYS, can neither be compared with such tools nor with DBS.

On one hand, our KBMS approach firstly surpasses existing tools by means of the concepts underlying the KRISYS object-centered representation model. KOBRA offers an integrated framework of mixed knowledge representation capabilities which is not usually found in existing tools. Whereas tools emphasize either a declarative, procedural, or structural view of the world, KOBRA remains neutral, equally focusing on all of them. For this reason, it may combine different concepts integrating all different aspects of knowledge and consequently obtaining the powerful framework necessary to enable a natural and accurate modeling of all aspects of every application world. Secondly, KRISYS supports knowledge independence, allowing for its continuous amelioration without affecting its applications. Finally, our KBMS outstrips existing tools since its usage is not restricted to sizes of virtual memories.

On the other hand, KRISYS firstly surpasses DBS by means of the expressiveness, flexibility, and rich constructs of the KOBRA model as well as of the mechanisms provided for reasoning and for guaranteeing the KB integrity. These constructs and mechanisms allow for the integration of a much higher degree of application's semantics into the model, thereby showing several significant advantages when compared to data models:

- Structural object-orientation (i.e., the representation of complex objects) is supported by means of the abstraction concept of aggregation.

- Behavioral object-orientation is achieved by the integration of procedural knowledge into the object description (methods).

- Data-orientation is provided by the concept of demons allowing for the specification of reactions to certain events.

- Intensional knowledge may be represented by rules (also by demons) in order to dynamically derive new knowledge.

- Organizational principles are provided in an integrated fashion by the abstraction concepts of classification, generalization, element- and set-association, and element- and component-aggregation. The semantics of these concepts are incorporated into the system via built-in reasoning facilities, which guarantee the structural and application-independent semantic integrity of the KB.

- Application-dependent semantic integrity is explicitly specified and maintained via aspects, demons, and rules.

Secondly, the knowledge independent interface KOALA provides mechanisms not usually supported by DBS languages: user-defined predicates for object qualification, general recursion, qualified projections, etc. Furthermore, it allows the user to see a KB in an abstract, functional way defined by means of the two operations TELL and ASK. To modify a KB, the user merely tells KRISYS facts about the world by specifying the new knowledge state found in his application domain without any hints as to how this state can be achieved. Since he may be completely unaware of the actual state of the KB, the system decides whether, for example, an insert, modify, or delete operation is necessary to achieve the new state. The same occurs when knowledge is requested. In an ASK operation, he does not have to know how the required knowledge is represented (e.g., extensionally or intensionally) nor about the way it has to be retrieved (e.g., KB access, deduction, or computation). Therefore, our knowledge independence approach completely isolates the user from the actual representation of knowledge and from the operations performed to fulfil the required tasks. A DB-user, on the other hand, cannot be wholly isolated from these aspects. In spite of supporting data independence, DBS obligate their users to exactly know the actual state of the DB in order to be able to precisely specify the way to achieve the new state found in the application world. In other words, our knowledge independence concept subsumes data independence.

Finally, KRISYS eliminates the difference between information and meta-information, which is apparent in existing data models. Our KBMS approach integrates meta-information into the KB and allows the user to access it at the same level as the "usual" information. For this reason, the user may apply the same flexible and powerful operations to manipulate meta-information as he does to information, thereby eliminating the difference between KB design and KB manipulation, which is necessary to support an incremental development process. The strict separation of DB design and DB manipulation, which is required by existing DBS, does not reflect the real world situation, where changes that affect the application model may also occur. It even neglects the needs of KS and some other complex applications, where an incremental design process is required. KRISYS, on the other hand, allows for an integration of KB design and manipulation, providing a knowledge model and a language that harmonize these activities in one single process. For this reason, KBMS, and with this also KRISYS, should not only be seen as systems for the management of KB but also as powerful modeling tools that permit a flexible manipulation, extension, modification, and restructuring of the user's conceptualization of the application world, i.e., the model of expertise represented as KB contents.

Here, it is important to emphasize what we have been affirming right from the very first pages of this work: It is necessary to reevaluate the development of knowledge-based applications in order to view it basically as a KB construction task. In this new software development paradigm, KBMS will provide the necessary modeling and management environment for carrying out this task.

"... I believe that it is time to reconsider the software development paradigm in favour of one that views software development primarily as knowledge-base construction. This shift of viewpoint is bound to have a tremendous impact on large established research areas within Computer Science concerned with software development. Moreover, the shift can only come about when KBMSs become widely available." ([My86, p. 8]).

Appendix

The ASK-statement

```
<ask-statement> ::= '('ASK [ '('{<projection>}+')' ] [ <selection> ]')'
<selection> ::= <formula>
<formula> ::= predicate> |
              '('(AND|OR) <formula> {<formula>}+')' |
              '('EXIST {<query-variable>}+ <formula>')' |
              '('FORALL {<query-variable>}+WITH <selection> <formula>')'
<predicate> ::= <is-a-pred> | <possible-val-pred> | <possible-card-pred> |
                <number-comp-pred> | <is-in-pred> | <equivalence-pred> |
                <equality-pred> | <abstraction-pred> | <message-pred> | <path-pred>
<is-a-pred> ::= '('[NOT-]   (IS-SCHEMA | IS-METHOD |
                            IS-SLOT | IS-ASPECT ) <cond-atom-term> ')'
<possible-val-pred> ::= '('[NOT-]IS-POSSIBLE-VALUE      <number-schema-term>
                                                       <possible-val-term>')'
<possible-card-pred> ::= '('[NOT-]IS-POSSIBLE-CARD      <number-atom-term>
                                                       <possible-card-term>')'
<number-comp-pred> ::= '(' ('='|'<>'|'<'|'<='|'>'|'>=')   <number-atom-term>
                                                       <number-atom-term>')'
<equivalence-pred> ::= '('[NOT-]EQUIV <list-term> <list-term>')'
<is-in-pred> ::= '('[NOT-]IS-IN <element-term> <list-term>')'
<equality-pred> ::= '('[NOT-]EQUAL <general-term> <general-term>')'
<abstraction-pred> ::= '('[NOT-]   (IS-INSTANCE | IS-SUBCLASS | IS-ELEMENT |
                                  IS-DIRECT-INSTANCE | IS-DIRECT-SUBCLASS |
                                  IS-DIRECT-ELEMENT | IS-SUBSET |
                                  IS-DIRECT-SUBSET) <schema-name-atom-term>
                                                   <schema-name-atom-term>')'
<message-pred> ::= '('[NOT-]MESSAGE  <method-name-atom-term>
                                     <schema-name-atom-term>
                                     <parameter> ')'
<path-pred> ::= '(' PATH {<query-variable>}*   <link-clause> [ <definitions-clause >
                                               [<make-clause>] [<choose-clause>]]
                                               [<restrictions-clause>]]')'
<link-clause> ::= '('LINK <formula> ')'
```

<definitions-clause> ::= '('DEFINITIONS { ('('EQUAL <query-variable>
                                                          <general-term> ')' |
                                        '('IS-IN <query-variable>
                                                          <general-term>')') }+ ')'

<restrictions-clause> ::= '('RESTRICTIONS <formula> ')'

<choose-clause> ::= '('CHOOSE {(<choose-cond> |
                         '('AND {<choose-cond>}+ ')') }+ ')'

<make-clause> ::=

    '('MAKE { '('<query-variable> '(' (MIN-PATH | MAX-PATH |
                                     SUM-PATH | PROD-PATH |
                                     AVG-PATH | COUNT-PATH |
                                     UNION-PATH |
                                     INTERSECTION-PATH) <query-variable> ')' ')' }+ ')'

<choose-cond> ::='(' (MINIMAL | MAXIMAL | ANY) <query-variable> ')'

<cond-atom-term> ::= <schema-name-atom-term> | <method-name-atom-term> |
                      <slot-name-atom-term> | <aspect-name-atom-term>

<list-term> ::= <schema-name-list-term> | <slot-name-list1-term> |
                <number-list-term> | <aspect-name-list-term> |
                <aspect-val-list-term> | <method-name-list1-term> |
                <set-op-list-term> | <list-op-list-term> | <query-variable>

<element-term> ::= <list-term> | <atomic2-term>

<general-term> ::= <atomic1-term> | <list-term> | <method-code-lambda-term> |
                    <aspect-val-posval-term> | <aspect-val-card-term>

<atomic1-term> ::= <atomic2-term> | <slot-type-atom-term> |
                <method-type-atom-term>

<atomic2-term> ::=<schema-name-atom-term> | <slot-name-atom-term> |
                <aspect-name-atom-term> | <number-atom-term> |
                <method-name-atom-term>

<aspect-name-atom-term> ::= <aspect-name> | <method-result-term> | <query-variable>

<aspect-name-list-term> ::= method-result-term> |
                '('{<aspect-name>}+')' |
                '('(ALL-ASPECTS |
                    STANDARD-ASPECTS |
                    USERDEFINED-ASPECTS)
                                <slot-or-method-name-atom-term>
                                <schema-name-atom-term>')'

<aspect-val-posval-term> ::=

              '('ASPECTVALUE POSSIBLE-VALUE   <slot-name-atom-term>

                                    <schema-name-atom-term>')'

<aspect-val-card-term> ::= '('ASPECTVALUE CARDINALITY   <slot-name-atom-term>

                                      <schema-name-atom-term>')'

<aspect-val-list-term> ::= '('ASPECTVALUE   <aspect-name-atom-term>

                                    <slot-or-method-name-atom-term>

                                    <schema-name-atom-term>')'

<possible-card-term> ::= <aspect-val-card-term> | <cardinality-intervall>

<possible-val-term> ::= <aspect-val-posval-term> | <possible-values-form>

<slot-type-atom-term> ::= '('SLOTTYPE   <slot-name-atom-term>

                                    <schema-name-atom-term>')'

<slot-origin-atom-term> ::= '('SLOTORIGIN   <slot-name-atom-term>

                                    <schema-name-atom-term>')'

<slot-name-atom-term> ::= <slot-name> | <query-variable> | <method-result-term>

<slot-name-list1-term> ::=   <method-result-term> |

                    '('{<slot-name>}+')' |

                    '('ALL-SLOTS <schema-name-atom-term>')' |

                    '('INHERITED-SLOTS

                                    <schema-name-atom-term>

                                    (<schema-name-atom-term> |

                                    '('SUPERS<schema-name-atom-term>')')]')' |

                    '('NOT-INHERITED-SLOTS <schema-name-atom-term>')' |

                    '('INSTANCE-SLOTS <schema-name-atom-term>')' |

                    '('OWN-SLOTS <schema-name-atom-term>')' |

                    '('STANDARD-SLOTS <schema-name-atom-term>')' |

                    '('USERDEFINED-SLOTS <schema-name-atom-term>')'

<slot-val-list-term> ::= '('SLOTVALUES   <slot-name-atom-term>

                                    <schema-name-atom-term>')'

<slot-val-element-term> ::= '('SLOTVALUE   <slot-name-atom-term>

                                    <schema-name-atom-term>')'

<method-type-atom-term> ::= '(' METHODTYPE   <method-name-atom-term>

                                    <schema-name-atom-term> ')'

<method-origin-atom-term> ::= '('METHODORIGIN   <method-name-atom-term>

                                    <schema-name-atom-term>')'

```
<method-result-term> ::= '('METHODRESULT   <method-name-atom-term>
                                  <schema-name-atom-term> <parameter>')'
<method-name-atom-term> ::= <method-name> | <method-result-term> | <query-variable>
<method-name-list1-term> ::=   <method-result-term> |
                      (' {<method-name>}+')' |
                      '(' ALL-METHODS <schema-name-atom-term> ')'
                      '(' INHERITED-METHODS
                              <schema-name-atom-term>
                              [ (<schema-name-atom-term> |
                                '(' SUPERS <schema-name-atom-term>')')]')' |
                      '(' NOT-INHERITED-METHODS
                                  <schema-name-atom-term>')' |
                      '(' INSTANCE-METHODS <schema-name-atom-term> ')' |
                      '(' OWN-METHODS <schema-name-atom-term> ')' |
                      '(' USERDEFINED-METHODS <schema-name-atom-term> ')'
<method-code-lambda-term> ::= '(' METHODCODE   <method-name-atom-term>
                                  <schema-name-atom-term> ')'
<closure-list-term> ::= (SLOTVALUES ('*' | <intnum> )<slot-name-atom-term>
                              <schema-name-atom-term> ')'
<schema-name-atom-term> ::=   <schema-name> | <query-variable> |
                          <slot-val-element-term> | <slot-origin-atom-term> |
                          <method-result-term> | <method-origin-atom-term>
<schema-name-list-term> ::=   '(' {<schema-name>}+ ')' | <aspect-val-list-term> |
                          <closure-list-term> | <method-result-term> |
                          <slot-val-list-term> | <slot-val-element-term> |
                          '('(UNION | INTERSECTION | DIFFERENCE)
                                  <schema-name-list-term>
                                  <schema-name-list-term>')' |
                          '('CONCAT   <schema-name-list-term>
                                  <schema-name-list-term>')' |
                          <query-variable>| '(' ALL <schema-name-atom-term>')'
<number-atom-term> ::= <number> | <query-variable> |
                      <slot-val-element-term> | <method-result-term> |
                      '(('+'|'-'|'*'|'/'|'DIV'|'MOD')   <number-atom-term>
                                      <number-atom-term>')' |
                      '(('SUM'|'AVG'|'MIN'|'MAX'|'PROD') <number-list-term>')'
```

```
                              '('COUNT <list-term>')'
<number-list-term> ::= '(' {<number>}+ ')' | <slot-val-list-term> |
                       <slot-val-element-term> | <aspect-val-list-term> |
                       <method-result-term> | <query-variable> |
                       '('(UNION | INTERSECTION | DIFFERENCE)   <number-list-term>
                                                              <number-list-term>')' |
                       '('CONCAT <number-list-term> <number-list-term>')'|
                        '('ALL <number-atom-term>')'
<parameter> ::= '(' { <general-term> }* ')'
<set-op-list-term> ::= '('(UNION | INTERSECTION | DIFFERENCE) <list-term> <list-term>')'|
                       '('ALL <general-term>')'
<number-schema-term> ::=  <number-or-schema-atom-term> |
                          <number-or-schema-list-term>
<number-or-schema-atom-term>    ::=   <schema-name-atom-term>   |   <number-atom-term>
<number-or-schema-list-term> ::=
                              <schema-name-list-term> | <number-list-term> |
                              '('ALL <number-or-schema-atom-term>')'|
                              '('(UNION | INTERSECTION |
                              DIFFERENCE | CONCAT)  <number-or-schema-list-term>
                                                    <number-or-schema-list-term>')'
<slot-or-method-name-atom-term> ::=   <slot-name-atom-term> |
                                      <method-name-atom-term>
<possible-values-form> ::= NO-VALUES | <log-condition>
<log-condition> ::= <condition> | <neg-condition> |
                    '(' ( AND | OR )  <log-condition>
                                 { <log-condition> }+ ')'
<neg-conditon> ::= '(' NOT-ONE-OF <condition> ')'
<condition> ::= <list-of-values> |
                '(' SUBCLASS-OF <schema-name> ')' |
                '(' INSTANCE-OF <schema-name> ')' |
                '(' ELEMENT-OF <schema-name> ')' |
                '(' SUBSET-OF <schema-name> ')' |
                '(' DIRECT-SUBCLASS-OF <schema-name> ')' |
                '(' DIRECT-INSTANCE-OF <schema-name> ')' |
                '(' DIRECT-ELEMENT-OF <schema-name> ')' |
                '(' DIRECT-SUBSET-OF <schema-name> ')' |
```

```
                    '(' REAL ')' | '(' INTEGER ')' |
                    '(' INTERVALL <intervall-term> ')' |
<list-of-values> ::= 'list'
<intervall-term> ::= ('<'|'>') <number1> <number2> ('<'|'>')
<number> ::= <intnum> | <realnum>
<intnum> ::= [<sign>] {<digit>}+
<realnum> ::=[<sign>] {<digit>}+ '.' {<digit>}+
                    [E [<sign>] {<digit>}+]
<digit> ::= '0' | '1' | '2' | '3' | '4' | '5' | '6' | '7' | '8' | '9'
<sign> ::= '+' | '-'
<cardinality-intervall> ::= '[' <intnum> (<intnum> | '!') ']'
<query-variable> ::= '?'<name>


<projection> :: =<query-variable> |
                    '('{<query-variable>|<schema-name>}+ <projection-clause> ')'
<projection-clause> ::= SCHEMA | <attribute-clause>
<attribute-clause> ::= <slot-clause> | <method-clause>
<slot-clause> ::= <slot-selection> [<slot-projection>] [<aspect-clause>] |
                    { SLOT {(<query-variable> | <slot-name>)}+
                    [<slot-projection>] [<aspect-clause>] }+
<slot-selection> ::= ALL-SLOTS |
                    INHERITED-SLOTS [ ( <schema-name> |
                        '(' SUPERS <schema-name> ')' ) ] |
                    NOT-INHERITED-SLOTS | INSTANCE-SLOTS |
                    OWN-SLOTS | STANDARD-SLOTS | USERDEFINED-SLOTS
<slot-projection> ::= [SLOTNAME] [SLOTVALUES]
                    [SLOTTYPE] [SLOTORIGIN]
<method-clause> ::= <method-selection> [<method-projection>] [<aspect-clause>] |
                    {METHOD {(<query-variable> | <method-name>)}+
                    [<method-projection>] [<aspect-clause>] }+
<method-selection> ::= ALL-METHODS |
                    INHERITED-METHODS [ (<method-name> |
                        '('SUPERS <method-name> ')' ) ] |
                    NOT-INHERITED-METHODS |INSTANCE-METHODS |
                    OWN-METHODS | USERDEFINED-METHODS
<method-projection> ::= [METHODNAME] [METHODCODE]
```

[METHODTYPE] [METHODORIGIN]

<aspect-clause> ::= <aspect-selection> [<aspect-projection>] |

    { ASPECTS {(<aspect-name> | <query-variable>)}+

     <aspect-projection> }+

<aspect-selection> ::= ALL-ASPECTS | STANDARD-ASPECTS | USERDEFINED-ASPECTS

<aspect-projection> ::= [ASPECTNAME] [ASPECTVALUE]

The Tell-statement

<tell-statement> ::= '(' TELL {assertion}+ [WHERE <selection>] ')'

<assertion> ::= <abstraction-assertion> |

   <is-schema-assertion> |

   <assign-assertion> |

   <is-in-assertion> |

   <message-pred>

<abstraction-assertion> ::= '(' [NOT-] (IS-DIRECT-INSTANCE |

      IS-DIRECT-SUBSET |

      IS-DIRECT-ELEMENT |

      IS-DIRECT-SUBCLASS)

        <schema-name-atom-term>

        <schema-name-atom-term>')'

<is-schema-assertion> ::= '('[NOT-]IS-SCHEMA <schema-name-atom-term> ')'

<assign-assertion> ::= <assign-slot-val-atom> |

    <assign-slot-val-list> |

    <assign-aspect-val-card> |

    <assign-aspect-val-posval> |

    <assign-aspect-val-list> |

    <assign-method-code-lambda>

<assign-slot-val-atom> ::= '(' EQUAL <slot-val-element-term>

      <number-schema-term> ')'

<assign-slot-val-list> ::= '(' EQUAL <slot-val-list-term>

      <number-schema-list-term> ')'

<assign-aspect-val-card> ::= '(' EQUAL <aspect-val-card-term>

      <possible-card-term> ')'

<assign-aspect-val-posval> ::= '(' EQUAL <aspect-val-posval-term>

      <possible-val-term> ')'

<assign-aspect-val-list> ::= '(' EQUAL   <aspect-val-list2-term>
                                             <list-term> ')'
<assign-method-code-lambda> ::= '(' EQUAL   <method-code-lambda-term>
                                             (<method-code-lambda-term> |
                                              <lambda-expression>) ')'
<is-in-assertion> ::= <is-in-slot> |
                      <is-in-aspect> |
                      <is-in-slot-val> |
                      <is-in-aspect-val> |
                      <is-in-method-val>
<is-in-slot> ::= '('[NOT-]IS-IN   <slot-name-atom-term>
                                   <slot-name-list2-term> ')'
<is-in-aspect> ::= '(' [NOT-]IS-IN   <aspect-name-atom-term>
                                      <aspect-name-list2-term> ')'
<is-in-method> ::= '(' [NOT-]IS-IN   <method-name-atom-term>
                                      <method-name-list2-term> ')'
<is-in-slot-val> ::= '('[NOT-]IS-IN   <number-schema-term>
                                       <slot-val-list-term> ')'
<is-in-aspect-val> ::= '(' [NOT-]IS-IN <element-term> <aspect-val-list2-term> ')'
<aspect-val-list2-term> :== '(' ASPECTVALUE   <aspect-name-atom-term>
                                               <slot-or-method-name-atom-term2>
                                               <schema-name-atom-term> ')'
<slot-or-method-name-atom-term2> ::=   <slot-name-atom-term> |
                                        <method-name-atom-term> |
                                        '(' (INSTANCESLOT | OWNSLOT)
                                          <slot-name-atom-term> ')' |
                                        (' (INSTANCEMETHOD | OWNMETHOD)
                                          <method-name-atom-term> ')'
<lambda-expression> ::= Lambda-Expression in LISP
<slot-name-list2-term> ::= '('   (INSTANCE-SLOTS | OWN-SLOTS)
                                   <schema-name-atom-term> ')'
<aspect-name-list2-term> ::= '('USERDEFINED-ASPECTS
                                     <slot-or-method-name-atom-term2>
                                     <schema-name-atom-term> ')'
<method-name-list2-term> ::=   '(' (INSTANCE-METHODS | OWN-METHODS)
                                   <schema-name-atom-term>

List of Figures

List of Tables

References

[Ab74]   Abrial, J.R.: Data Semantics, in: Data Management Systems, (eds.: Klimbie, J.W., Koffeman, K.L.), North-Holland Publ. Comp., Amsterdam, Netherlands, 1974.

[AB85]   Appelrath, H.-J., Bense, H.: Two Steps for Making PROLOG Programming Systems Better: DB Support and Metainterpreter (in German), in: Proc. of the GI-Conference on Database Systems for Office, Engineering and Science Environments, IFB 94, Springer-Verlag, Karlsruhe, March 1985, pp. 161-176.

[AKSF82]   Aikins, J., Kunz, J., Shortliffe, E.H., Fallat, R.: PUFF: An Expert for Interpretation of Pulmonary Function Data, Memo-HPP-82-13, Stanford, 1982.

[An85]   Anderson, J.R.: Cognitive Psychology and Its Implications, 2nd ed., Freeman, San Francisco, CA, 1985.

[As76]   Astrahan,M.M., et al.: System R: Relational Approach to Database Management, in: ACM Transactions on Database Systems, Vol. 1, No. 1, June 1976, pp. 97-137.

[Ba85]   Bayer, R.: Database Technology for Expert Systems, in: Proc. GI-Conference "Knowledge-based Systems", IFB 112, Springer-Verlag, Munich, Oct. 1985, pp. 1-16.

[Ba87a]   Banerji, R.B.: Minimax Procedure, in: [Sh87], pp. 614-617.

[Ba87b]   Bauer, S.: A PROLOG-based Deductive Database System (in German), Undergraduation Final Work, University of Kaiserslautern, Computer Science Department, Kaiserslautern, 1987.

[Ba88]   Bancilhon, F.: Object-Oriented Database Systems, in: Proc. 7th ACM SIGART-SIGMOD-SIGACT Symposium on Principles of Database Systems, Austin, Texas, March 1988.

[BALLS85] Blaser, A., Alschwee, B., Lehmann, Hein, Lehmann, Hubert, Schönfeld, W.: An Expert System for Law with Natural Language Dialog - A Project Report (in German), in: Proc. GI-Conference "Knowledge-based Systems" IFB 112, Springer-Verlag, Munich, October 1985, pp. 42-57.

[BB75]   Brown, J.S., Burton, R.R.: Multiple Representations of Knowledge for Tutorial Reasoning, in: Representation and Understanding: Studies in Cognitive Science (eds.: Bobrow, D.G., Collins, A.), Academic Press, New York, 1975, pp. 311-349.

[BBA75]   Barr, A., Beard, M., Atkinson, R.C.: A Rationale and Description of a CAI Program to Teach the BASIC Programming Language, in: Instruc. Science, Vol. 4, 1975, pp. 1-31.

[BBB74]   Brown, J.S., Burton, R.R., Bell, A.G.: SOPHIE: A Sophisticated Instructional Environment for Teaching Electronic Troubleshooting [an Example of AI in CAI], Bolt. Beranek & Newman, Tech. Rep. No. 2790, Cambridge, Mass., 1974.

[BBK82]   Brown, J.S., Burton, A.G., deKleer, J.: Pedagogical Natural Language and Knowledge Engineering Techniques in SOPHIE I, II and III, in: Intelligent Tutoring Systems (eds.: Sleeman, D., Brown, J.), Academic Press, New York, 1982, pp. 227-282.

[BC75]   Bobrow, D., Collins, A. (eds.): Representation and Understanding, Academic Press, New York, 1975.

[Be84a]   Beeler, J.: Expert Systems Inching into Business, in: Computerworld, May 7, 1984.

[Be84b]   Begg, V.: Developing Expert CAD Systems, Kogan Page, London, 1984.

[BF78]   Buchanan, B.G., Feigenbaum, E.A.: DENDRAL and Meta-DENDRAL: Their Appli-
             cation Dimension, in: Artificial Intelligence, Vol. 11, No. 1, 1978, pp. 5-24.

[BFL83]   Brachman, R.J., Fikes, R.E., Levesque, H.J.: KRYPTON: A Functional Approach to
             Knowledge Representation, in: Computer, Vol. 16, No. 10, Oct. 1983, pp. 67-73.

[BH81]   Bennet, J.S., Hollander, C.R.: DART - an Expert System for Computer Fault Diag-
             nosis, in: Proc. 7th International Joint Conference on Artificial Intelligence, Van-
             couver, Canada, 1981, pp. 843-845.

[BL85]   Brachman, R.J., Levesque, H.J. (eds.): Readings in Knowledge Representation,
             Morgan Kaufmann, Los Altos, California, 1985.

[BM86]   Brodie, M.L., Mylopoulos, J. (eds.): On Knowledge Base Management Systems
             (Integrating Artificial Intelligence and Database Technologies), Topics in Informa-
             tion Systems, Springer-Verlag, New York, 1986.

[BMS84]   Brodie, M.L., Mylopoulos, J., Schmidt, J.W. (eds.): On Conceptual Modelling
             (Perspectives from Artificial Intelligence, Databases, and Programming Languag-
             es), Topics in Information Systems, Springer-Verlag, New York, 1984.

[BMW82]   Beetem, A., Milton, J., Wiederhold, G.: Performance of Database Management
             Systems in VLSI Design, in: IEEE Database Engineering, Vol. 5, No. 2, June
             1982, pp. 15-20.

[BMW84]   Borgida, A., Mylopoulos, J., Wong, H.K.T.: Generalization/Specialization as a Basis
             for Software Specification, in: [BMS84], pp. 87-114.

[Bo83]   Borrmann, H.-P.: MODIS - An Expert System for Supplying Repair Diagnosis of
             the Otto-Motor and its Aggregates (in German), Research Report No. 72/83, Uni-
             versity of Kaiserslautern, Computer Science Department, Kaiserslautern, 1983.

[Bo86]   Borgida, A.: Survey of Conceptual Modeling of Information Systems, in: [BM86],
             pp. 461-470.

[BOR81]   Bartels, U., Olthoff, W., Raulefs, P.: APE: An Expert System for Automatic Pro-
             gramming, in: Proc. 7th International Joint Conference on Artificial Intelligence,
             Vancouver, Canada, 1981, pp. 1037-1043.

[Br79]   Brachman, R.J.: On The Epistemological Status of Semantic Networks, in: [Fi79],
             pp. 3-50.

[Br81]   Brodie, M.L.: Association: A Database Abstraction for Semantic Modelling, in:
             Proc. 2nd Int. Entity-Relationship Conference, Washington, D.C., Oct. 1981.

[Br83]   Brachman, R.J.: What IS-A Is and Isn't: An Analysis of Taxonomic Links in Seman-
             tic Networks, in: IEEE Computer, Vol. 16, No. 10, Oct. 1983, pp. 30-36.

[Br84]   Brodie, M.L.: On the Development of Data Models, in: [BMS84], pp. 19-47.

[BR86]   Bancilhon, F., Ramakrishnan, R.: An Amateur's Introduction to Recursive Query
             Processing Strategies, in: Proc. ACM SIGMOD '86, Washington, May 1986,
             pp. 16-52.

[BS79]   Bradley, R., Swartz, N.: Possible Worlds: An Introduction to Logic and its Philoso-
             phy, Basil Blackwell, Oxford, 1979.

[BS83]   Bobrow, D.G., Stefik, M.: The LOOPS Manual, Xerox PARC, Palo Alto, CA, 1983.

[BS84]   Buchanan, B.G., Shortliffe, E.H.: Rule-Based Expert Systems: The MYCIN Experi-
             ments of the Stanford Heuristic Programming Project, Addision-Wesley Publ.

[BS85]   Brachman, R.J., Schmolze, J.G.: An Overview of the KL-ONE Knowledge Repre-
           sentation System, in: Cognitive Science, Vol. 9, No. 2, 1985, pp. 171-216.

[BSF69]   Buchanan, B.G., Sutherland, G., Feigenbaum, E.A.: Heuristic DENDRAL: A Pro-
           gram for Generating Explanatory Hypotheses in Organic Chemistry, in: Machine
           Intelligence, Vol. 4, (eds.: Meltzer, B., Michie, D.), Elsevier, New York, 1969.

[BW77]   Bobrow, D., Winograd, T.: An Overview of KRL, A Knowledge Representation
           Language, in: Cognitive Science, Vol. 1, No. 1, January 1977, pp. 3-46.

[Ca84]   Campbell, A.: Implementations of PROLOG, Ellis Horwood Limited, Chichester,
           1984.

[Ca87]   Carnegie Group Inc.: Knowledge Craft CRL Technical Manual, Version 3.1, Carn-
           egie Group, 1987.

[CDV88]   Carey, M.J., DeWitt, D.J., Vandenberg, S.L.: A Data Model and Query Language
           for EXODUS, in: Proc. of the ACM SIGMOD Conf., Chicago, 1988, pp. 413-423.

[Ch76]   Chamberlin, D.D., et al.: SEQUEL 2: A Unified Approach to Data Definition, Ma-
           nipulation and Control, in: IBM Journal of Research and Development, Vol. 20,
           No. 6, 1976, pp. 560-575.

[Ch79]   Chandrasekaran, B., et al.: An Approch to Medical Diagnosis Based on Conceptu-
           al Structures, in: Proc. 6th International Joint Conference on Artificial Intelligence,
           Tokyo, 1979, pp. 134-142.

[Ch83]   Chomicki, J.: A Database Support System for PROLOG, in: Proc. of Logic Pro-
           gramming Workshop '83, Portugal, 1983.

[Ch84]   Chandrasekaran, B.: Expert Systems: Matching Techniques to Tools, in: Artificial
           Intelligence Applications for Business (editor: Reitman, W.), Ablex Publishing Cor-
           poration, Norwood, New Jersey, 1984.

[CJM76]   Chilausky, R., Jacobson, B., Michalski, R.S.: An Application of Variable-Valued Log-
           ic to Inductive Learning of Plant Disease Diagnostic Rules, in: Proc. 6th Annual In-
           ternational Symp. Multiple-Valued Logic, Tokyo, Aug. 1976, pp. 645-655.

[CJV83]   Clifford, J., Jarke, M., Vassiliou, Y.: A Short Introduction to Expert Systems, in:
           Database Engineering, Vol. 3, No. 4, December 1983, pp. 3-16.

[CK88]   Crasemann, C., Krasemann, H.: Presented for Discussion: Engineer - a New Hat
           on Old Heads (in German), in: Informatik-Spektrum, Vol. 11, No. 1, February
           1988, pp. 43-48.

[Cl79a]   Clancey, W.J.: Tutoring Rules for Guiding a Case Method Dialogue, in: Internation-
           al Journal of Man-Machine Studies, Vol. 11, No. 1, 1979, pp. 25-49.

[Cl79b]   Clancey, W.J.: Dialogue Management for Online Tutorials, in: Proc. 6th Internation-
           al Joint Conference on Artificial Intelligence, Tokyo, 1979, pp. 155-161.

[Cl83]   Clancey, W.J.: GUIDON, in: Journal of Computer Based Instruction,   Vol. 10,
           No. 1 and 2, 1983, pp. 8-15.

[Cl85]   Clayton, B.D.: Inference ART Programming Tutorial, Volume 1 Elementary ART
           Programming, Volume 2 A First Look At Viewpoints, Volume 3 Advanced Topics in
           ART, Los Angeles, CA, 1985.

[CL71]   Chang, C.-L., Lee, R.C.-T.: Symbolic Logic and Mechanical Theorem Proving, Aca-
           demic Press, New York, 1971.

[CM81]   Clocksin, W.F., Mellish, C.S.: Programming in Prolog, Springer-Verlag, Berlin,
           1981.

[CM83]   Chandrasekaran, B., Mittal, S.: Conceptual Representation of Medical Knowledge for Diagnosis by Computer: MDX and Related Systems, in: Advances in Computers, Vol. 22, 1983, pp. 217-293.

[CM88]   Computer Magazin, Vol. 17, No. 9, 1988, pp. 37-44.

[CMT82]   Chakravarthy, U.S., Minker, J., Tran, D.: Interfacing Predicate Logic Languages and Relational Data Bases, in: Proc. of the 1st Int. Logic Programming Conf., Marseille, Sept. 1982.

[Co70]   Codd, E.F.: A Relational Model of Data for Large Shared Data Banks, in: Communications of the ACM, Vol. 13, No. 6, June 1970, pp. 377-387.

[Co78]   Cohen, P.R.: On Knowing What to Say: Planning Speech Acts, Ph.D. Thesis (TR-118), Univ. of Toronto, Dept. of Computer Science, Toronto, 1978.

[Co79]   Codd, E.F.: Extending the Database Relational Model to Capture More Meaning, in: ACM Transactions on Database Systems, Vol. 4, No. 4, Dec. 1979, pp. 397-434.

[CSB79]   Clancey, W.J., Shortliffe, E.H., Buchanan, B.G.: Intelligent Computer-aided Instruction for Medical Diagnosis, in: Proc. 3rd Annual Symposium on Computer Applications in Medical Care, 1979, pp. 175-183.

[Da81]   Davis, R., et al.: The Dipmeter Advisor: Interpretation of Geological Signals, in: Proc. 7th International Joint Conference on Artificial Intelligence, Vancouver, Canada, Aug. 1981, pp. 846-852.

[Da83]   Date, C.J.: An Introduction to Database Systems, Vol. 1 and Vol. 2, 3rd edition, Addison-Wesley Publishing Company, Reading, Mass., 1983.

[Da84]   Date, C.J.: Some Principles of Good Language Design, in: ACM SIGMOD Record, Vol. 14, No. 3, Nov. 1984, pp. 1-7.

[Da86]   Dadam, P., et al.: A DBMS Prototype to Support Extended NF^2-Relations: An Integrated View on Flat Tables and Hierarchies, in: Proc. ACM SIGMOD Conf., Washington, D.C., 1986, pp. 356-367.

[Da87]   Date, C.J.: A Guide to INGRES, Addision-Wesley Publishing Company, Reading, Mass., 1987.

[DBS77]   Davis, R., Buchanan, B.G., Shortliffe, E.H.: Production Rules as a Representation for a Knowledge-based Consultation Program, in: Artificial Intelligence, Vol. 8, No. 1, 1977, pp. 15-45.

[DD86]   Dittrich, K.R., Dayal, U. (eds.): Proc. Int. Workshop on Object-Oriented Database Systems, Pacific Grove, 1986.

[De88]   Deßloch, S.: KOALA - The Design of a Knowledge Independent User Interface for the KBMS KRISYS (in German), Undergraduation Final Work, University of Kaiserslautern, Computer Science Department, Kaiserslautern, 1988.

[Di86]   Dittrich, K.R.: Object-oriented Database Systems: the Notion and the Issues, in: [DD86], pp. 2-4.

[Di87]   Dittrich, K.R.: Object-Oriented Database Systems - A Workshop Report, in: Proc. 5th Int. Conference on Entity-Relationship Approach, Dijon, France, North-Holland Publishing Company, 1987, pp. 51-66.

[dK86]   de Kleer, J.: An Assumption-based Truth Maintenance System, in: Artificial Intelligence, Vol. 28, No. 2, January 1986, pp. 127-162.

[DM89]   Deßloch, S., Mattos, N.M.: KOALA - an Interface for Knowledge Base Manage-
           ment Systems, Research Report, University of Kaiserslautern, 1989, submitted for
           publication.

[DN66]   Dahl, O.J., Nygaard, K.: SIMULA an Algol-based Simulation Language, in: Commu-
           nications of the ACM, Vol. 9, No. 9, 1966, pp. 671-678.

[Do79]   Doyle, J.: A Truth Maintenance System, in: Artificial Intelligence, Vol. 12, No. 3,
           1979, pp. 231-272.

[DR84]   Duda, R.O., Reboh, R.: AI and Decision Making: The PROSPECTOR Experience,
           in: Artificial Intelligence Applications for Business (editor: Reitman, W.), Ablex Pub-
           lishing Corporation, Norwood, New Jersey, 1984.

[DS86]   Dayal, U., Smith, J.M.: PROBE: A Knowledge-Oriented Database Management
           System, in: [BM86], pp. 227-257.

[Ea80]   Eastman, C.M.: System Facilities for CAD-Databases, in: Proc. 17th Design Auto-
           mation Conf., Minneapolis, 1980, pp. 50-56.

[EC75]   Eswaran, K.P., Chamberlin, D.D.: Functional Specifications of a Subsystem for
           Database Integrity, in: Proc. of the 1st Conference on Very Large Data Bases,
           1975, pp. 48-68.

[EHLR80]   Erman, L.D., Hayes-Roth, F., Lesser, V., Reddy, D.: The Hearsay II Speech-Under-
           standing System: Integrating Knowledge to Resolve Uncertainty, in: Computer
           Surveys, Vol. 12, No. 2, 1980, pp. 213-253.

[EN69]   Ernst, G.W., Newell, A.: GPS: A Case Study in Generality and Problem Solving,
           Academic Press, New York, 1969.

[ES85]   ESPRIT'84 - Status Report, North-Holland Publ. Comp., Amsterdam, 1985.

[Fa79]   Fahlman, S.E.: NETL: A System for Representing and Using Real-World Knowl-
           edge, MIT Press, 1979.

[Fa80]   Fagan, J.M.: VM: Representing Time-dependent Relations in a Medical Setting,
           Doctoral Thesis, Stanford University, Computer Science Department, Stanford,
           California, June 1980.

[FBL71]   Feigenbaum, E.A., Buchanan, B.G., Lederberg, J.: Generality and Problem Solving:
           A Case Study Using the DENDRAL Program, in: Machine Intelligence 6 (eds.:
           Meltzer, D., Michie, D.), Edinburgh University Press, 1971, pp. 165-190.

[Fe77]   Feigenbaum, E.A.: The Art of Artificial Intelligence: I. Themes and Case Studies of
           Knowledge Engineering, in: Proc. 5th International Joint Conference on Artificial
           Intelligence, Cambridge, Mass., August 1977, pp. 1014-1029.

[Fi79]   Findler, N.V. (editor): Associative Networks: Representation and Use of Knowl-
           edge by Computer, Academic Press, New York, 1979.

[Fi83]   Fischer, W.E.: Database Systems for CAD-Workstations (in German), Doctoral
           Thesis, IFB70, Springer-Verlag, Karlsruhe, 1983.

[Fi88]   Filman, R.E.: Reasoning with Worlds and Truth Maintenance in a Knowledge-based
           Programming Environment, in: Communications of the ACM, Vol. 31, No. 4, April
           1988, pp. 382-401.

[FK85]   Fikes, R., Kehler, T.: The Role of Frame-based Representation in Reasoning, in:
           Communications of the ACM, Vol. 28, No. 9, Sept. 1985, pp. 904-920.

[FKFO79]   Fagan, L.M., Kunz, J.C., Feigenbaum, E.A., Osborn, J.J.: Representation of Dy-
           namic Clinical Knowledge: Measurement Interpretation in the Intensive Care Unit

in: Proc. 6th International Joint Conference on Artificial Intelligence, Tokyo, Aug. 1979, pp. 260-262.

[FLK83]   Fox, M., Lowenfeld, S., Kleinosky, P.: Techniques for Sensor-based Diagnosis, in: Proc. 8th International Joint Conference on Artificial Intelligence, Karlsruhe, 1983, pp. 158-163.

[FM83]   Feigenbaum, E.A., McCorduck, P.: The Fifth Generation: Artificial Intelligence and Japan's Computer Challenge to the World, Addison-Wesley Publ. Comp., Reading, Mass., 1983.

[FN71]   Fikes, R.E., Nilsson, N.J.: STRIPS: A New Approach to the Application of Theorem Proving to Problem Solving, in: Artificial Intelligence, Vol. 2, No. 3, 1971, pp. 189-208.

[FN78]   Fenves, S.J., Norabhoompipat, T.: Potentials for Artificial Intelligence Applications in Structural Engineering Design and Detailing, in: Artificial Intelligence and Pattern Recognition in Computer-aided Design (editor: Latombe, J.C.), in: Proc. IFIP Working Conference, Grenoble, France, 1978, pp. 105-119.

[Fo80]   Forgy, C.L.: The OPS 5 User's Manual, Tech. Report, Carnegie-Mellon University, Pittsburgh, 1980.

[Fr79]   Friedland, P.: Knowledge-Based Experiment Design in Molecular Genetics, Doctoral Thesis, Memo-HPP-79-29, Stanford University, Stanford, California, Oct. 1979.

[Fr86]   Frost, R.A.: Introduction to Knowledge Base Systems, Collins Professional and Technical Books, London, 1986.

[FWA85]   Fox, M., Wright, J., Adam, D.: Experience with SRL: an Analysis of a Frame-based Knowledge Representation, Technical Report CMU-CS-81-135, Carnegie-Mellon University, Pittsburgh 1985.

[Ga82]   Gaschnig, J.: PROSPECTOR: An Expert System for Mineral Exploration, in: Introdutory Readings in Expert Systems (editor: Michie, D.), Gordon and Beach Publishers, New York, 1982, pp. 47-64.

[GD87]   Graefe, G., DeWitt, D.J.: The EXODUS Optimizer Generator, in: Proc. ACM SIGMOD International Conference on Management of Data, San Francisco, 1987, pp. 160-172.

[Ge79]   Geutner, D.: Toward an Intelligent Tutor, in: Procedures for Instructional Systems Development (editor: O'Neil, H.F.O.), Academic Press, New York, 1979.

[Ge82]   Gershman, A.: Building a Geological Expert System for Dipmeter Interpretation, in: Proc. European Conference on Artificial Intelligence, Orsay, France, 1982, pp. 139-140.

[Ge87]   Gevarter, W.B.: The Nature and Evaluation of Commercial Expert System Building Tools, in: IEEE Computer, Vol. 20, No. 5, May 1987, pp. 24-41.

[GH86]   Glass, A.L., Holyoak, K.J.: Cognition, 2nd ed., Random House, New York, 1986.

[GM78]   Gallaire, H., Minker, J. (eds.): Logic and Databases, Plenum, New York, 1978.

[GMD87]   Gesellschaft für Mathematik und Datenverarbeitung mbH: BABYLON, Reference and User Manual (in German), GMD, Bonn, 1987.

[GMN84]   Gallaire, H., Minker, J., Nicolas, J.-M.: Logic and Databases: A Deductive Approach, in: ACM Computing Surveys, Vol. 16, No. 2, June 1984, pp. 153-185.

[GN87]   Gallaire, H., Nicolas, J.-M.: Logic Approach to Knowledge and Data Bases at ECRC, in: Bull. Data Engineering, Vol. 10, No. 4, Dec. 1987, pp.

[GP77]   Goldstein, I., Papert, S.: Artificial Intelligence, Language and the Study of Knowl-
            edge, in: Cognitive Science, Vol. 1, No. 1, January 1977, pp. 84-123.

[GP83]   Gründig, L., Pistor, P.: Land Information Systems and Their Requirements on Da-
            tabase Interfaces (in German), IFB 72, Springer-Verlag, 1983, pp. 61-75.

[GR77]   Goldstein, I., Roberts, R.B.: NUDGE: A Knowledge-Based Scheduling Program,
            in: Proc. of the 5th International Joint Conference on Artificial Intelligence, Cam-
            bridge, Mass., August 1977, pp. 257-263.

[GR83]   Goldberg, A., Robson, D.: Smalltalk-80 - The language and Its Implementation, Ad-
            dison-Wesley Publ. Comp., Reading, Massachusetts, 1983.

[Gr88]   Grasnickel, A.: Implementation of a NDBS-Kernel for the KBMS Prototype KRI-
            SYS (in German), Undergraduation Work, University of Kaiserslautern, Computer
            Science Department, Kaiserslautern, 1988.

[GS82]   Guttman, A., Stonebraker, M.: Using a Relational Database Management System
            for Computed Aided Design Data, in: IEEE Database Engineering, Vol. 5, No. 2,
            June 1982, pp. 21-28.

[GWCRM86]   Groß, E., Walter, J., Christaller, T., Rome, E., Müller, B.S.: Software Design and
            Implementation of the Expert System Tool BABYLON Using Object-Oriented Pro-
            gramming (in German), in: Proc. GI 16th Conference, IFB 126, Springer-Verlag,
            Berlin, 1986, pp. 180-194.

[Ha74]   Hayes, P.J.: Some Problems and Non-Problems in Representation Theory, in:
            Proc. of the Summer Conference of the Society for the Study of Artificial Intelli-
            gence and Simulation of Behavior, Essex University, 1974.

[Ha84]   Hayes-Roth, F.: The Knowledge-Based Expert System: A Tutorial, in: IEEE Com-
            puter, Vol. 17, No. 9, September 1984, pp. 11-28.

[Ha85]   Hayes-Roth, B.: A Blackboard Architecture for Control, in: Artificial Intelligence,
            Vol. 26, 1985, pp. 251-321.

[Ha87]   Hayes-Roth, F.: Expert Systems, in: [Sh87], pp. 287-298.

[Hä88a]   Härder, T. (ed.): The PRIMA Project Design and Implementation of a Non-Stan-
            dard Database System, SFB 124 Research Report No. 26/88, University of
            Kaiserslautern, Kaiserslautern, 1988.

[Hä88b]   Härder, T.: A DB-based Architecture for Knowledge Base Management Systems
            (in German), ZRI Research Report No. 4/88, University of Kaiserslautern, Kaisers-
            lautern, 1988.

[Hä89a]   Härder, T.: Non-Standard DBMS for Support of Emerging Applications - Require-
            ment Analysis and Architectural Concepts, in: Proc. Hawaii Int. Conf. on System
            Sciences, Hawaii, Jan. 1989.

[Hä89b]   Härder, T.: Classical Data Models and Knowledge Representation (in German), in:
            Informationstechnik, Vol. 2, 1989.

[HDE78]   Hart, P.E., Duda, R.O., Einaudi, M.T.: PROSPECTOR: A Computer-based Consul-
            tation System for Mineral Exploration, Tech. Report, SRI International, Menlo
            Park, California, 1978, in: Math Geology, Vol. 10, No. 5, pp. 589-610.

[He71]   Hewitt, C.: Procedural Embedding of Knowledge in PLANNER, in: Proc. of 2nd
            International Joint Conference on Artificial Intelligence, London, August 1971, pp.
            167-182.

[He72]   Hewitt, C.: Description and Theoretical Analysis (Using Schemata) of PLANNER: A Language for Proving Theorems and Manipulating Models in a Robot, Ph.D. Thesis, MIT, Dept. of Mathematics, 1972.

[He75]   Hendrix, G.: Expanding the Utility of Semantic Networks through Partitioning, in: Proc. 4th Int. Joint Conf. on Artificial Intelligence, Tbilisi, USSR, Sep. 1975, pp. 115-121.

[He87]   Heuschen, L.: Reasoning, in: [Sh87], pp. 822-827.

[HK87]   Hull, R., King, R.: Semantic Database Modeling: Survey, Applications, and Research Issues, in: ACM Computing Surveys, Vol. 19, No. 3, September 1987, pp. 201-260.

[HM78]   Hammer, M., McLeod, D.: The Semantic Data Model: A Modelling Mechanism for Data Base Applications, in: Proc. of the ACM SIGMOD, Int. Conf. on Management of Data, 1978, pp. 26-36.

[HMM87]   Härder, T., Mattos, N., Mitschang, B.: Mapping Frames with New Data Models (in German), in: Proc. German Workshop on Artificial Intelligence GWAI'87, Springer Verlag, Geseke, 1987, pp. 396-405.

[HMMS87]   Härder, T., Meyer-Wegener, K., Mitschang, B., Sikeler, A.: PRIMA - A DBMS Prototype Supporting Engineering Applications, SFB 124 Research Report No. 22/87, University of Kaiserslautern, 1987; in: Proc. 13th VLDB Conf., Brighton, UK, 1987, pp. 433-442.

[HMP87]   Härder, T., Mattos, N.M., Puppe, F.: On Coupling Database and Expert Systems (in German), in: State of the Art, Vol. 1, No. 3, pp. 23-34.

[Ho87]   Holyoak, K.: Cognitive Psychology, in: [Sh87], pp. 115-120.

[HR83a]   Härder, T., Reuter, A.: Concepts for Implementing a Centralized Database Management System, in: Proc. of the International Computing Symposium 1983 on Application Systems Development, Nürnberg, Teubner-Verlag, March 1983, pp. 28-59.

[HR83b]   Härder, T., Reuter, A.: Database Systems for Non-Standard Applications, Research Report No. 54/82, University of Kaiserslautern, Computer Science Department, 1982, in: Proc. International Computing Symposium 1983 on Application Systems Development, Nürnberg, Teubner Verlag, 1983, pp. 452-466.

[HR85]   Härder, T., Reuter, A.: Architecture of Database Systems for Non-Standard Applications (in German), in: Proc. GI-Conference on Database Systems for Office, Engineering and Science Environments, IFB 94, Springer-Verlag, Karlsruhe, 1985, pp. 253-286.

[HS88a]   Hübel, C., Sutter, B.: Experiences in Supporting an Engineering Application by PRIMA, in: [Hä88a], pp. 117-140.

[HS88b]   Hörth, S., Schneider, P.: Implementation of the User Interface of the KBMS KRISYS (in German), Undergraduation Final Work, University of Kaiserslautern, Computer Science Department, Kaiserslautern, 1988.

[HWL83]   Hayes-Roth, F., Waterman, D.A., Lenat, D.B. (eds.): Building Expert Systems, Volume 1, Addison-Wesley Publishing Company, Reading, Mass., 1983.

[In84]   IntelliCorp Inc.: The Knowledge Engineering Environment, IntelliCorp, Menlo Park, California, 1984.

[In87a]   Inference Corporation: ART Reference Manual, Version 3.0, Inference Corporation, Los Angeles, CA, 1987.

[In87b]   IntelliCorp Inc.: KEEconnection: A Bridge Between Databases and Knowledge Bases, IntelliCorp., Technical Article, Menlo Park, California 1987.

[JCV84]   Jarke, M., Clifford, J., Vassiliou, Y.: An Optimizing PROLOG Front End to a Relational Query System, in: Proc. ACM SIGMOD Conference, Boston, June 1984, pp. 296-306.

[JS85]   Johnson, W.L., Soloway, E.: Proust, in: Byte, April 1975.

[Jü87]   Jüttner, G.: The Development of a Knowledge-based Learning System for the Construction of Thesauruses for Information Retrieval Systems (in German), Doctoral Thesis, Technical University of Munich, Munich, 1987.

[JV84]   Jarke, M., Vassiliou, Y.: Coupling Expert Systems with Database Management Systems, in: Artificial Intelligence Applications for Business (ed.: Reitman, W.), Ablex Publ. Comp., Norwood, New Jersey, 1984, pp. 65-85.

[Ke81]   Keller, A.M.: Updates to Relational Databases Through Views Involving Joins, Research Report RJ 3282, IBM Research Laboratory, San Jose, California, 1981.

[Ke86]   Kerschberg, L. (editor): Proceedings from the First International Workshop on Expert Database Systems, Kiawah Island, South Carolina, October 1984, Benjamin/Cunnings Publ. Comp., Menlo Park,CA., 1986.

[KM87]   Kramer, B.M., Mylopoulos, J.: Knowledge Representation, in: [Sh87], pp. 882-890.

[Kn88]   Knecht, C.: The Intregration of Concepts for Knowledge Processing in a Frame-Model-Analysis, Design, and Implementation (in German), Undergraduation Final Work, University of Kaiserslautern, Computer Science Department, Kaiserslautern, 1988.

[Ko74]   Kowalski, R.: Predicate Logic as a Programming Language, in: Proc. IFIP Congress, Stockholm, Sweden, 1974, pp. 569-574.

[Ko79]   Kowalski, R.A.: Logic for Problem Solving, North-Holland, New York, 1979.

[Ko87]   Korf, R.E.: Heuristics, in: [Sh87], pp. 376-380.

[KW82]   Kulikowski, C., Weiss, S.: Representation of Expert Knowledge for Consultation: The Casnet and Expert Projects, in: Artificial Intelligence in Medicine (editor: Szolovits, P.), AAAS Selected Symposium 51, 1982.

[KY82]   Kunifuji, S., Yokota, H.: PROLOG and Relational Data Bases for Fifth Generation Computer Systems, in: Workshop on Logical Bases for Data Bases, Toulouse, Dec. 1982.

[La83]   Lafue, G.M.E.: Basic Decisions about Linking an Expert System with a DBMS: A Case Study, in: Database Engineering, Vol. 6, No. 4, Dec. 1983, pp. 56-64.

[LB86]   Levesque, H.J., Brachman, R.J.: Knowledge Level Interfaces to Information Systems, in: [BM86], pp.13-34.

[LBFL80]   Lindsay, R., Buchanan, B.G., Feigenbaum, E.A.., Lederberg, J.: Application of Artificial Intelligence for Organic Chemistry: The DENDRAL-Project, McGraw-Hill Book Company, New York, 1980.

[Le83]   Leith, P.: Hierarchically Structured Production Rules, in: The Computer Journal, Vol. 26, No. 1, 1983, pp. 1-5.

[Le88]   Leick, F.J.: The Design and Implementation of a Rule-based Programming Enviroment for Processing and Modeling Expert Knowledge (in German), Undergraduation Final Work, University of Kaiserslautern, Computer Science Department, Kaiserslautern, 1988.

[LFL88]   Lee, M.K., Freytag, J.C., Lohman, G.M.: Implementing an Interpreter for Function-
           al Rules in a Query Optimizer, Research Report RJ 6125 (60619), IBM Research
           Laboratory, San Jose, CA, March 1988.

[Li85]   Lichten, L.: Development of a Special Application Computer-aided Design System,
           Am Machine, Vol. 129, No. 104, January 1985.

[Li87]   Lieberman, H.: Object Oriented Languages, in: [Sh87], pp. 452-456.

[LK84]   Lorie, R., Kim, W., et al.: Supporting Complex Objects in a Relational System for
           Engineering Databases, IBM Research Laboratory, San Jose, CA, 1984.

[LLB79]   Lachman, J.L., Lachman, R., Butterfield, E.C.: Cognitive Psychology and Informa-
           tion Processing: An Introduction, Erlbaum Association, Hillsdale, NJ, 1979.

[LM89]   Leick, F.J., Mattos, N.M.: A Framework for an Efficient Processing of Knowledge
           Bases on Secondary Storage, Research Report, University of Kaiserslautern,
           1989, in: Proc. 4th Brazilian Symposium on Data Bases, Campinas - Brazil, April
           1989.

[LMP86]   Lindsay, B., McPherson, J., Pirahesh, H.: A Data Management Extension Architec-
           ture, IBM Almaden Research Center, San Jose, CA, 1986.

[Lo76]   Lowerre, B.T.: The HARPY Speech Recognition System, PhD. Thesis, Carnegie-
           Mellon University, Computer Science Department, Pittsburgh, 1976.

[Lo78]   Loveland, D.: Automated Theorem Proving, North Holland Publ. Comp., Amster-
           dam, 1978.

[Lo81]   Lorie, R.A.: Issues in Databases for Design Applications, in: Proc. IFIP Conf. on
           CAD Data Bases, File Structures and Data Bases for CAD, (eds.: Encarnacao, J.,
           Krause, F.L.), North-Holland Publ. Comp., 1981, pp. 214-222.

[Lo83]   Lohman, G., et al.: Remotely-Sensed Geophysical Databases: Experience and Impli-
           cations for Generalized DBMS, in: Proc. of the SIGMOD'83 Conference, San Jo-
           se, 1983, pp. 146-160.

[Lo85]   Lockemann, P.C.; et al.: Requirements of Technical Applications on Database Sys-
           tems (in German), in: Proc. GI-Conference on Database Systems for Office,
           Engineering and Science Environments, IFB 94, Springer-Verlag Karlsruhe, 1985,
           pp. 1-26.

[LS87]   Lockemann, P.C., Schmidt, J.W. (eds.): Datenbank-Handbuch, Springer-Verlag,
           Berlin, 1987.

[LSG82]   Lenat, D.B., Sutherland, W.R., Gibbons, J.: Heuristic Search for New Microcircuit
           Structures: An Application of Artificial Intelligence, in: AI Magazine, Vol. 3,
           pp. 17-33.

[Ma77]   Martin, N., et al.: Knowledge-Base Management for Experiment Planning in Molec-
           ular Genetics, in: Proc. 5th International Joint Conference on Artificial Intelligence,
           Cambridge, Mass., August 1977, pp. 882-887.

[Ma83]   Masunaga, Y.: A Relational Database View Update Translation Mechanism, Re-
           search Report RJ 3742, IBM Research Laboratory, San Jose, California, 1983.

[Ma86a]   Mattos, N.M.: Concepts for Expert Systems and Database Systems Integration
           (in German), Research Report No. 162/86, University of Kaiserslautern, Computer
           Science Department, Kaiserslautern, 1986.

[Ma86b]   Mattos, N.M.: Mapping Frame Concepts with the MAD model (in German), Research Report No. 164/86, University of Kaiserslautern, Computer Science Department, Kaiserslautern, 1986.

[Ma87]   Marsland, T.A.: Computer Chess Methods, in: [Sh87], pp. 159-171.

[Ma88a]   Mattos, N.M.: Abstraction Concepts: the Basis for Data and Knowledge Modeling, ZRI Research Report No. 3/88, University of Kaiserslautern, in: 7th Int. Conf. on Entity-Relationship Approach, Rom, Italy, Nov. 1988, pp. 331-350.

[Ma88b]   Mattos, N.M.: KRISYS - A Multi-Layered Prototype KBMS Supporting Knowledge Independence, ZRI Research Report No. 2/88, University of Kaiserslautern, in: Proc. Int. Computer Science Conference - Artificial Intelligence: Theory and Application, Hong Kong, Dec. 1988, pp. 31-38.

[MB84]   McDermott, J., Bachant, J.: R1 Revisited: Four Years in the Trends, in: AI-Magazine, Fall 1984, pp. 21-32.

[Mc80a]   McDermott, J.: R1: An Expert in the Computer Systems Domain, in: Proc. First Annual National Conference on Artificial Intelligence, Stanford University, 1980, pp. 269-271.

[Mc80b]   McDermott, D.: The PROLOG-Phenomenon, in: SIGART Newsletter, No. 72, July 1980, pp. 16-20.

[Mc82]   McDermott, J.: R1: A Rule-based Configurer of Computer Systems, in: Artificial Intelligence, Vol. 19, 1982, pp. 39-88.

[Mc83]   McDermott, D.: Contexts and Data Dependencies: A Synthesis, in: IEEE Trans. Pattern Anal. Mach. Intell., Vol. 5, No. 3, May 1983, pp. 237-246.

[Me64]   Mendelson, E.: Introduction to Mathematical Logic, Van Nostrand, New York, 1964.

[Me87]   Mettrey, W.: An Assessment of Tools for Building Large Knowledge-Based Systems, in: AI Magazine, Vol. 8, No. 4, Winter 1987, pp. 81-89.

[Mi75]   Minksy, M.: A Framework for Representing Knowledge, in: The Psychology of Computer Vision (editor: Winston, P.H.), McGraw-Hill, New York, 1975, pp. 211-277.

[Mi79]   Miller, M.L.: A Structural Planning and Debugging Environment for Elementary Programming, in: Proc. 1st International Joint on Man-Machine Studies, 1979, pp. 79-95.

[Mi88a]   Mitschang, B.: A Molecule-Atom Data Model for Non-Standard Applications - Requirements, Data model Design, and Implemlentation Concepts (in German), Doctoral Thesis, University of Kaiserslautern, Computer Science Department, Kaiserslautern, 1988.

[Mi88b]   Mitschang, B.: Towards a Unified View of Design Data and Knowledge Representation, in: Proc. of the 2nd Int. Conf. on Expert Database Systems, Tysons Corner, Virginia, April 1988, pp. 33-49.

[Mi89]   Michels, M.: The KBMS KRISYS from the Viewpoint of Diagnosis Expert Systems (in German), Undergraduation Final Work, University of Kaiserslautern, Computer Science Department, Kaiserslautern, 1989.

[ML84]   Mylopoulos, J., Levesque, H.J.: An Overview of Knowledge Representation, in: [BMS84], pp. 3-17.

[MM88]   Mattos, N.M., Michels, M.: Modeling Knowledge with KRISYS: the Design Process of Knowledge-Based Systems Reviewed, Research Report, University of Kaiserslautern, 1988, submitted for publication.

[MMJ84]   Marque-Pucheu, G., Martin-Gallausiaux, J., Jomier, G.: Interfacing PROLOG and Relational Data Base Management Systems, in: New Applications of Data Bases (eds. Gardarin, G., Gelenbe, E.), Academic Press, London, 1984, pp. 225-244.

[Mo88]   Mohr, F.: A Frame Model for Knowledge Representation and Organization - Analysis, Design, and Implementation (in German), Undergraduation Final Work, University of Kaiserslautern, Computer Science Department, Kaiserslautern, 1988.

[MPM82]   Miller, R., Pople, H. Myers, J.: INTERNIST1, An Experimental Computer-Based Diagnostic Consultant for General Internal Medicine, in: New England Journal of Medicine, Vol. 307, No. 8, Aug. 1982, pp. 468-476.

[MS81]   McDermott, J., Steele, B.: Extending a Knowledge Based System to Deal with Ad Hoc Constraints, in: Proc. 7th International Joint Conference on Artificial Intelligence, Vancouver, Canada, 1981, pp. 824-828.

[MS83]   Martins, J.P., Shapiro, S.C.: Reasoning in Multiple Belief Spaces, in: Proc. 8th International Joint Conference on Artificial Intelligence, Karlsruhe, 1983, pp. 370-372.

[MW84]   Missikoff, M., Wiederhold, G.: Towards a Unified Approach for Expert and Database Systems, in: [Ke86], pp. 383-399.

[My80]   Mylopoulos, J.: An Overview of Knowledge Representation, in: Proc. of the Workshop on Data Abstraction, Databases and Conceptual Modelling, Pingree Park, Colorado, June 1980, pp. 5-12.

[My86]   Mylopoulos, J.: On Knowledge Base Management Systems, in: [BM86], pp. 3-8.

[Na83]   Nau, D.S.: Expert Computer Systems - Special Feature, in: IEEE Computer, Vol. 16, No. 2, Feb. 1983, pp. 63-85.

[Ne67]   Neisser, U.: Cognitive Psychology, Prentice-Hall, Englewood Cliffs, NJ, 1967.

[Ni80]   Nilsson, N.J.: Principles of Artificial Intelligence, Tioga, Palo Alto, CA, 1980.

[NS63]   Newell, A., Simon, H.A.: GPS: A Program that Simulates Human Thought, in: Computers and Thought (eds.: Feigenbaum, E.A., Feldman, J.A.), McGraw-Hill, New York, 1963, pp. 279-296.

[OL82]   Olson, J.P., Ellis, S.P.: PROBWELL - An Expert Advisor for Determining Problems with Producing Wells, in: IBM Scientific/Engineering Conference, Poughkeepsie, New York, Nov. 1982.

[Os79]   Osborn, J., et al.: Managing the Data from Respiratory Measurements, in: Medical Instrumentation, Vol. 13, No. 6, Nov. 1979.

[Pa83]   Parsaye, K.: Logic Programming and Relational Databases, in: Database Engineering, Vol. 6, No. 4, Dec. 1983, pp. 20-29.

[PGKS76]   Pauker, S., Gorry, G., Kassirer, J., Schwartz, W.: Towards the Simulation of Clinical Cognition: Taking the Present Illness by Computer, in: American Journal of Medicine, Vol. 60, 1976, pp. 981-996.

[PM88]   Peckham, J., Maryanski, F.: Sematic Data Models, in: ACM Computing Surveys, Vol. 20, No. 3, September 1988, pp. 153-189.

[PMM75]   Pople, H.E., Myers, J.D., Miller, R.A.: Dialog Internist: A Model of Diagnostic Logic for Internal Medicine, in: Proc. 4th International Joint Conference on Artificial Intelligence, Tbilisi, USSR, Sep. 1975, pp. 849-855.

[Po77]   Pople, H.E.: The Formation of Composite Hypotheses in Diagnostic Problem Solving: An Exercise in Synthetic Reasoning, in: Proc. 5th International Joint Conference on Artificial Intelligence, Cambridge, Mass., August 1977, pp. 1030-1037

[Po82]   Pople, H.: Heuristic Methods for Imposing Structure on ILL-Structured Problems, in: Artificial Intelligence in Medicine (editor: Szolovits, P.), AAAS Selected Symposium 51, Nestview Pr., Boulder, Colo., 1982, pp. 119-190.

[PSSWD87]   Paul, H.-B., Schek, H.-J., Scholl, M.H., Weikum, G., Deppisch, U.: Architecture and Implementation of the Darmstadt Database Kernel System, in: ACM SIGMOD Conf., San Francisco, 1987, pp. 196-207.

[Pu83]   Puppe, F.: MED1: a Heuristic-based Diagnosis System with an Efficient Control Structure (in German), Research Report No. 71/83, University of Kaiserslautern, Computer Science Department, Kaiserslautern, 1983.

[Pu84]   Puppe, B.: The Development of Computer Applications in Medicine and MED1: an Expert System for Breast Pain Diagnosis (in German), Doctoral Thesis, University of Freiburg, Freiburg, 1984.

[Pu85]   Puppe, F.: Experiences from 3 Projects for Applications of MED1 (in German), GI-Conference "Knowledge-based Systems", IFB 112, Springer-Verlag, Munich, 1985, pp. 234-245.

[Pu86a]   Puppe, F.: Diagnostic Problem Solving with Expert Systems (in German), Doctoral Thesis, University of Kaiserslautern, Computer Science Department, Kaiserslautern, 1986.

[Pu86b]   Puppe, F.: Expert Systems (in German), in: Informatik Spektrum, Vol. 9, No. 1, February 1986, pp. 1-13.

[Py84]   Pylyshyn, Z.: Computation and Cognition: Toward a Foundation for Cognitive Science, MIT Press, Cambridge, MA, 1984.

[Ra82]   Raulefs, P.: Expert Systems (in German), in: Artificial Intelligence Spring School, Teisendorf, March 1982, pp. 61-98.

[Re78]   Reiter, R.: On Closed World Databases, in: [GM78], pp. 56-76.

[Re80]   Reggia, J., et al.: Towards an Intelligent Textbook of Neurology, in: Proc. 4th Annual Symposium on Computer Applications in Medical Care, Washington, District of Colombia, 1980, pp. 190-199.

[Re87]   Reuter, A.: Coupling Database and Expert Systems (in German), in: Informationstechnik , Vol. 29, No. 3, 1987, pp. 164-175.

[RHMD87]   Rosenthal, A., Heiler, S., Manola, F., Dayal, U.: Query Facilities for Part Hierarchies: Graph Traversal, Spatial Data, and Knowledge-Based Detail Supression, Research Report, CCA, Cambridge, MA, 1987.

[Ri86]   Richter, M.H.: An Evaluation of Expert System Development Tools, in: Expert Systems, Vol. 3, No. 3, July 1986, pp. 166-182.

[RKB85]   Roth, M.A., Korth, H.F., Batory, D.S.: SQL/NF: A Query Language for $\neg$ 1NF Relational Databases, TR-85-19, Univ. of Texas at Austin, Dept. Comp. Sciences, 1985.

[Ro65]   Robinson, J.A.: A Machine Oriented Logic Based on the Resolution Principle, in: Journal of the ACM, Vol. 1, No. 4, 1965, pp. 23-41.

[RS87]   Rowe, L.A., Stonebraker, M.R.: The POSTGRES Data Model, in: Proc. 13th VLDB Conference, Brighton, 1987, pp. 83-96.

[Sa74]   Sacerdoti, E.D.: Planning in a Hierarchy of Abstraction Spaces, in: Artificial Intelligence, Vol. 5, No. 2, 1974, pp. 115-135.

[Sa77]   Sacerdoti, E.D.: A Structure for Plans and Behavior, American Elsevier, New York, 1977.

[SA77]   Schank, R.C., Abelson, R.P.: Scripts, Plans, Goals and Understanding, Erlbaum Association, 1977.

[SB82]   Sleeman, D., Brown, J.S. (eds.): Intelligent Tutoring Systems, Academic Press, New York, 1982.

[SB83]   Smith, R.G., Baker, J.D.: The Dipmeter Advisor System: A Case Study in Commercial Expert System Development, in: Proc. 8th International Joint Conference on Artificial Intelligence, Karlsruhe, 1983, pp. 122-129.

[SB86]   Stefik, M., Bobrow, D.G.: Object-Oriented Programming: Themes and Variations, in: AI-Magazine, Vol. 6, No. 4, Winter 1986, pp. 40-62.

[Sc75]   Schank, R.: Conceptual Information Processing, North Holland Publ. Comp., Amsterdam, 1975.

[Sc76]   Schubert, L.: Extending the Expressive Power of Semantic Networks, in: Artificial Intelligence, Vol. 7, No. 2, 1976, pp. 163-198.

[Se73]   Senko, M.E., et al.: Data Structures and Accessing in Data Base Systems, in: IBM Systems Journal, Vol. 12, No. 1, 1973, pp. 30-93.

[SG84]   Stoyan, H., Görz, G.: LISP - An Introduction in the Programming (in German), Springer-Verlag, Berlin, 1984.

[Sh76]   Shortliffe, E.H.: Computer-based Medical Consultations: MYCIN, American Elsevier, New York, 1976.

[Sh87]   Shapiro, S.C. (editor): Encyclopedia of Artificial Intelligence, Vol. 1 and Vol. 2, John Wiley & Sons, New York, 1987.

[SHM77]   Szolovits, P., Hawkinson, L., Martin, W.A.: An Overview of OWL, A Language for Knowledge Representation, MIT/LCS/TM-86, MIT Laboratory for Computer Science, 1977.

[Si80]   Sidle, T.W.: Weakness of Commercial Data Base Management Systems in Engineering Application, in: Proc. 17th Design Automation Conf., Minneapolis, 1980, pp. 57-61.

[Si89]   Sikeler, A.: Implementation Concepts for Non-Standard Database Systems - Illustrated by Means of the DBS-kernel PRIMA (in German), Doctoral Thesis, University of Kaiserslautern, Computer Science Department, Kaiserslautern, 1989.

[Sm84]   Smith, J.M.: Expert Database Systems: A Database Perspective, in: [Ke86] , pp. 3-15.

[So83]   Soloway, E., et al.: Meno-II: An AI Based Programming Tutor, in: Journal of Computer Based Instruction, Vol. 10, No. 1 and 2, 1983, pp. 20-34.

[SR86]   Stonebraker, M., Rowe, L.A.: The Design of POSTGRES, in: Proc. ACM SIGMOD Conf., Washington, D.C., 1986, pp. 340-355.

[SS77a]   Stallman, R.M., Sussman, G.J.: Forward Reasoning and Dependency-Directed Backtracking in a System for Computer-Aided Circuit Analysis, in: Artificial Intelligence, Vol. 9, 1977, pp. 135-196.

[SS77b]   Smith, J.M., Smith, D.C.P.: Database Abstractions: Aggregation and Generalization, in: ACM Transactions on Database Systems, Vol. 2, No. 2, June 1977, pp. 105-133.

[SS86]   Schek, H.-J., Scholl, M.H.: The Relational Model with Relation-Valued Attributes, in: Information Systems, Vol. 11, No. 2, 1986, pp.137-147.

[St78]   Stefik, M.J.: Inferring DNA Structures from Segmentation Data, in: Artificial Intelligence, Vol. 11, 1978, pp. 85-114.

[St81a]   Stefik, M.J.: Planning with Constraints (MOLGEN: Part 1), in: Artificial Intelligence, Vol. 16, No. 2, 1981, pp. 111-140.

[St81b]   Stefik, M.J.: Planning and Meta-planning (MOLGEN: Part 2), in: Artificial Intelligence, Vol. 16, 1981, pp. 141-170.

[St82]   Stefik, M.J., et al.: The Organization of Expert Systems, A Tutorial, in: Artificial Intelligence, Vol. 18, 1982, pp. 135-173.

[St83]   Stefik, M.J., et al.: Basic Concepts for Building Expert Systems, in: [HWL83], pp. 59-86.

[St86]   Stauffer, R.: Database Support Concepts for the Expert System MED1 (in German), Undergraduation Final Work, University of Kaiserslautern, Computer Science Department, Kaiserslautern, 1986.

[STW84]   Schrefl, M., Tjoa, A.M., Wagner, R.R.: Comparison-Criteria for Semantic Data Models, in: Proc. IEEE 1st Int. Conf. on Data Engineering, Los Angeles, 1984, pp. 120-125.

[SWKH76]   Stonebraker, M., Wong, E., Kreps, P., Held, G.: The Design and Implementation of INGRES, in: ACM TODS, Vol. 1, No. 3, 1976, pp. 189-222.

[Sz82]   Szolovits, P.: Artificial Intelligence in Medicine, Westview, Boulder, 1982.

[Sz86]   Szolovits, P.: Knowledge-Based Systems: A Survey, in: [BM86], pp.339-352.

[Te85]   Teknowledge: S1 Users Guide, Teknowledge, 1985.

[Th87]   Thomczyk,C.: Concepts for Coupling Expert and Database Systems - an Analysis Based on the Diagnose Expert System MED1 and the Database System INGRES (in German), Undergraduation Work, University of Kaiserslautern, Computer Science Department, Kaiserslautern, 1987.

[Ul82]   Ullman, J.D.: Principles of Database Systems, 2nd edition, Computer Science Press, London, 1982.

[Va85]   Vassiliou, Y.: Integrating Database Management and Expert Systems, in: Proc. GI-Conference on Database Systems for Office, Engineering and Science Environments, IFB 94, Springer-Verlag, Karlsruhe, March 1985, pp. 147-160.

[VCJ83]   Vassiliou, Y., Clifford, J., Jarke, M.: How Does an Expert System Get Its Data, in: Proc. of the 9th VLDB Conf., Florence, October 1983, pp. 70-72.

[VCJ84]   Vassiliou, Y., Clifford, J., Jarke, M.: Access to Specific Declarative Knowledge by Expert Systems, in: Decision Support Systems, Vol. 1, No. 1, 1984.

[vEK76]   van Emden, M.H., Kowalski, R.A.: The Semantics of Predicate Logic as a Programming Language, in: Journal of the ACM, Vol. 23, No. 4, 1976, pp. 733-742.

[vM79]   van Melle, W.: A Domain-Independent Production Rule System for Consultation Programs, in: Proc. 6th International Joint Conference on Artificial Intelligence, Tokyo, 1979, pp. 923-925.

[WABGO86]   Wall, R.S., Apon, A.W., Beal, J., Gately, M.T., Oren, L.G.: An Evaluation of Commercial Expert System Building Tools, in: Data & Knowledge Engineering, Vol. 1, 1985, pp. 279-304.

[We78]   Weiss, S.M., et al.: A Model-Based Method for Computer-Aided Medical Decision-Making, in: Artificial Intelligence, Vol. 11, No. 2, 1978, pp. 145-172.

[WH79]   Waterman, D., Hayes-Roth, F.: Pattern-Directed Inference Systems, Academic Press, New York, 1979.

[Wi75]   Winograd, T.: Frame Representation and the Declarative-Procedural Controversy, in: [BC75], pp. 185-210.

[Wi84a]   Winston, P.H., Horn, B.K.P.: LISP, 2nd ed., Addison-Wesley Publishing Company, Reading, Mass., 1984.

[Wi84b]   Williams, C.: ART the Advanced Reasoning Tool: Conceptual Overview, Inference Corporation, Los Angeles, 1984.

[WK79]   Weiss, S., Kulikowski, C.: EXPERT - a System for Developing Consultation Models, in: Proc. 6th International Joint Conference on Artificial Intelligence, Tokyo, 1979, pp. 942-947.

[WOLB84]   Wos, L., Overbeek, R., Lusk, E., Boyle, J.: Automated Reasoning: Introduction and Applications, Prentice-Hall, Englewood Cliffs, NJ, 1984.

[Za86]   Zaniolo, C.: Safety and Compilation of Non-recursive Horn Clauses, in: Proc. First Int. Conf. on Expert Database Systems, Charleston, South Carolina, April 1986, pp. 167-178.

Lecture Notes in Artificial Intelligence (LNAI)

Lecture Notes in Computer Science